HESS

HUGH THOMAS

HESS

A TALE OF TWO MURDERS

Hodder & Stoughton

LONDON SYDNEY AUCKLAND TORONTO

British Library Cataloguing in Publication Data

Thomas, Hugh
   Hess: a tale of two murders.
   I. Title
   823′.914[F]

   ISBN 0-340-48869-7 (cased)
         0-340-49056-X (paperback)

First printed 1979 under the title
The Murder of Rudolf Hess. This
revised edition first printed 1988.

Published by Hodder and Stoughton,
a division of Hodder and Stoughton Ltd,
Mill Road, Dunton Green, Sevenoaks, Kent TN13 2YE
Editorial Office: 47 Bedford Square, London WC1B 3DP

Photoset by Rowland Phototypesetting Ltd,
Bury St Edmunds, Suffolk

Printed in Great Britain by Mackays of Chatham Ltd,
Chatham, Kent.

Contents

Illustrations

Acknowledgments

1   D. Herbert Schob and Motorbuch Verlag
2   Imperial War Museum
3   Rex Features

Line Illustrations

Foreword

THE FIRST EDITION of this book was published in 1979 under the title *The Murder of Rudolf Hess*. I wrote it because I considered that a very great injustice had been done to the last, lonely inmate of Spandau Gaol, Allied Prisoner No. 7, known to the world as Rudolf Hess. I believed then that he was not Hess at all, but an impostor who was thrust upon, or infiltrated by, the British in 1941. I conceived it my duty, as a doctor, to obtain restitution for someone who had been dreadfully wronged.

Nine years ago I was very much afraid that when the prisoner finally died, his body would be cremated, and the physical evidence of his identity destroyed. Fortunately, that did not happen. After his sudden death on August 17th, 1987, two separate post mortem examinations of his body were made, one by a leading British pathologist, one by a German.

Having studied both their reports, and made my own investigation of events that day in Spandau, I am more convinced than ever that the man was not Hess. Further, the forensic evidence shows unequivocally that he did not hang himself, as both unofficial rumours and official statements claimed, but that he was murdered.

To be brutally strangled after forty-seven years in gaol is a dismal fate for any man. Why should this one have suffered it? And why should the British Government still be putting out mendacious statements about him nearly half a century after he arrived in Scotland?

I cannot answer by any means all the questions I have raised. But I hope that my own research will provoke other historians, both amateur and professional, to ferret tirelessly after the truth.

HUGH THOMAS
March 1988

Acknowledgments

FIRST, I SHOULD like to thank Frau Ilse Hess and her son Wolf Rüdiger, who answered what obviously were extremely disturbing questions with patience and good temper.

I am also indebted to the following, for information, advice and assistance: The American Mission, Berlin (the late Mr Richard Bauer); Beaumount Aviation Literature; Mr J. Clifford; Mr Sidney Clifford; Mr Alan Cooper; Mr J. H. Everett; the German Federal Archives (Koblenz); Mr Roger Grant; Dr Ben Hurewitz; the Imperial War Museum (Mr McCann, Head of Exhibits Section; Mr David Penn, Head of Firearms Department; the Keeper of the Department of Photographs); the Institute for Jewish Affairs, London; Mrs Ellis Jones; Mr James Leasor; Mr Douglas McRoberts; Messerschmitt Historical Section (Herr Ebert); the Meteorological Office, Bracknell; Radio Signals of Belfast (Mr Lyons); Mr James Reigate; the Royal Aeronautical Society (Mr Fitzgerald); the Royal Air Force, Hendon and Farnborough; also pilots of Strike Command; the Rumanian Embassy, London; the Soviet Embassy, London; Dr Maurice N. Walsh; the West German Embassy, London (Military Attaché). The lines from "Hess" by A. P. Herbert are quoted by permission of the estate of A. P. Herbert.

1

The Discovery

EVER SINCE A German pilot came to earth in Scotland on the night of May 10th, 1941, claiming to be Hitler's deputy, Rudolf Hess, in search of peace with England, the man and his case have remained disturbingly enigmatic. It is true that the man who arrived bore a striking physical resemblance to the Deputy Führer; yet his confused and pathetic character seemed strangely unlike that of the formidably efficient officer who until the day before had been at Hitler's right hand, directing the affairs of the Third Reich.

During his initial imprisonment in Britain, then at the Nuremberg war trials, and later during his long incarceration in Spandau Gaol, the man's behaviour was always erratic. He appeared to lose his memory, then admitted that the loss had been feigned. He refused to see Frau Hess, her son or any other relative until 1969 – twenty-eight years after he had been captured. At Nuremberg he did not recognise either of the two secretaries who had worked for Hess during the war. When an Allied officer came to question him in his cell at Nuremberg, he said, "Sir, there is no such person as Hess here. But if you are looking for Convict Number 125 – then I'm your man."[1] His behaviour always presented an uncomfortable number of inconsistencies.

Although, like most people in Britain, I was vaguely familiar with the story, I had never studied it closely until I became directly involved with the last, lonely inmate of Spandau. But then, in October 1972, I was posted to Berlin as Consultant in General Surgery to the British Military Hospital.

My principal duty, I knew, would be to treat members of the numerous military garrison and their families, and until I arrived in Germany I did not realise that Spandau's Prisoner No. 7 – then aged seventy-nine – might come under my care. Then, however, I learnt that I might have to treat him, so I began to read up his background and medical history, as any doctor does when he has taken on a new patient.

In a garrison library I found *The Case of Rudolf Hess*, a symposium edited by the late J. R. Rees, the Army psychiatrist who had been nominally in charge of the prisoner for most of his time in England. The book was mainly a detailed record of the subject's peculiar behaviour in British hands between 1941 and 1945, and then at the Nuremberg trial; but Rees also gave a brief account of Hess's early life and career up to the moment of his historic flight. One sentence of particular interest to me recorded that in the First World War Hess "fought on the Western Front and was wounded twice, in 1916, and again in 1917, when he had a gunshot wound of the chest which injured his lung".[2]

As a military surgeon who had been seconded to Belfast for four months during a bloody outbreak of I.R.A. violence, I was already familiar with chest wounds caused by high-velocity bullets. I knew the effect of wounds involving ribs and lung both clinically and radiologically, and exactly the kind of scars that such wounds leave. To me – as to any surgeon – scars are of immediate interest, since to the trained eye they tell an explicit tale: one can read at a cursory glance the injuries or operations a person has had. Nor do scars ever disappear: though they whiten and fade with age, it is a simple biological fact that they never go away. Thus I was naturally curious to see what scars Prisoner No. 7 carried as a result of his First World War wounds. The question was not whether he would have any scars or not, but where and what shape the scars would be. From their nature and position I should, I thought, be able to deduce many of the circumstances of his various woundings, and also of any surgery he had received.

As a matter of course I went through his medical file, and in it I found a document which struck me as slightly odd. This was a report on the prisoner's physical condition made by Captain Ben Hurewitz, the American doctor who examined him when he was brought to Nuremberg in 1945.[3] The report appeared to have been compiled with great care: it recorded the patient's condition in detail, down to the fact that he had a patch of chronic dermatitis an inch square on his left calf. Yet the only scars which Hurewitz reported were two small linear marks, the first an inch long and the other three-quarters of an inch, on the patient's chest, and "the faint markings of a scar" half an inch long on his left index finger. The chest marks, it was well known, had been caused by one of the prisoner's alleged attempts at suicide: he had pushed a long, thin kitchen knife through his skin. Yet apart from these small defects, Hurewitz recorded no scars at all. Surely, I thought, he must have missed some?[4]

My chance to examine the prisoner thoroughly did not come for nearly a year. I saw him once or twice at the monthly meetings held in

Spandau, yet these occasions were anything but suitable for making a full survey. The professed object of the meetings was to check on Prisoner No. 7's welfare, but so elephantine and farcical was the administration of the gaol that the meetings invariably became social rather than medical occasions. Each of the occupying powers – Britain, the United States, France, and Russia – had charge of the gaol for a month at a time, and at the monthly meeting each in turn vied with its predecessor in laying on a lavish lunch. The prisoner was examined, it is true; but only very briefly, and as a kind of prelude to the party. After the inspection, which took place in No. 7's stark cell, everyone withdrew to the more civilised atmosphere of the ante-room and drank deep to the remarkable continuing fitness of the prisoner. The German cooks faithfully bent their efforts to lend the month a suitable national flavour: on the appropriate days consommé gave place to bortsch, corned-beef hash to steak-and-kidney pudding, and so on.

At most of these meetings in late 1972 and early 1973 the atmosphere became decidedly mellow. On one occasion, however, the normal conviviality failed to develop. The reason was simple: Colonel Phillips, the officer commanding the British Military Hospital, made a suggestion deeply offensive to the Russians – that No. 7 should be admitted to the hospital for a series of specialist X-rays to determine his internal condition. The prisoner had not shown any particular symptoms of disease in recent months: Phillips's aim was merely to take what he regarded as a sensible precaution.

Four years earlier, in 1969, No. 7 had almost died as a result of a perforated (or burst) duodenal ulcer. The crisis had been precipitated by two factors: first by the intransigence of the Russians, who during their month of duty at Spandau at first refused to release the prisoner to hospital, even though he was clearly in a bad way; and second, the dubious quality of the medical treatment which he received in Spandau. It was Phillips's anxiety to prevent another such fiasco, and the knowledge that few proper medical tests had ever been carried out on No. 7, that made him suggest the examination.

It was rumoured that, to ensure Allied support, he held a series of informal meetings, one of them in the library of the British Military Hospital. The aim was to present a united front to the Russians. But the Soviet reaction proved to be as childish as it was predictable: using the fact of the "clandestine" gatherings as an excuse, the Russians walked out of the next four-power meeting. Later, however, realising the size of the propaganda weapon which the West would possess if anything happened to No. 7 because of their opposition, they agreed

that the examination should take place. By then Phillips had moved
on elsewhere and had been succeeded at the British Military Hospital
by Colonel John Edgington.

The examination took place in September 1973. The German press
and television had somehow got wind of the fact that the prisoner was
to be moved from Spandau to the hospital, some two miles along
Heerstrasse, and all that day the approaches to the hospital were alive
with reporters and cameramen, cruising up and down in cars, festoon-
ing the trees, crawling about the undergrowth, jockeying for position
so that they could get one glimpse or a photograph of Spandau's last
survivor as he emerged from the ambulance. Even if there had been
no leak to the press, the level of security precautions would itself have
betrayed the fact that a very important patient was about to arrive:
soldiers armed with sub-machine guns patrolled the grounds and
swung in the trees not occupied by newsmen, and as the prearranged
hour approached they cleared Dickensweg, the street leading to the
gates.

The ambulance, escorted by a motor cavalcade, arrived soon after
five p.m., and the patient was transferred – unseen by the outside
world – into the spacious, airy modern hospital, which had been
completed only a few years before and formed a striking contrast to
the high-vaulted, iron-bulwarked, dark and dirty Spandau.

Needless to say, all four occupying powers had to be represented at
the examination, and what should have been purely a medical event
inevitably became a social gathering. Quite properly, John Edgington had asked all his specialists to be present, ready to give advice,
when the patient was brought in. In terms of medical experience I was
the senior person in the place, and although the patient had been
officially admitted under the care of the Commanding Officer, I knew
only too well who would bear immediate as well as ultimate responsibility if anything went wrong during the examination, or if any serious
abnormality was found.

Yet besides the doctors actually needed, there also assembled a
number of hangers-on who had come mainly for the party: other
members of the hospital staff, the officers commanding the other
Allied hospitals, members of the British Military Government, and
officials from Spandau, not least Voitov, acting commandant of the
Russian Garrison in the gaol.

Voitov was a character both sinister and absurd. He had come to
Spandau as a prison warder, set to spy on the suspect commandant of
the day, but by sheer assiduity he had worked his way to the top of the
Russian hierarchy in the gaol. He terrorised his colleagues, and at

meetings he could make them crumple up with one glare across the table. To us, however, he looked like a hack cartoonist's idea of a typical K.G.B. agent: the single button which held the jacket of his bright blue suit together threatened constantly to do horrible damage to his sagging pot-belly, and if anyone ever showed Prisoner No. 7 the slightest sign of human kindness – even reaching out to give him a helping hand – he would yell out (in Russian) like a parrot, "*Stop! That is contrary to the Nuremberg agreement!*" or, "*No comfort! It is against the spirit of the convention!*" So precisely similar were all his protests that even people who spoke no Russian knew what they meant before the interpreter translated them. A further element of farce was added by the fact that the Russian doctor, who anyway looked like Charlie Chaplin with his glossy black hair, small moustache and baggy clothes, had on this occasion broken his leg. The rocker on his plaster-cast had been set at the wrong angle, so that as he hobbled about, leaning on a cane, his foot stuck out sideways at two o'clock.

All these people, together with sundry interpreters, had gathered on the ground floor of the hospital for the arrival of No. 7. More than twenty of them crowded into the three small rooms at the end of the wing – the radiologist's office, the tea-room and the secretary's office, where drink and salmon sandwiches were lavishly displayed. I myself do not like drinking while on duty, so I confined myself to the sandwiches, which were excellent.

The patient spent the first forty-five minutes with the ophthalmic surgeon, Colonel Dowson, who gave his eyes the most careful examination they had had since the war, and confirmed that the glasses he had been wearing were worse than useless. Encouraged by the care and consideration which Dowson accorded him, No. 7 emerged looking cheerful, and went through into the X-ray room to change out of his loose grey suit into a white hospital shift, a garment which is put on from the front and fastened with strings behind one's back.

He then had a barium meal, so that a thorough X-ray examination could be made of his stomach and intestines. (When a solution of barium sulphate fills the stomach, it shows up clearly on an X-ray machine. The stomach is outlined, and any defects, such as ulcer-craters or tumours, become apparent. Much depends on the skill of the radiologist, who rolls the patient back and forth on the table, watching continuously through the X-ray machine, and taking a photograph whenever he sees a view that looks likely to yield information.)

On this occasion the radiologist was Major Bill Leach, a quiet and efficient operator who was expert at his job. As usual, the examination was conducted in darkness, with Leach wearing his infra-red eye-shield between screening sessions, to keep his eyes acclimatised to the dark, so that he could see into the machine with better definition. He also wore a lead gown to protect him from reflected X-rays. I, too, wore a lead gown and infra-red glasses, and hovered between the X-ray room and the adjoining darkroom to make sure that everything went smoothly and the patient did not suddenly become distressed, as he had in 1969. Voitov – rigid with suspicion, as always – also hovered to make sure no one gave the patient any succour. But the wretched Russian was also extremely nervous, for not being a doctor he had no lead gown and feared for the safety of his reproductive organs; as a result, whenever his conscience allowed him to, he headed back to the vodka and whisky sour.

The first phase of the examination was successful and relatively quick. In half an hour or so, Bill Leach put up a series of photographs on the viewing-screen in the radiologist's office, and the assembled forces took a few minutes off from their party to look at them. After some discussion it was agreed that although the patient's stomach and duodenum exhibited certain irregularities attributable to his age, and scarring from past ulceration, there was no tumour or active ulcer. The small intestine was also normal, though rather clumped together in the middle of the abdomen.

The second phase of the examination took much longer. For nearly two hours everyone waited in vain for the barium to empty into the large intestine, so that that too could be examined. The patient was given a drug called Maxolon, but it had no effect. Someone then suggested that we should give him something to eat, to see if food would produce a gastro-colic reaction. A bowl of cold salmon was therefore produced – and even at that stage, with my slender knowledge of No. 7 and his background, I was amazed by the way he despatched it. To say he wolfed the salmon gives scarcely any indication of the speed at which the fish disappeared. He held the bowl close under his chin with one hand, and with the other spooned the food furiously into his mouth as if it had been soup. The salmon vanished almost as fast as a live fish would have jumped back into the river. It struck me as odd, even then, that a man who was supposed to have been a fastidious vegetarian should gobble food so compulsively.

In any case, the salmon produced the required result. Some twenty minutes later the barium began moving down the large intestine, and in due course good pictures were obtained of most of the rest of the bowel. Again, these confirmed that everything was in as good shape as it could be for a man of almost eighty.[5]

My chance to look at his torso did not come until almost at the end of the session. Voitov hung around the X-ray room interminably, with his jacket button straining at his stomach just as hard as he himself was straining to be officious. As long as he remained in sight, I could not even approach No. 7 closely, let alone get a look at him naked.

At last, however, the moment came. Bill Leach stuck his head round the corner of the darkroom and told the patient that the final pictures were all right: he could go. No. 7 got off the X-ray table and moved across to the changing-cubicle in the corner of the room. Sergeant Stuart McClean, the young radiographer, who had been present throughout, was already in front of the cubicle and began helping the patient off with his shift.

My opportunity arose when Voitov vanished for a moment. I went across and stood close to No. 7 as he took off the shift forwards, sliding it away from his body, down his arms. For a few seconds he was stark naked, standing side-on to me. Then he reached his arm backwards, feeling for the sleeve of his dressing-gown. As he did that, he exposed the whole of his torso to my close-up scrutiny.

I looked in bewilderment. I saw at once the two small linear scars reported by Hurewitz, and also a small scar on one wrist; *but apart from these marks there was no trace of any former wound.* For an instant I froze in disbelief. Then I put out a hand and held the dressing-gown, in the pretence of helping but in reality to have another, longer, absolutely clear view of his torso. Neither chest nor arms carried any wound-scars whatever. Satisfied with my scrutiny, I let the dressing-gown go and muttered something like, "*Es tut mir Leid*" (I'm sorry). No. 7 probably thought I was just being clumsy in helping him on with the gown.

For the rest of the evening I felt stunned. This man had *not* been shot in the chest during the First World War, or at any other time. Nor had he been wounded in the arm. Perhaps, I thought, there was a persistent mistake running all through his records. Perhaps Rudolf Hess never *had* been wounded, as the book claimed.

In any case, the session ended in characteristic fashion, with John Edgington extending the patient a friendly hand, to wish him well, and Voitov screaming out, "No physical comfort!" and claiming that the gesture violated the Nuremberg sentence. At eight forty-five p.m. the patient was driven back to his cell at Spandau.

Even that session of almost four hours did not quench the local passion for socio-medical occasions featuring Berlin's star patient, and it was decided to bring No. 7 back to the hospital a few days later for a barium enema and X-ray examination of the one part of his intestinal tract that had escaped scrutiny – his lower bowel and rectum. On purely medical grounds, Bill Leach and I were opposed to the return visit. We felt satisfied from what we had already seen that there was nothing seriously wrong with the patient's large bowel, and that nothing would be gained diagnostically by bringing him in again for a barium enema. By then, however, my personal instincts were at war with my professional ones, for I greatly wanted to look at his chest again: a return visit would give me a second opportunity, and so I did not press my professional opinion too hard. Perhaps this was just as well, for the administrators as usual knew better than the specialists advising them, and decided that No. 7 was to come in again anyway.

The return visit took place on September 25th, 1973. This time there was no security leak, and in consequence no milling throng of pressmen. The ambulance drove to the hospital with only a modest escort and arrived unobtrusively at about the same time as before, five thirty p.m. Even the hangers-on had thinned out for the second performance: the cocktail party was a good deal smaller.

During the interval I had done some research on No. 7's X-rays – both those from a few days earlier and the ones taken during the crisis of 1969. Both sets included clear pictures of the patient's chest, and again there was no trace of any wound-damage. As I shall explain in detail later, even if a rifle bullet passes *between* two ribs, without touching either, the shock of its passage leaves visible damage on both the ribs nearest to its path. If the bullet damages a lung, one long-term effect is a clearly visible track. Yet in none of the X-rays of No. 7 was there *any* sign of damage to be seen.

I was already aware of the enormity of the fact on which I seemed to have stumbled. This man had been convicted of being a Nazi war criminal, and had already spent more than thirty-two years in prison. For thirty-two years the world had believed he was Rudolf Hess. Yet now I knew that unless the historical records were wrong, he could not be.

My doubts had been increased by a curious passage in Rees's book, which I had read again. It seemed that Dr H. V. Dicks, one of the psychiatrists who cared for the prisoner in England between 1941 and 1945, had known Hess's brother, Alfred, before the war, and had been told by him that when Hess had been wounded, the doctor who operated on him had been the celebrated pioneer of thoracic (or chest) surgery, Ferdinand Sauerbruch.

Rees related how, in 1944, when the prisoner seemed to have lost his memory, an attempt was made to restore it by administering the narcotic Evipan. During the experiment the patient appeared to become drowsy, as he was supposed to; but afterwards, in a letter home, he boasted that he had been in full conscious control all the time. Throughout the session the doctors' questions produced nothing but negative or incoherent replies, *until one of them asked about the war wound and the great surgeon Sauerbruch*. At that point, according to the official report, two of the doctors noticed "a quick gleam of recognition". Soon afterwards, the patient sat up and called for water.[6]

In other words, the question about the wound quickly made him abandon the pose of unconsciousness which until then he had maintained. Later, in Britain and at the Nuremberg trial, he admitted that his various losses of memory had also been faked. Thus it seemed that mention of the wound had touched on a subject too risky for him to discuss.

In an attempt to make further checks, I had again gone carefully through a second book on the subject, *Hess*, by Roger Manvell and Heinrich Fraenkel, two authors well versed in Nazi history. They, too, mentioned Hess's First World War injuries, recording that in 1917 he was "seriously injured in the lung".[7] Yet they produced no evidence or reference to back up their assertion. Still I thought that some extraordinary mistake had been made.

So that I should miss no chance of further discovery, I made quite certain that I was present throughout the second examination. Again Voitov lurked about, but only intermittently. The main difference between this and the first occasion was in the demeanour of the patient. A week ago No. 7 had arrived in sullen and uncooperative mood; today he was all smiles and taking a keen interest in everything that went on. He seemed particularly pleased with all the attention being paid him, and his face was suffused by the inane grin that he habitually wore at moments of pleasure. As he sat on a chair in the X-ray room waiting for the final preparations to be made, he seemed full of bonhomie, and kept making pleasant small-talk in his excellent English, "Is this what I take?" "Is that how you do it?" and so on. I answered him in a friendly but non-committal way: I could not put the questions I would have liked, as Voitov was waiting to pounce on any irregularity.

At last we got down to business. The barium enema was administered, the X-ray room darkened. Bill Leach began to screen and take photographs. Voitov hastily withdrew to keep his manhood out of danger.

After a comparatively brief session Leach decided he had taken enough pictures. There followed a short wait, during which the films were being processed. With the light in the X-ray room on again, the patient sat up on the edge of the table, still happy and relaxed. Then someone called out that the films were all right, and that No. 7 could get dressed. At once he slipped off his shift – still sitting on the edge of the table – and began to pull on the warmer dressing-gown. As he did so, I again had a clear view of his chest. I stepped forward and pointed at it, saying in a friendly, straightforward voice, *"Was ist passiert mit den Kriegsunfällen? Nicht hauttief?"* ("What happened to your war-wounds? Not even skin-deep?")

Even in my primitive German, the question had a startling effect. The patient's manner changed instantly. From being in a sunny, cheerful mood, he turned chalk-white and began to shake. For an instant he stared at me in what appeared bewilderment or even utter disbelief. Then he looked down and avoided my eyes. After what felt like ages he muttered, *"Zu spät, zu spät"* ("Too late, too late").

He was shaking so violently that I was afraid he might have a heart attack, so I murmured something inconsequential and stepped quietly backward. No. 7 stood up and shuffled across the room towards the changing-cubicle, releasing as he went a flood of barium and diarrhoea which spread across the floor.

McClean, the sergeant radiographer, saw the sudden change in the patient and helped him towards the cubicle, taking the shift from him, handing him towels, and throwing others on the floor to mop up the mess. But then, for the next ten minutes, No. 7 remained shut into the cubicle, ignoring the ever-efficient McClean's offers of further help and refusing to come out. When he did re-emerge, fully dressed again in his old grey suit, he was still severely distressed. He obviously wanted nothing to do with me. Fearing that he might collapse, I thought it better not to approach him. I therefore stood still and let him make a wide berth round me, out into the passage. I myself was glad to escape into the anonymity of the darkroom, where I spent some time poring over the new X-ray photographs.

The second examination was over much sooner than the first, and by seven o'clock the patient was on his way back to Spandau. The incident left me profoundly shaken. Looking back over it, as I have done a thousand times, I accept that No. 7's sudden breakdown *could* be attributed to purely physical causes. It may be that he was merely overtaken by a sudden irresistible urge to empty his bowel. McClean, who did not then speak much German, and in any case had not fully heard my question since I was facing away from him, thought the words "*Zu spät, zu spät*" referred to the patient's need to reach a lavatory.

At the time I said nothing about the incident to McClean, but while I was doing research for this book, in 1978, he confirmed the fact that the patient's whole manner had suddenly changed – that he looked shaky and sullen, and refused to leave the cubicle in spite of the solicitous overtures from outside.[8] I could not accept at the time – and I cannot now – that shame at making a mess of himself was the sole reason for the instantaneous collapse of his morale.

As I had expected, the new X-rays showed no trace of any abnormality, and thereafter the prisoner was allowed to resume his life in Spandau undisturbed. After many more rounds of drinks, representatives of the four powers signed a slip of paper announcing that the various tests had been carried out to their satisfaction.

2

The Surgical Evidence

IT MAY BE said that I should have made my discovery known at once. The reason I did not was that I myself was then an Army officer and knew the military mind: any discovery I claimed to have made would have been quickly swept under the carpet and buried for another thirty years.

Instead of enlisting help, I continued my own enquiries. I did not see No. 7 again during the rest of my two-year tour, but in an attempt to discover more about his background I used an intermediary – one of the prison warders – to ask oblique and apparently innocent questions on my behalf. Scarcely any of these produced solid information, and sometimes I had the distinct feeling that the prisoner was playing with me. He seemed to know what was going on and fed my intermediary deliberately misleading answers.

Then, in Manvell and Fraenkel's book, I found a note saying that a record of Rudolf Hess's First World War service was preserved in the Bundesarchiv, the Federal German Archives, in Koblenz. This information proved wrong, but a courteous note from the Bundesarchiv directed me to the Berlin Document Centre – also known as the American Mission – in the former capital.

The Document Centre is an immense and extraordinary underground stronghold. Once the fortified headquarters of Hermann Goering, it now houses hundreds of thousands of documents captured from the Germans at the end of the Second World War. Recently it has come to light that thousands of Nazi records have disappeared from the Centre; but in 1973 the archive was, so far as I know, intact. From this bunker came the document that seemed to clinch my belief: a photostat copy of Hess's service record for the First World War. As far as I know, no other author writing about Hess had then used, or even *seen*, this tell-tale document. It had certainly never been published.

It is written in beautiful old German script, with many of the words compressed into abbreviations. To make sure that it was genuine, and

Kriegs-Rangliste

der

bayer. Flieger-Ersatz-Abteilung I

für

Ltn. d. Res. (1.F.R.) Rudolf Heß.

8.8.17   bei der Erstürmung des Ungureana pfo. erwundet
         (Gew.-Geschoß – Linge lks)
         9.8.17 ins Kriegsbez. 21.c/Bezdiuasarhely,
         25.8.17 ins Kriegsbez. B Alt.21/Sepsiszentgyörgi,
         11.9.17 auf Transport,
         17.9.17 ins Res.-Laz. Meißen / So.,
         25.10.17 ins Res.-Laz. Alexandersbad,

F. d. R.

München, den 23.11.1937

Heller

Oberregierungsrat.

Excerpts from Hess's War Record (see text pp. 28–9).

to be certain that I did not misinterpret any of the entries, I sent it for translation to a German friend who had served as a medical orderly in the First World War. To him, it was as if a long-lost letter from the past had suddenly come to light, and he fell on it with delight, exclaiming with joy at the copperplate *Schrift*, which he had not seen used for years.

Stamped in Munich on November 23rd, 1937, the document is a summary of Lieutenant Hess's military service, a digest of earlier records such as was made for every officer after his active career had ceased. Its authenticity was confirmed by the late Richard Bauer, then Deputy Director of the Berlin Document Centre and an acknowledged expert on Nazi records in general.

Besides noting Hess's date and place of birth (April 26th, 1894, in Alexandria) the sheets give details of his religion, parents, marital status, orders and decorations, and so on. They also record his various postings, and every occasion on which he reported sick, even with a sore throat. The entries of particular relevance read as follows:

12.6.16	Wounded near Douaumont, artillery missile left hand and upper arm.
13.6.16	Into the reserve hospital, Bad Homburg v.d.H.
28.6.16	Into the reserve hospital, Ilsenburg Harz.
14.7.16	To the reserve troops.
25.7.17	Wounded in the hills between Ojtoztal and Slanic (left upper arm). Remained with unit.
8.8.17	Severely wounded in the storming of the Ungüreana (rifle bullet – left lung).
9.8.17	Into the war hospital, 21c/Bezdivasarhely.
25.8.17	Into the war hospital, B department, Sepsiszentgyörgi.
11.9.17	Evacuation.
17.9.17	The reserve hospital, Meissen, Saxony.
25.10.17	The reserve hospital, Alexandersbad.
10.12.17	To the reserve troops.
11.12.17–31.12.17	On leave to Reicholdsgrün [the Hess family home].
22.1.18–4.2.18	On leave to Reicholdsgrün.
20.8.18–26.8.18	Convalescent leave.
27.11.18	On leave to Reicholdsgrün until discharged.

Here was clear evidence of three separate woundings. The first, on June 12th, 1916, sounds moderately serious. Hess was hit in the left hand and upper arm by shrapnel from an artillery shell, and although there is no mention of bone fractures, one can surmise that he must have suffered severe lacerations – otherwise he would not have spent more than a month in hospital and then been transferred to the reserve. In the middle of the war the hospitals were obviously under pressure to discharge patients as soon as possible: they must have got rid of Hess the moment his recovery allowed. Thus a month in hospital must represent a substantial wound.

The record does not show when he returned to active service; but he sustained his next wound in the Rumanian campaign during the summer of 1917 – another injury to the left arm, received on July 25th. This was obviously slight, as he remained with his unit.

Yet the next wound, sustained on August 8th, was of such severity that it effectively put an end to his active service in the infantry. Not only did he spend *four months* in various hospitals (August 9th to December 10th), but even when discharged, he went only to the reserve, and he spent until February 1918 convalescing. Moreover, as the record shows, in July 1918 he was awarded a "Dull White Battle Wound Badge", a wounded man's honourable discharge from the infantry.

Now, in those six words of compressed German script, I seemed to have final proof that Prisoner No. 7 could not be Rudolf Hess: *Schw. [Schwer] Verwundet (Gew. [Gewehr] Geschoss – Lunge lks [links])*. Severely wounded (rifle bullet – left lung). The absence of scars proved that No. 7 had never been wounded in the chest on this scale. Nor had he been wounded in the upper arm. The arm wound, however, although positive proof in itself, nevertheless seemed relatively unimportant: it was the lung wound which provided the most devastating and conclusive evidence, and thus fascinated me most.

By the time I made this breakthrough I was back in Belfast, dealing almost every day with wounds caused by rifle bullets. I was therefore again confronted, in daily experience, with the typical damage that high-velocity rounds cause. To gain a clearer picture of the original incident I began to research the Rumanian campaign of 1917.[1] The storming of "the Ungüreana", it turned out, was so small an incident as not to have been chronicled in detail by the victorious Germans. According to the Rumanians, the position fell in only four days before the remorseless German advance. There were, however, heavy casualties on both sides.

The Rumanians, I found, were using an 1893-model Mannlicher rifle of 6.5 mm calibre. Despite an indifferent cartridge, the muzzle velocity was between 2,500 and 2,700 feet-per-second, and the rifle could kill a man at 2,500 yards. The bullets were long and had good penetration.

The Rumanians also had some Russian rifles – Moisin-Nagants – of a larger calibre (7.62 mm) dating from 1891. These fired a better cartridge than the Mannlicher (the Spitzer) and threw a 150-grain bullet at 2,800 feet-per-second muzzle velocity. The bullet was shorter and more accurate than that of the Mannlicher, with equal stopping-power.

The overwhelming probability is that Hess was hit by one or other of these bullets. There is also a chance, however, that he was shot by one of his own men, or by one of the enemy using a captured rifle. If this had happened, he would have been hit by a 7.9 mm Mauser, with a stopping-power equal to that of the Moisin-Nagant.

From my own work, and from a study of recent research,[2] I could form a clear idea of the sort of chest wound that any of these bullets would have created. (It is evident that the wound was not caused just by a glancing blow: if Hess had been merely grazed, he would not have needed an operation or spent so long recovering.[3] Nor would he have been left permanently short of breath while climbing hills in later life. Obviously the injury caused substantial damage to the left lung.)

Even if the bullet had entered his chest *between* two ribs, without touching either, and had gone out between two ribs, again without touching bone, it still would have left permanent evidence, both on the bones and in the lung. Not only would it have made a hole approximately the size of the rib-space, which would have had to be sewn up: it would also have deformed both pairs of bones between which it passed, because the kinetic energy imparted by a high-velocity bullet inevitably damages the periosteum, or lining of the bone. It is this lining which causes the growth of the bone, and if it is disrupted, new bone forms over the place, with periosteum on top of it, producing a hard lump known as a callus. It is my own experience – and that of countless other military surgeons, including Sauerbruch – that ribcages penetrated by rifle bullets invariably suffer periosteal damage. The *minimal* effect of a rifle-wound in the chest is therefore a heaping of the bones on either side of the point of injury, and a consequent narrowing of the intercostal space.

Moreover, a bullet passing through the lung inevitably leaves what is known as soft-tissue track. The missile itself destroys the lung-tissue in its path, and the accompanying kinetic energy destroys or severely bruises the tissue surrounding the actual track. The diameter of the core destroyed by a high-velocity bullet is generally about two inches, and old-fashioned bullets such as those used in the First World War tended to cause greater disruption than modern ones.[4]

When the lung heals, the dead matter is replaced by fibrous tissue. Both this and the pneumonic consolidation left by the collapse of the surrounding part of the lung show up clearly on X-rays.

This, then, is the absolute *minimum* long-term damage likely to have been suffered by Rudolf Hess: a thickening of the ribs and a track through the left lung. In practice, however, the chance of a bullet passing into the chest and out again without striking a rib at all is exceedingly small, partly because the intercostal gaps are narrow, and partly because the ribs are not set horizontally or opposite each other, front and back. If a round does strike a rib on entry, it shatters the bone and imparts such kinetic energy to the pieces that they themselves become missiles and are driven on through the chest, causing even greater damage. Because of this tendency of the bullet to harness fragments of the body as further missiles, and itself to break up, the exit-wound is almost always larger than the entrance.

A certain amount must depend on the range from which Hess was shot. If – as seems likely in the storming of a fortified position – he was hit from close range, say a hundred metres, and the bullet passed through his chest, the minimum result of a rib-strike would have been an entrance-wound one inch in diameter and an exit-wound – depending on how many ribs had been shattered – between an inch-and-a-half and two inches across. If he was hit from farther off, say up to 800 metres, the bullet would have caused much the same sort of wound, though possibly with less extensive bone damage. If the bullet was tumbling, it would have caused a large, jagged entrance-wound at least two inches across. If the round had arrived at terminal velocity, it would have been tumbling violently, and so would have slashed a large entrance-hole, as well as causing extensive rib damage. Besides, an operation to extract the bullet would have been necessary, if it had not come out on the other side.

The final possibility is that the bullet only grooved the side of the thorax (although severely enough to damage the lung). Even if this had happened, it would still have made an entrance-hole at least an inch long and an exit-hole of two inches or more. Also, the two holes would have been linked by a subcutaneous tunnel.

Accounts of the incident describe Hess falling unconscious from loss of blood, and nearly dying when his wound-dressing came off as he was carried down from the front. Most authors call the wound a *Durchschuss*, or through-shot, though some describe it as a *Steck-*

schuss, or shot that lodges in the body. Either would have needed corrective surgery. After a *Steckschuss*, the surgeon would obviously have had to open the chest to remove the bullet, and even a *Durchschuss* would have made an operation necessary. At the very least the surgeon would have had to sew up the entrance- and exit-holes. It is also highly probable that he would have had to open up the wounds further to extract pieces of bone, cloth and other debris sucked in by the bullet. Any such incision would have left a scar at least four inches long, and in the long term a rather horrific scar at that, raised, puckered, and not at all like that of a clean knife-cut.

In his own definitive work *Die Chirurgie der Brustorgane*, first published in 1918, Sauerbruch admitted to a forty per cent mortality rate among soldiers with rifle-wounds of the lung. The main reason was that the dirt and debris pulled in by the suction effect of the bullet almost always set up an infection, the trouble often being exacerbated by the considerable delay between the time at which a man was wounded and his admission to a hospital equipped to give him active treatment.

It seems that Hess fell victim to just such a delay. According to the record, he was shot on August 8th but did not reach hospital until the 9th. Thus he must have waited at least twelve hours, or perhaps as long as twenty-four, for treatment. Today, even with the advantages of modern chemotherapy, a delay of *two* hours is considered greatly to impair the chances of a wound healing cleanly. A delay of twelve hours is considered gross. If a patient has to wait a whole day for treatment, his wound will almost certainly become infected: either the track will suppurate, or an abscess called an empyema will form in the pleural space next to the lung. This may or may not drain through the chest wall.

It seems certain that in 1917, with no antibiotics available, and at least a twelve-hour delay, Hess must have developed a suppurative wound. His long stay in hospital and protracted convalescence strongly suggest that this happened. They suggest, moreover, that the wound did not heal particularly well.

In his book, Sauerbruch made no mention of treating Hess: the work is not memoirs, but a technical exposition. Yet because the surgeon described the techniques which he employed, we can see that in many ways they are extraordinarily similar to those in use today. Sauerbruch was years ahead of his time: in spite of the problems caused by the lack of antibiotics, he was an aggressive surgeon, always willing to operate if he saw the chance of saving a man's life. He would cut across the ribs more than we do today, and if necessary he would excise part of a rib altogether, leaving a gap filled only by skin and muscle. Although we do not know the exact nature of the operation performed on Hess, the wounds caused by bullet and scalpel must have left him with at least one large, unsightly scar, probably with two.

All these possibilities have taken some time to explain. But to me, when I saw Hess's war record, they were evident in a flash, and they added up to one simple fact, that unless the record is false, Spandau's Prisoner No. 7, who bore no wound scars at all, was not Rudolf Hess. Perhaps I should emphasise that this is not a matter of personal opinion, but of straightforward medical fact. Any surgeon with experience of gunshot wounds will agree with me.

In theory, it is of course possible that the war record was falsified by order of Hess himself, in an attempt at self-glorification. Yet this seems improbable. The real Hess was not at all a vainglorious person. Nor, in 1937, when the record was stamped, had he any need to inflate his own military reputation. At that stage he was securely placed as Hitler's right-hand man. His service career was nearly twenty years behind him, and he had no immediate military ambitions. There would have been no point, at that late stage, in faking details of his distant past.

Besides, "details" is the appropriate word. The nature of the record itself, with its minutiae of illnesses and postings, has the ring of absolute authenticity.

Once I had seen the prisoner and the document, I scarcely knew what to believe. The medical evidence was absolute. Spandau's Prisoner No. 7 had never been wounded seriously. I therefore knew either that he was not Hess, or that the medical records for the real Hess were nonsense.

Then, in the autumn of 1978, I met Frau Ilse Hess at her home in the Bavarian Alps. She professed herself astonished by my doubts, and told me she had never had the faintest suspicion that the man in Spandau might not be her husband. Yet, equally, she confirmed that her husband *had* been seriously wounded during the First World War. More than that: she told me, in a letter, that the wound had been a *Lungendurchschuss*, or a shot through the lung; that it effectively ended her husband's career in the infantry; that when walking uphill he felt its effects only during the first thousand metres of a climb; and that in normal life the only thing which reminded him of the wound were *the scars which he bore on his body, front and back*.

There, then, was the essential collaboration of the original war records. Hess – his own wife confirmed – had scars on his chest and his back. The rifle bullet, as I had expected to find, passed right through his chest. Prisoner No. 7 had never been shot in this way. Therefore I knew for certain that he was not Rudolf Hess.

3

The Flight

THE REAL RUDOLF HESS took off from Augsburg, about forty miles north-west of Munich, at five forty-five p.m. on Saturday, May 10th, in a Messerschmitt Bf 110, a twin-engined, twin-tailed fighter commonly known as the *Zerstörer*, or Destroyer. At ten ten p.m. the same evening coastal radars near Holy Island in Northumberland picked up a single aircraft coming in from the North Sea. The track was designated "Raid 42", and in a few minutes the plane was correctly identified as a Messerschmitt 110 by members of the Royal Observer Corps.

Until now, it has always been assumed that the plane which reached Scotland was the one that left Bavaria earlier the same day. In fact, clear evidence exists to show that it was not. Moreover, although both *ends* of the story are well vouched for – the take-off from Augsburg and the arrival in Scotland – the central section has never been satisfactorily explained. Research conducted over ten years makes it possible to demonstrate two novel facts: first, that two different aircraft were involved; and second, that an elaborate plot was mounted to make it seem that only one aircraft had been used.

There is no doubt that the real Hess took off as history relates. His departure was witnessed and photographed by one of his adjutants, young Karlheinz Pintsch. The flight plan, which the pilot himself filed, described the mission as a training flight of the kind he had made many times before, and the north-westerly track of his aircraft was plotted by German radar stations all the way to the North Sea. After nearly 400 miles overland, the Messerschmitt crossed the coast north-east of Amsterdam just before seven thirty p.m. and faded from the screens as it continued out to sea.[1]

Nor is there any doubt about the details of the intruder which the British air-defence system designated "Raid 42". First spotted just after ten p.m., it was tracked continuously by Royal Observer Corps posts and R.A.F. stations until it crashed almost exactly an hour later. As the pilot reached the coast he dived to pick up speed, and roared across the Border country at tree-top level, doing more than 300 m.p.h. and leaving outpaced a Boulton Paul Defiant which had been scrambled in an attempt at interception.[2]

Flying almost due west, the Messerschmitt stormed on over Kilmarnock, some twenty-five miles south of Glasgow, to the west coast. When it reached the sea the pilot turned south and followed the coast for a few miles before heading back inland. By then the R.A.F. no longer derided the Observer Corps' identification; at first the professional airmen had refused to believe that the plane could be an Me 110, on the grounds that such an aircraft would not have enough fuel to return from Scotland to Germany. But when they found out how fast it was travelling, they changed their minds.

The pilot's aim was to land in, or drop by parachute into, the grounds of Dungavel House, the home of the Duke of Hamilton, but although he flew almost over the house on his westward pass, he missed it by some thirty miles as he came back on his second run. What happened then is a matter of some doubt. By the pilot's own account – which is extremely suspect – he took the aircraft back up to 6,500 feet, extricated himself from the cockpit with some difficulty, and parachuted down, to land near the village of Eaglesham, where he was soon arrested by a ploughman, David McLean. The aircraft crashed nearby at 11.09 p.m. This is the traditional version of the story, told and re-told ever since; yet recent research, not least by the aviation expert Douglas McRoberts, suggests that the pilot did not bale out at all, but managed a controlled crash-landing.

The evening of May 10th was warm and clear, and in that northern latitude darkness did not fall until very late. Official lighting-up time was 11.16 p.m. – *after* the crash – and as the Messerschmitt roared in circles overhead, people came out of their houses to watch it. None got a better view than the families living in the eight houses that made up the hamlet of Watersfoot: they saw the plane make three circuits – one very low, one higher, and another low. On the last pass (by their account) it came in on a straight approach and made a controlled belly-landing some twenty yards to the right of the Humbie road, which runs between Floors Farm and Bonnyton Farm. Having skidded a hundred yards or so on its belly, it hit a hump, lifted off briefly again, plunged into a dip, and came to rest when it met a second rise in the ground.

The pilot, the watchers presumed, was flung clear. When first found, he gave his name as Hauptmann (or Captain) Alfred Horn, and demanded to be taken to the Duke of Hamilton; later he claimed to be Rudolf Hess, Hitler's Deputy, and he was identified as such by a diplomat who had seen Hess several times in Germany before the war. I shall return to the identification later; but first let us concentrate on the flight, and in particular on the plane.

As I studied the published records, I suddenly realised that one simple but conclusive fact appears to prove the existence of two separate aircraft. The photograph taken by Pintsch (and reproduced opposite page 64) shows clearly that Hess's Messerschmitt *was not fitted with auxiliary fuel-tanks beneath its wings*. The aircraft that reached Scotland *did* have such tanks, one of which was recovered from the Clyde next day. Even if Hess had landed somewhere en route to refuel – and there is no record that he did – it is inconceivable that auxiliary tanks would have been fitted in the middle of his journey. This being the case, it immediately seems clear that two different aircraft were involved.

The fact cannot be conclusively established by the absence of wing-tanks alone, for there is no positive evidence to show that the take-off portrayed was that of May 10th, 1941. The airfield is certainly the one at Augsburg, for the buildings in the background are recognisable, but there is nothing to identify the date. For the fact that this *was* the vital take-off and not an earlier one, we have only the word of Pintsch, who as an old man told the author James Leasor that he had taken the photograph on the day of Hess's final departure.[3] The fact that he did take pictures on May 10th was confirmed by a surviving witness of the scene, Helmut Kaden, who at the time was assistant to Piehl, the airfield manager.[4]

Two further facts seem to confirm that the pictures *were* taken that day. Pintsch recorded that May 10th was fine and sunny, and the pictures of Hess's departure were certainly taken on a day of bright sun. Moreover, the slanting, angled shadows show that the take-off occurred late in the afternoon. (Summer-time had started in Germany on April 1st, and by May 10th darkness did not fall in Bavaria until after eight p.m.) Even so, the point must remain open, the strong probability being that the take-off shown in the photograph was the historic one.

Next it seemed vital to establish precisely what kind of aircraft the real Hess had flown, as several different types of Messerschmitt 110 had been in use during 1941 and each had a different flight range. I therefore visited Messerschmitt headquarters outside Munich. To my surprise, I found that *no record exists* of what type of plane the Deputy Führer had taken. Although Herr Ebert, director of the firm's historical section, was helpfulness itself, he could not answer my question, for the simple reason that *the relevant files were missing*.

Although the factory still had the files on every Messerschmitt 109 which it produced (an individual dossier for every plane), and those on the types which came later, including the first jets and rocket-planes, all the files on the 110s mysteriously disappeared towards the end of the war.

Nevertheless, I had a clue to help me. In one of Pintsch's photographs (reproduced opposite page 65) the serial number of Hess's plane is visible: it is 3526/52. Fortunately another photograph survives in Messerschmitt's files which positively identifies aircraft No. 3996 as a Mark E2. From the numbers, one can see that Hess's plane came off the production line 470 units before the E2. Messerschmitt's records show that the total of E types produced was 400. Thus even if the E2 photographed had happened to be the *last* of the E series, the figures would still put Hess's plane squarely in the middle of the D series production run. His plane was therefore a D type, and since the rates of production are known for 1940 and 1941, one can tell that it came off the line in October or November 1940. (The figure 52, after the oblique stroke, refers to the production-batch, but cannot now be matched with any original record.)

So much for the myth, fostered by numerous writers, that the aircraft Hess flew was a brand-new secret model. Far from being new or secret, the 110s were several years old. The first prototype had flown on May 12th, 1936; the first pre-production aircraft had been rolled out at Augsburg in August 1937, and in August 1938 the aircraft, its assembly line and even its fire-power had been demonstrated in a show of force specially laid on for General Vuillemin, the French Chief of Air Staff. The exercise, devised by the Head of the Luftwaffe, was a typically devious attempt to impress foreigners: only a few aircraft were available, but as they took off and landed at intervals and made wide taxiing circuits on the ground out of sight, it seemed as if a continuous stream of fighters was taking part.[5]

The curse of the 110, though, was its lack of endurance. The maximum range of the early models was only 680 miles. For the C series, the introduction of better engines – Daimler Benz 601As – and extra fuel-tanks in the wings outboard of the engines raised the maximum range to 876 miles. Then, however, the attempt to provide some armoured protection for the pilot and gunner increased the weight by nearly 500 pounds, thereby reducing performance again.

The Norwegian campaign in the first half of 1940 soon showed that the 110Cs had too little endurance for the long-distance cover which the Germans needed to protect their convoys. Highest priority was therefore given to the development of a *langstrecken Zerstörer*, or long-range destroyer. First the 110 was fitted with a single, 264-gallon tank made of wood and canvas and mounted beneath the front of the fuselage, which caused it to be nicknamed *Dackelbauch*, or dachshund-belly. Not only did the plane look – and fly – as if it was pregnant: it was also highly dangerous, as petrol vapour frequently ignited in the tank, which was, in theory, jettisonable but in practice often failed to detach itself when empty, especially if the air temperature was very low.

This version was soon scrapped, and another produced with shackles beneath the wings, outboard of the engines, for carrying twin, jettisonable tanks, as well as with "wet-points" through which the extra fuel could be pumped to the engines. The drop-tanks could be of either sixty-six gallons (300 litres) each or 198 gallons (900 litres) each; the larger version gave the aircraft a maximum range under optimum conditions of 1,200 miles. The plane naturally handled better with no drop-tanks fitted, but without them its practical range was limited to 850 miles. The D series plane in which Hess took off from Augsburg on May 10th, 1941, must have had the fittings for drop-tanks, but according to the photograph carried none. Its maximum endurance was therefore about 850 miles.

Optimum conditions, however, did not prevail by any means all the way to Scotland. To achieve its maximum range, a 110D had to cruise at 217 m.p.h. and at a height of 13,200 feet. Yet Hess was obliged to fly at three different altitudes during his transit of Germany alone. The reason was the security system used to control German air-space throughout the war. The whole country was divided up into square zones, and all pilots were required to fly at heights which varied not only from one zone to the next, but also according to the time of day. The zoning times and heights were changed each month – or, in times of crisis, more frequently still – and it was every pilot's duty to make certain that he had an up-to-the-minute *Fliegekarte* (flight map) showing the day's requirements before he set out on a flight. Any aircraft not flying at the correct height would be challenged from the ground, and if the pilot gave no satisfactory response, a fighter would very soon be up alongside, ready to shoot him down.

Hess, in his flight from Augsburg, took off in the Munich zone, passed into the Cologne zone, and thence into the Amsterdam zone. He thus had to change height twice, a process which always increases fuel consumption.

A far greater increase in consumption must have resulted from the low-level, high-speed dash across country made by the Messerschmitt that reached Scotland. By diving to ground level as soon as he crossed the coast, and going at full throttle through the Border hills, the pilot certainly burnt up a great deal more fuel than if he had been cruising normally. It is not possible to estimate the extra consumption exactly, but the high-speed run lasted more than half an hour, with the aircraft doing over 300 m.p.h. all the way. Its speed and lack of altitude must have raised consumption very sharply.

Even if a 110D without drop-tanks had flown from Augsburg to Dungavel by the shortest possible route (while skirting the English coast for safety), it still would have been hard pressed to complete the course, for the distance is nearer 900 miles than 850. But the pilot who landed in Scotland did *not* fly straight. Not only did he fly on past Dungavel to the west coast and then turn south before heading inland again, thus adding nearly 100 miles to his route. He also, by his own account, followed a most eccentric course over the North Sea, twisting and turning back and forth before he made for the coast of Northumberland (see diagram on page 43).

The prisoner was exceedingly proud of his flight, regarding it as a supreme personal achievement and describing it readily whenever anybody showed interest. He himself, while in British hands, drew the map on which the diagrams in this book are based. (The letters A B C D have been added for ease of reference on the diagram on page 49. The other letters and timings are the pilot's own.)[6]

According to his own account, immediately after crossing the coast of the North Sea, he turned ninety degrees to starboard (at the point marked A) and flew a north-easterly leg of thirty minutes. Then, at point B, he turned ninety degrees to port and flew on his original heading (but on a course parallel to it) the leg B–C. Then he turned ninety degrees to port again, and flew three times back and forth, C–D, D–C, C–D, before heading in for the coast of Northumberland. The effect of all this manoeuvring would have been to add one leg of thirty minutes and three legs of twenty minutes to his journey. In other words, he increased the time he had to stay in the air by ninety minutes.

From the timing of the leg across Germany, observed from the ground stations, and from the dimensions of the North Sea rectangle, it can be deduced that the pilot was flying at, or maybe just over, the aircraft's most efficient cruising speed. At 220 m.p.h., the extra ninety minutes meant that he had to fly another 330 miles.

Availing myself of the best possible expert advice, I got master navigators serving in the R.A.F. Strike Command to compute the total distance that an aircraft flying from Augsburg to Dungavel, via the mysterious North Sea rectangle, would have had to travel. The answer, allowing for twists and turns to avoid airfields in Germany, and the final diversion out over the Clyde, was 1,260 statute miles. Since a Messerschmitt 110D without drop-tanks was capable of less than 900 miles, there is no chance whatever that one could have flown the course which the pilot who parachuted into Scotland claimed to have followed. Even if the Messerschmitt *had* started with auxiliary fuel-tanks, its maximum range – considering the necessary changes of height over Germany and the high-speed dash across the Border country – could not have been more than 1,150 miles, so that it would have run out of fuel more than a hundred miles short of its destination. Whether Hess's aircraft started with drop-tanks or not, the flight described by the pilot who reached Scotland was a physical impossibility.

After the first publication of this book, Herr Ebert tried to shoot down my claims by maintaining that the Messerschmitt could have managed the flight; but he undermined himself by failing to realise how far the pilot said he had flown. Thus in 1982 he sent the Scottish aviation expert Doug McRoberts an exploded diagram of a 110D or E, showing all its fuel tanks, and wrote on it: "With this fuel-capacity, including the two drop-tanks and under best conditions, the Me 110 D/E could fly over a distance of c. 1,400 km (870 miles) ferry range. The distance Augsburg–Cologne–den Haag–Glasgow is 1,335 km or 830 miles." It may or may not be significant that after the book came out a copy of the photograph of Hess taking off was removed from the wall behind Herr Ebert's desk.

It should also be emphasised that the pilot who reached Scotland displayed extraordinary incompetence. First, he arrived with his auxiliary wing-tanks still in place. Had he come on a genuine long-distance flight, he would have jettisoned them hours earlier, because the aircraft handled far better without them: it was standard practice on lengthy sorties to use the outboard fuel first and get rid of the tanks as soon as possible, after about 300 miles. On the kind of low-level, high-speed run which the Messerschmitt performed over Scotland, they would have been a severe handicap, adding greatly to the drag and reducing manoeuvrability.

Second, the pilot approached the coast of Northumberland at the worst possible altitude (from his own point of view): at 12,000 feet the defensive radars could hardly fail to pick him up. Anyone with good flying sense and experience would have slipped in at sea-level, beneath the radar screen.

Third, by roaring across Scotland at high speed, he put himself at maximum disadvantage – both by inevitably attracting the attention of everyone on the ground, and by making his own identification of landmarks far more difficult. Altogether, his approach suggests that he was an inexperienced pilot, and poorly briefed.

The account which the prisoner gave was false in several ways; but, beyond the discrepancies which the British might have noticed, there was one of which they could not be aware at the time. Although German radar stations tracked Hess's plane as far as point A, they did *not* track it flying off the Dutch coast from A to B. Yet the coast there was watched continuously by a formidable array of radar stations, both on the mainland and on the chain of islands a few miles out to sea. Hess's aircraft was plotted from the island of Terschelling as it headed out to sea. It did not turn right, but carried straight on. Neither Hess, nor the pilot who flew to Scotland, nor anyone else covered the leg A to B at the time claimed that evening. Had any aircraft flown that course, the radars could not have missed it.[7]

In a way the picture of the flight that emerges is unsatisfactory, for it consists almost entirely of negatives. It may be as well to list these:

1. The 110D that left Augsburg apparently carried no underwing fuel-tanks.
2. It could not have reached Dungavel even by the direct route.
3. Still less could it have reached Dungavel by the route the pilot claimed to have flown.
4. Even a 110D with drop-tanks could not have completed the claimed route.
5. The pilot did not fly at least one of the legs (A–B) which he claimed to have flown.
6. He did not, as he claimed, feather his propellers before baling out. The aircraft came down under full power.

Thus one is left with a collection of pieces which do not seem to fit together. One is also left with the obvious fact that the pilot had not done what he said he had. Why did he lie? (Later in the war it was noticeable that although the man enjoyed boasting about his flight, if anyone showed too close an interest he would suddenly clam up and close his atlas with a snap, refusing to discuss the matter any further.[8])

A certain amount of information can be gleaned from the wreckage of the plane, even though it was roughly handled. When a crew from No. 63 Maintenance Unit reached it at midnight, it was still more or less intact, except that a fuel fire had ignited the oxygen bottles at the back of the cockpit and burnt out or melted part of the central section.

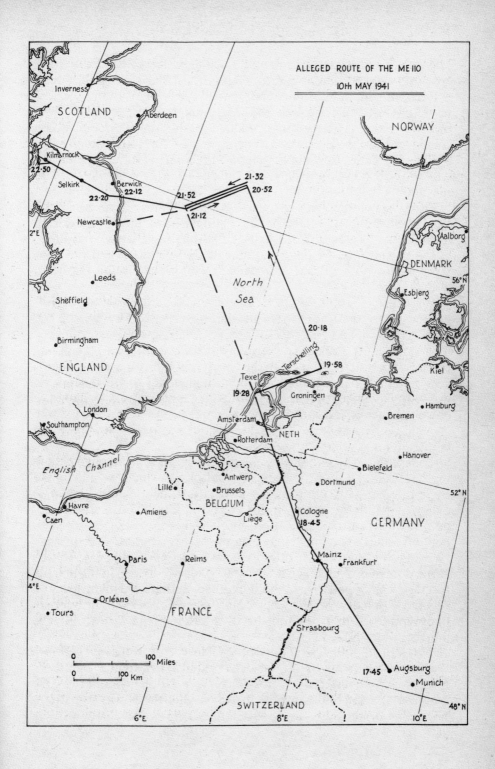

ALLEGED ROUTE OF THE ME 110
10th MAY 1941

The fact that the airframe was little damaged certainly supports the account of a crash-landing, rather than that of a dive from altitude.

Returning in the morning, and treating the remains of the Messer-schmitt as an ordinary wreck, the crew drained off the remaining fuel from the tanks inside the wings and then cut the wings off, so that they could transport the plane to their depot at Carluke, some fifteen miles to the east. There they dumped it on a great pile of other wreckage – only to receive urgent orders, a couple of days later, to recover and reassemble it.

From the records that survive, it is certain that the aircraft was not a *Dackelbauch*, but a 110D or possibly 110E. One of the two underwing drop-tanks was recovered from the Clyde on May 11th by a freighter, but both must have fallen into the estuary together when the pilot jettisoned them, for the release mechanism in the aircraft detached both at once.

One curious feature was that the aircraft's guns had their barrels packed with grease. At the time this was taken to show that the plane's mission had been one of peace. In retrospect it seems insane that the Deputy Führer of Germany should have been denied any chance of defending himself in the air. Surely even on training-flights he would have been furnished with normal means of self-defence. It was always possible that he might meet an enemy aircraft, and to have had no chance of shooting back would have been suicidal. To me, the greased-up barrels suggest that the aircraft was brand new, and had been sent into the air at very short notice.

Today, the only major parts in official hands are the engines and the fuselage section, from cockpit to tail-plane, which are kept in the Imperial War Museum's hangar at Duxford, near Cambridge. The engine block numbers are 01 301 0031 and 3205 4; but these do not help towards our identification, since Daimler Benz, the makers, kept no record matching engine-numbers to airframes. The fuselage markings, by contrast, do offer a clue as to where the plane was based at the time of its flight. The first visible letter was torn in half when the fuselage was ripped apart, and it had been tentatively identified as a severed V or half a W. Yet when I saw the wreckage itself, rather than photographs of it, I realised that this letter was in fact an N. The marking reads NJ + OQ.

When the fighters came out of the factory, they were marked with "VJ", and when an aircraft was delivered to a nightfighter squadron, the V was changed to an N (for *Nachtjäger*, or night-hunter) by the addition of a single downward stroke, so that the N was sometimes not quite upright.

The point has often been made that the letters OQ are not by any means ideal for aircraft on active service, since they are similar enough to each other (and to G) to make quick identification in bad light or bad weather uncertain – and sure enough, they were *not* used by the Luftwaffe for operational aircraft. The designation NJ + OQ was one of the *delivery codes* used for new aircraft being sent to forward bases. Further, it is now known that all the designations between NJ + OA and NJ + OX were delivered to Aalborg, in Denmark, and that those between NJ + OK and NJ + OX were sent there from October 1940 onwards at the urgent order of Air-General Udet, Quartermaster-General of the Luftwaffe, since the long-range fighters were urgently needed for convoy defence in the far north. Some of the planes were based at Stavanger and Trondheim, but Aalborg became the centre of operations, and it was to Aalborg that the Scottish aircraft, NJ + OQ, had been delivered. It was so new, in fact, that only one side of its fuselage had been given its finishing coat of paint: the other was covered with grey factory primer. Had it ever gone into active service, its fuselage number would have been changed, probably to NJ + C and a number.[9]

The aircraft which Hess habitually flew from Augsburg, and in which he took off on May 10th, 1941, was NJ + C11. This was the number which Helmut Kaden, assistant manager of the airfield, noted in his diary at the time, the number which he gave in a television interview during the 1970s (before he realised what markings the Scottish plane carried) and the number which he confirmed to me on the telephone. Later, when he saw my evidence, he suddenly decided that his contemporary note, made forty years earlier, must have been wrong, and changed his story; but he has changed his story so often since then that I do not have much faith in his later utterances. One certain fact is that after May 10th NJ + C11 was never seen again.

In spite of numerous loose ends, the clear fact emerges that two different Messerschmitts were involved in the Hess affair. The one which crashed in Scotland took off – possibly – from Aalborg and flew via part, at any rate, of the route that the pilot described. (His drawing of the approach from point D to the English coast and route across country corresponded precisely with the plots made by the ground stations.) The aircraft that left Augsburg crossed the Dutch coast near the island of Terschelling and disappeared out to sea.

What happened to it? There was one man, I thought, who might still be able to provide the answer, or at least throw light on the question. That was Adolf Galland, the former ace fighter-pilot who in May 1941 was in command of the Luftwaffe Me 109 fighter squadrons along that part of the North Sea coast. Years after the event, he revealed in his memoirs, *The First and the Last* (first published in Germany in 1953), that "early in the evening" of May 10th he got an extraordinary telephone call from Goering, who sounded "very agitated" and ordered Galland to take off immediately with his entire wing.[10] When Galland pointed out that there were no reports of any enemy aircraft flying in, Goering shouted, "Flying in? What do you mean by flying in? You're supposed to stop an aircraft flying out! The Deputy Führer has gone mad and is flying to England in an Me 110. He must be brought down."

According to Galland, he thought the order crazy, not least because, he says, "There were about ten minutes left till dark." Even so, "just as a token", he ordered a take-off, each squadron being told to send up one or two planes. He claims that he gave the pilots no reason for the take-off, and that later, when he rang Goering back, he "reported the failure of our mission".

To Galland, it seemed that "someone had made a last-minute attempt to pull the emergency cord of a fast train speeding over the wrong points". He described the whole incident as "one of the most mysterious affairs" of the war. That seems to me an understatement. To be rung up suddenly by the Reichsmarschall commanding the air force and ordered to shoot down the Deputy Leader of the country must have been an astonishing experience, and Galland's published account of it is far from satisfactory. Yet when I tried to interview Galland to glean more information, it was made clear to me that my enquiries were not welcome.[11]

Goering's telephone call on the evening of May 10th, 1941, is in itself extremely suspicious. Next day, when summoned to Hitler's mountain headquarters, the Berghof, he pretended to know nothing about Hess's departure. Yet, according to Galland, he did know about it. Not only was he aware of Hess's flight on the evening of the 10th, he had positively ordered the Luftwaffe to shoot the Deputy Führer down. This alone argues the existence of a plot. How did Goering know that Hess was about to do a bunk? Who had told him? How *long* had he known? On whose orders, or with whose consent, did he command the Deputy Führer's assassination? So desperate an action would surely have needed the direct approval of Hitler himself. Yet Goering did not even tell the Führer what was happening, let alone seek his consent. And why, when Goering did call Galland, was he in such a panic? His haste suggests that he feared part of the plot had misfired.[12]

The timing of the telephone call also seems odd. Galland says it came only about ten minutes before dark. Yet on the north coast of Germany darkness did not fall until after nine p.m. that evening. By nine p.m. Hess – supposing he had carried straight on – would have been at least ninety minutes, or some 300 miles, beyond the coast, and far beyond the reach of any fighters based on the Continent. If Goering knew the time of Hess's take-off, he must have realised this. There would therefore have been no point in telephoning just before dark. Could the call have come through much earlier than Galland relates?

According to Willi Messerschmitt, head of the aircraft firm, Goering also telephoned *him* on the evening of the 10th, ringing him at about ten p.m. and demanding "in an excited manner" that Messerschmitt should present himself for interview in Munich at the first possible moment.[13] Again, it sounds as if Goering was in a panic. Perhaps some part of the plot had gone wrong, or there had been a failure in communications.

In purely mechanical terms, the German aircraft guarding the north coast would have had no difficulty in shooting down Hess's plane if they had intercepted it. An Me 110 cruising at about 220 m.p.h. would have been easy meat for Me 109s, which, as the British knew to their cost, were very fast into the air and, at that stage of their development, capable of about 340 m.p.h. in level flight, and much more in a dive.

I assume that Hess *was* shot down into the sea, and I believe that one can pinpoint within a narrow bracket the time at which the shooting down took place. Hess crossed the coast just before seven twenty-eight p.m. On a normal training-flight he would have flown about fifty miles out to sea, turning all the time in a right-handed arc, which would have brought him back to the coast some thirty minutes later. It was therefore between seven twenty-eight and seven fifty-eight that the attack must have been made.[14]

I therefore assume that Hess was shot down, beyond the reach of the radar screens, at about seven forty-five p.m. I also assume that the man who arrived in Scotland – Hess's double, except that he was much thinner – was then ordered to take off from Aalborg, and was given Hess's times over Germany and the North Sea coast so that he could write them on his own map and correlate his alleged route and timings accordingly.

Only a sequence of events like this makes sense of the strange rectangle which the pilot drew. If he had come from Augsburg, as he claimed, there would have been no point whatever in flying from A to B and then three times back and forth between C and D. Such manoeuvring would have achieved nothing but a lethal expenditure of fuel. The obvious course to follow was the straight one, from A to D. Even on this line there would have been no danger of being spotted by British radar or intercepted by fighters cruising off the coast. The course A–D lay more than 120 miles out from the English coast all the way, and was well beyond the range of radar, which even in the best possible conditions could not scan much beyond sixty miles.

According to one report, the pilot who landed in Scotland claimed that his manoeuvrings were designed to waste time: he had failed to realise that darkness fell later in the far north, he said, and so had reached the middle of the North Sea much too early. This explanation seems totally implausible. Hess was a meticulous planner, and would never have made so gross an error as to forget the late northern light. It would have been just as easy for him to take off an hour later.

As I see it, the rectangle had only one purpose, and that was to act as a flexible buffer which would absorb any discrepancies that might develop between one part of the plan and the other, and be spotted either in England or in Germany. Obviously it was hard to get one man shot down, another into the air from a base in another country, and the timing so well correlated that the plane which reached Scotland did not arrive impossibly early or suspiciously late. I believe that the rectangle, whether or not it was flown, was a device invented to waste time deliberately, if need be, and to graft the flight from Aalborg on to the track of the one from Augsburg, the two coinciding at Point C or Point D. If the pilot of NJ + OQ needed to waste time, he could have done it nearly as well by flying round in circles; this, however, would have presented greater navigational problems, and to fly straight back and forth between C and D was simpler. Coming from Aalborg, which was little over two hundred miles from Point C, he would certainly have had plenty of fuel to cruise spare minutes away.

Looking back, it seems incredible that no one spotted the glaring discrepancies in the account which the prisoner himself gave. When he landed, he still carried his flight map with his alleged route, including the rectangle, superimposed on the transparent cover. From the start the map was in British hands, yet no one seems to have looked at it critically. Later, while in captivity at Abergavenny, the prisoner re-drew his route for Dr Rees, the psychiatrist in charge of him, and presumably Rees showed it to the authorities ultimately in charge. The map was reproduced in Rees's book, published in 1947.

Yet every author since Rees has slavishly trotted out the fact that the prisoner did brilliantly well to fly nearly 900 miles. It occurred to no one to measure the distance which he himself said he had flown. If anyone had done so, it would have become evident that his alleged route was not 900 miles, but nearer 1,300 miles.

In a letter to Frau Hess written in 1947 he said he had flown direct "except for the diversions I made in order to hoodwink our friends the British".[15] How would flying back and forth three times between points C and D have hoodwinked anybody, especially when the aircraft was out of range of any radar observation?

On the map which he drew for Rees, the pilot made some faint marks beside the principal features. These are reproduced on the diagram below. It is tempting to try to work out what his real route must have been, and even if one cannot reach any definite conclusions, one can point out several suggestive facts.

One is that the line drawn above the O points straight in the direction of Aalborg. Another is that the distance from Point O to Aalborg is the same as that from Point B to Point C – 200 miles, or some fifty-four minutes' flying time at the plane's economical cruise-speed. In other words, if the second aircraft *did* come from Aalborg, it could easily have reached Point C within an hour of take-off.

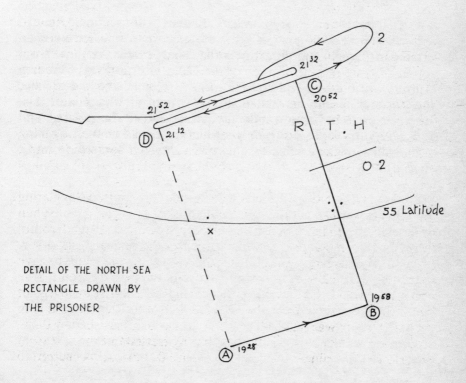

DETAIL OF THE NORTH SEA
RECTANGLE DRAWN BY
THE PRISONER

If the second pilot took off in good time, he may indeed have cruised back and forth between Points C and D, as he later claimed. But if (as Goering's panic suggests) there was some sort of hitch, and the second aircraft was late into the air, the pilot may have flown to Point O or Point D and straight on in the direction of Northumberland.

It was noticeable, but hardly surprising, that afterwards, whenever the prisoner described his flight and dwelt on the glory of it, he never referred to the part that carried him over his Fatherland. Though he eulogised the beauties of the North Sea (which he certainly saw, wherever he came from) and recorded how grateful he was to find white mist (which would give him cover) shrouding the shores of England, he never uttered one word about flying over Germany.

The idea of the two aircraft, the assassination of Hess and the substitution of a double, presupposes – I am well aware – a plot of fantastic complexity. Yet the plot met with equally fantastic success. Not only was Hess disposed of: the British public entirely failed to realise that it had been duped. Whether or not the British *Government* realised what had happened is another, and more dubious, question.

Even today, energetic research by amateur historians in Scotland is throwing up new discoveries – for instance that of an escape map, printed in German and showing Scotland and Scandinavia, which was retrieved from near the wreck of the Messerschmitt next morning. Another curious story is that of one of the soldiers who had guarded the prisoner during his first night. A couple of weeks later, two strange men from London suddenly arrived and interrogated him *for four hours*, trying to discover what had happened to the prisoner's cufflinks (which one must assume had contained something rather special).

4

The Real Hess

To DISENTANGLE THE circumstances of Hess's sudden departure from Germany, one must reach right back to the beginning of his life. He was born in 1894, the eldest son of a well-to-do businessman then trading in Alexandria, and he lived in Egypt until he was fourteen. The family house at Ibrahimieh was large, and so was the garden, in which Rudolf no doubt spent a good deal of time playing with his younger brother Alfred.

The boys' father disciplined them with old-fashioned rigidity. Meal times were invariable, and at table the children were not allowed to utter unless first spoken to by one of their parents.

Rudolf's first school was a German establishment in Alexandria, but in 1908 he was sent to board at the Evangelisches Paedogogium in Godesberg-am-Rhein. By then his father had bought an estate at Reicholdsgrün in Bavaria, and the family used to spend their summer holidays in the house he had built there. Hess's whole background was thus prosperous and upper middle class; later he became, as several commentators have remarked, one of "Hitler's gentlemen", in welcome and useful contrast to some of the common thugs by whom the Führer was surrounded.

In school he was quick and intelligent, and he showed a special interest in German history. He was also good at maths, physics, engineering and astronomy. But rather than going straight from school to university, as he would have liked, he humoured his father by agreeing to study business, first at a school in Switzerland, and then as an apprentice in a firm in Hamburg.

When the First World War broke out he promptly volunteered and joined the Sixteenth Bavarian Reserve Infantry Regiment, becoming a lieutenant.[1] As we have seen, his service record shows that he was wounded three times, the last time seriously. The most obvious physical effect of the lung-wound was that it left him permanently short of breath, especially when walking uphill, a deficiency about which he frequently complained to his family, his secretaries and his friends.

When he recovered from the lung injury, he volunteered to join the Imperial Flying Corps, then desperate for members, and in October 1918 he completed his training as an officer pilot. Within only a few days, however, the Armistice was signed, and in December he was demobilised.

Contemporary photographs show him as an attractive-looking young man, handsome in a rather heavy way, with his wide jawbones and thick black eyebrows almost meeting in the middle. Yet it does not sound as if he can ever have been a very lively or amusing companion. Already, in his early twenties, he had developed a prematurely middle-aged seriousness: he neither drank nor smoked, and disapproved of frivolities such as dancing.

After the war he plunged almost at once into the activity which was to dominate the rest of his life: politics. From the start he was an intensely political animal, and the collapse of the Imperial order in 1918 left Germany a fertile ground in which budding politicians could take root and flourish. By then the Communist revolution in Russia was well under way, and repercussions of it briefly shook many areas in Germany. Although the threat of a socialist takeover blew up and passed over very fast, it was enough to galvanise men with right-wing ideals into establishing the *Freikorps*, or Free Corps, a volunteer body whose aim was to prevent local build-ups of strength by the Left.

Hess served with the Free Corps between 1919 and 1920. In May 1919 he was wounded for the fourth time, in the leg, fighting in the streets of Munich during the skirmishes that brought about the overthrow of the short-lived Communist Government of Bavaria. From this period dated his fear and hatred of Communism, and in particular of Soviet Russia, which later became his main political obsession.

In 1920 he joined the University of Munich to read history, geography and politics. Even as a student he was politically active. In April he became Member No. 16 of the embryonic National Socialist German Workers' Party, which was already under the effective control of the young right-wing agitator Adolf Hitler.

Although he did not mention his name, Hess clearly had Hitler in mind when he won a university prize with an essay on the nature of the man who could lead the country back to its lost glory. "Where all authority has vanished," he wrote, "only a man of the people can establish authority . . . When necessity commands, he does not shrink before bloodshed. Great questions are always decided by blood and iron." In another sentence he gave a strange pre-echo of the position which he himself came to adopt. Instead of drinking his power to the dregs, he wrote, the dictator "sets it down and stands aside as a loyal adviser". The phrases described Hess's own career precisely: he seems never to have coveted supreme power himself; rather, he was content to become Hitler's shadow, his eternally loyal adviser.

By 1921 Hess was already close to Hitler. Not only did he discuss policy with Hitler, write important letters on his behalf and make Party speeches; he also fought physically in the ranks of the S.A. or *Sturm-Abteilung*, an organisation run by Hermann Goering ostensibly as an athletics group but in fact as the strong arm of the Party. It was during a brawl with the Communists at the Hofbräuhaus beerhall on November 4th, 1921, that he was hit on the head by a beer mug thrown at Hitler. Hess is said to have seen it coming and to have stood in its line deliberately. It is also said that the wound left a permanent scar, though no such scar was ever reported on the head of Prisoner No. 7.

Besides learning from these stimulating experiences in the front line, Hess had started to pick up ideas from a man who had a profound influence on the rest of his life: Professor-General Karl Haushofer, who in 1921 became Professor of Geopolitics at the University of Munich. Haushofer was an old-fashioned military aristocrat. Among his posts had been that of military attaché at the German Embassy in Tokyo, where he had served before the First World War, and his travels in the Far East and elsewhere helped to form his concept of the way a nation's political development is influenced by geographical factors.

In Munich, Haushofer expounded his theory that the age of the great sea empires (such as England's) had come to an end. Their place, he proclaimed, would be taken by land empires, and his dream was that Germany should take the lead in establishing some sort of united Europe. He believed that an Anglo-Saxon *Herrenvolk*, or master-race, could dominate the world if Germany and England joined forces. Given *Lebensraum*, or living-space, there was nothing that Germany would not achieve.

To an eager, ingenuous student like Hess, such talk of German expansion was heady stuff, and it further inflamed his political aspirations. He took a prominent part in the Munich Beerhall *Putsch* of 1923, when Hitler made an abortive attempt to seize power. When the coup failed, Hitler was arrested and imprisoned; Hess first escaped to Austria (helped by Haushofer) but later, hearing that his leader was in gaol, voluntarily returned and gave himself up. The result was that he joined Hitler for a short sentence, served in considerable comfort, in Landsberg Castle, some thirty miles from Munich. According to Ernst "Putzi" Hanfstaengl's memoir, *Hitler: The Missing Years*,

> He [Hitler] and Hess had not so much cells as a small suite of rooms forming an apartment. The place looked like a delicatessen store. You could have opened up a flower and a fruit and a wine shop with all the stuff stacked there.[2]

It must be borne in mind that Hanfstaengl was a bitchy and unreliable witness, who greatly disliked Hess and envied his easy way with Hitler. So perhaps Landsberg was not quite so sybaritic as he made out. In any case, it was in the gaol that the composition of Hitler's master-treatise, *Mein Kampf*, took place. Accounts differ as to the precise nature of Hess's involvement. Some say that he merely offered advice, passing on ideas planted by old Karl Haushofer; others that he took down the text of the book at Hitler's dictation and typed it out. Haushofer was certainly a frequent visitor at the prison, and Hess – whatever function he may have fulfilled – was closely involved with the crystallisation of Hitler's ideas. Hanfstaengl left a revealing snapshot of Hess in action:

> Hess was another whistler, like [Alfred] Rosenberg, to which he added the exasperating habit of fooling around with the chair he was sitting on. He would sit on it the wrong way round, pass it through his legs, sit on the back, twirl it on one leg, like an amateur acrobat trying to show off.
>
> He could not bear to see Hitler exposed to any views other than his own, and was always trying to distract attention. All Hess could do was talk in catch-phrases. "We must learn to be much more brutal in our methods. That is the only way to deal with our enemies . . ."[3]

To Hanfstaengl, Hess seemed a "moody introvert, jealously suspicious of anyone who approached Hitler too closely". Yet comparison with other contemporary accounts suggests that this description, while showing the closeness of the Führer and his right-hand man, was soured by personal envy. There is no reason to doubt that Hess whistled and fiddled with his chair in a maddening way. But to say that he could talk only in catch-phrases was an underestimation of his capabilities.

For example, when the newspaper editor Richard Breiting interviewed Hitler in 1931, Hitler clearly relied on Hess for countless organisational details and called him "my assistant of many years' standing".[4] Another contemporary, H. B. Gisevius, considered Hess "the hard man of the party",[5] and later, in November 1939, the experienced foreign correspondent William Shirer got the impression that Hess was "one of the few men he [Hitler] trusts with his innermost thoughts".[6] If one keeps strictly to these accounts, written without the benefit of hindsight, a far more forceful and pragmatic character emerges than the weakling disparaged in retrospect in 1941.

Certainly in the 1920s and 1930s nothing could disrupt the close bonds that had been forged during the Nazis' emergence between Hess and his leader. As Manvell and Fraenkel record, Hess was "at the administrative heart of the conspiracy for power" during the seven-year struggle which culminated in Hitler's seizure of office in 1933.[7] It was he, people said, who suggested the use of the title "Führer", or leader, after Mussolini's assumption of "Duce".

Hess was undoubtedly much influenced by Haushofer during this period of Nazi consolidation. At Munich he had sat at the professor's feet as an undergraduate; but now, as he gained political power, his role changed from that of student to that of protector. Karl Haushofer's wife Martha was half-Jewish, and when the Nazi persecution of the Jews began, it was Hess who protected her. Also during the early 1930s he became friends with one of the two Haushofer sons, Albrecht, a poet, a musician and, like his father, a politically-minded intellectual who hovered on the borderland between university and Government. In due course Hess arranged jobs for both Karl and Albrecht: the old professor in the various *Ausland* (or overseas) organisations which dealt with Germans living abroad, and Albrecht as professor of geopolitics at Berlin University.

In 1927 Hess married Ilse Pröhl, a blonde girl from Berlin, whom he had met seven years before when she too had been a student in Munich. Herself an early member of the Party, she knew Hitler well, and indeed had ridden in the ancient Mercedes which his friends hired to greet him when he was released from Landsberg Gaol. Thus Ilse too had made a positive contribution to the advancement of the Party; but when she married, her husband forbade her to take any further part in political activities.

It is said that the marriage was suggested by Hitler in a Munich restaurant, and certainly he was a witness at the wedding. Like the courtship, the union took a long time to bear fruit: the Hesses' only child – a son, Wolf Rüdiger – was not born until ten years later, in 1937.

Hess's rise to high office began in 1932, when Hitler made him head of a Central Party Commission. In effect this put him in control of all the Party's political activities, and he had a special brief to eliminate opposition. In 1933, when Hitler had become Chancellor, Hess became a member of the Reichstag (or Parliament) and then, on April 21st, the Führer's *Stellvertreter*, or Deputy. In theory he was responsible only for internal Party matters; in fact his grip extended far beyond Party bounds, and he had wide-reaching powers in the field of State. Not only did he prepare orders for Hitler to sign, and approve or disapprove of many public appointments: still more pernicious, he had the power to interfere with, or even initiate, new legislation, as well as to override sentences passed by courts if he thought them too lenient. According to William Shirer, he was "empowered to take 'merciless action' against defendants who in his opinion got off with too light sentences". He received a record of all those found guilty of attacking the Party, the Führer or the State, and many helpless victims disappeared promptly to concentration camps.[8]

By the early 1930s Hess had become a formidable figure. Kurt Lüdecke, who was then a supporter of Hitler, remembered meeting Hess in his office in Berlin during 1933:

> There sat a man not easy to read. Luxuriant dark hair crowned a strong, angular face; he had grey-green eyes under heavy, bushy brows; a fleshy nose, a firm mouth, and a square, determined jaw. Slender and clean-limbed, he was good-looking and rather Irish in appearance. There was a restrained fanaticism in his eyes, but his manner was collected and quiet. I recall him as a commanding presence, a compliment one can pay to only a few of the higher Nazi chiefs.
>
> Hess did not put me at my ease. I couldn't make him out and he didn't help me a bit. He was polite, too polite, very cool, and I couldn't get at him, couldn't draw anything out of him.[9]

During the 1930s, as the Nazi Party and the State became ever more synonymous, and Hitler began to govern more and more by decree, Hess, as his co-signatory, gained greater and greater power.

As Reichsminister without Portfolio he signed one decree after another that reflected the Nazis' hatred of Jews and the régime's bias against religion in general. It is enough, here, to list some of the decrees signed by him or, on his behalf, by Martin Bormann, his Chief of Staff:

March 16th, 1935	Decree for compulsory military service.
September 3rd, 1935	Party agencies ordered to report all persons criticising Nazi institutions or the Party to the Gestapo.
January 7th, 1936	Roman Catholic priests hostile to State or Party to be reported to the Gestapo.
March 13th, 1938	Law for reunion of Austria with German Reich.
May 20th, 1938	Jews deprived of right to vote or hold office.
July 25th, 1938	Jewish doctors forbidden to treat any but Jewish patients.
July 27th, 1938	Clergy prohibited from holding Party office.
September 27th, 1938	Jewish lawyers suppressed.
November 12th, 1938	Jews excluded from economic life.
April 30th, 1939	Eviction of Jewish tenants by landlords.
July 14th, 1939	Party members who became clergy or studied theology expelled.
September 1st, 1939	Decree incorporating Danzig in Reich.
October 8th, 1939	Decree incorporating Polish territories in Reich.

By the end of the 1930s Hess's power extended even beyond the frontiers of the country. One unit in his empire was the Party's *Ausland* Organisation, whose job was to maintain contact with nationals living outside Germany and keep them informed of the latest political developments at home. He also controlled the Party's *Aussenpolitisches Amt*, or foreign political department, and yet another organisation known as the People's League for Germans Abroad (of which Karl Haushofer became President). These various bodies enabled Hess to keep a check on German nationals living outside the Reich, and as the Second World War approached they gave him an ideal base from which to recruit secret agents. By 1939 he virtually had a secret service of his own, reporting to him personally. A further source of power was his control of the *Verbindungsstab*, an organisation that spied and reported on leading members of the Government and Civil Service.

In spite of his position, he remained, in personal terms, quiet and self-effacing. He lived without ostentation in Munich, and his only extravagance was a large brown Mercedes. He still neither drank nor smoked. Like Hitler, he was a vegetarian, fastidious about his food. To the Führer's supposed annoyance he even brought his own food with him when he lunched at the Chancellery in Berlin or the Berghof in Bavaria. He was always a bit of a crank, but no more cranky than a great many other Germans in an age when health fads were very much in vogue. As Frau Hess points out, her husband had inherited many of his ideas about natural food from his mother; they were not transient fads, but principles ingrained from childhood. It was his strong interest in health, and his desire to help others, that led him to establish the Rudolf Hess Hospital in Dresden.

Just as his character was systematically disparaged after his flight in 1941, so retrospective doubts were cast on his health, and in trying to assess how physically fit he was in the late 1930s, it is important to disentangle contemporary reports from reports made with the advantage of hindsight.

All we know for certain is that he had been diagnosed as suffering from a gall-bladder complaint in Munich, and that from the late 1930s he took homoeopathic drugs. There is no contemporary evidence of any kind that the gall-bladder complaint became suddenly worse, or that he increased his consumption of homoeopathic medicines before his flight. The one suggestion that he had some further disorder in 1940 comes from the fact that Himmler lent him his personal masseur, Felix Kersten, to help with stomach cramps. It is well known, however, that Himmler used Kersten as a personal secret agent, and loaned him to as many of his rivals as he could in attempts to glean information. It is thus perfectly possible that the masseur's visits to Hess were partly inspired by ulterior motives on Himmler's part.

Kersten found Hess "a good and helpful person, very modest in his way of life . . . quiet, friendly, and grateful".[10] In his office, too, the Deputy Führer was relaxed and easy-going with his staff. Ingeborg Sperr, a secretary who worked for him in Berlin, remembered him as being "very kind to all his co-workers and employees", demanding a lot from his colleagues but also "the utmost from himself". What impressed Fräulein Sperr most was his decency – "his marked 'inner cleanliness' and his willingness to help out other people . . . He was always polite and chivalrous to us ladies."

Looking back after the war, Fräulein Sperr did recall that his health had begun to deteriorate; but again it must be emphasised that there was no *contemporary* evidence for any such decline. All that can be said with certainty is that he was slightly hypochondriacal and believed in fringe medicine.[11]

Frau Hess emphatically denies that her husband had deteriorated in any way, mentally or physically, in the months before his departure. According to her, he was as vigorous and fully in control as he had ever been, and the day before his departure he jumped clean over one of the chairs in the house, out of sheer exuberance.[12]

Yet Hess's relatively gentle personal characteristics belied the steely toughness and determination with which he pressed home his political beliefs. The ruthless anti-Semitic decrees do not sound like the work of a quiet and friendly person. Another obsession of his, his hatred and fear of Communism, is not apparent in the pre-war legislation; but it burned in him all through the 1930s, frequently appearing in his speeches, and it came to the surface again when the nations began to align themselves in response to the conflagration that Hitler had started. As a member of the Secret Cabinet Council which planned the major acts of Nazi aggression, Hess played a leading part in the preparations for Operation Barbarossa, the invasion of Russia eventually launched in June 1941.

There was never any doubt of his patriotism, or of his devotion to Hitler; and yet, paradoxical though it sounds at first, there is no doubt, either, that in 1940 and early 1941 he became actively involved in attempts to make peace with England. His desire for peace was in no way treasonable. He had no knowledge of, or love for, the English. Rather, his manoeuvring was the result of purely practical considerations. If a settlement could be made with England, it would leave Germany free to tackle the *real* enemy, Soviet Russia.

His main agents in this context were the Haushofers, both of whom had friends in Britain and contacts in neutral countries such as Spain and Portugal.[13] On August 31st, 1940, Hess had an eight-hour meeting with Karl Haushofer at his home in Bavaria, from five p.m. till early morning. The two men spent three hours walking in the Grünwalder Forest as they discussed the possibilities of an English peace. But Albrecht Haushofer, whom Hess summoned to Bad Godesberg on September 8th, was far less optimistic than his father. He told Hess bluntly that "in the Anglo-Saxon world the Führer was regarded as Satan's representative on earth, and had to be fought. If the worst came to the worst, the English would rather transfer their whole Empire bit by bit to the Americans than sign a peace that left the National Socialist Government the masters of Europe."[14]

Hess seemed unable to understand why the English should not

have as good a special relationship with the Germans as they had with the Americans, and Albrecht tried to explain. Discussing possible middlemen, Albrecht suggested Sir Samuel Hoare, the British Ambassador in Madrid; Lord Lothian, the Ambassador in Washington and, as a final throw, his own friend the young Duke of Hamilton who, he said, had "access at all times to all important persons in London, even to Churchill and the King".[15] Albrecht's idea, outlined in a memorandum which he wrote to sum up the state of play a few days later, was that Hess might be able to meet the Duke "on neutral soil".

At that moment Albrecht Haushofer was "walking a tightrope", for he had also started to work for the German resistance to Hitler, of which Hess knew nothing.[16] Unlike his father, who had remained unswervingly loyal to the régime, Albrecht had become disgusted by the excesses of Nazi policy and believed that Hitler must somehow be removed. At the same time, thinking that any peace with Britain would be better than nothing, he reckoned it worth trying to open up a channel to England on Hess's behalf, "and he put forward Hamilton's name as a desperate man clutches at a straw". He knew perfectly well that the British were "in no mood for peace feelers", but nevertheless agreed to try this hundred-to-one chance. Haushofer gained the impression from his conversation with Hess that Hitler knew, in general terms, that his deputy was trying to set up peace initiatives.[17]

On September 10th, Hess wrote to Karl Haushofer saying that "it would be best to have the letter to the old lady [Mrs Roberts, a contact of the Haushofers in Lisbon] delivered through a confidential agent of the A.O. [*Ausland* Organisation]"; and on September 19th, in an immensely long-winded letter, Albrecht discussed the "technical route" by which a message from him would have to travel to reach the Duke of Hamilton.

He should, he suggested, send the Duke an apparently casual and unincriminating note, asking him to come to Lisbon. "I can write a few lines to him . . . in such a way that he alone will recognise that behind my wish to see him in Lisbon there is something more serious than a personal whim . . ."[18] The letter itself would travel through the Portuguese capital, via Mrs Roberts. With his letter to Hess, Albrecht included a draft of the note for Hamilton. This Hess evidently approved, for in due course the letter was sent. Yet, unlike an earlier missive which had reached Hamilton in the autumn of 1939, it was intercepted by the British Secret Service, who, having spent months trying to discover its provenance, and having mislaid it for some time, got the R.A.F. to confront the intended recipient with it in March 1941.

Thus for the moment nothing came of the Haushofer initiatives. But on April 28th, 1941, Hess sent Albrecht to Geneva to meet Dr Carl Burckhardt, President of the Swiss Red Cross, who had just returned from a visit to England. Burckhardt, who had been a diplomat and was widely experienced in international relations, took an even gloomier view than Albrecht of the possibilities of a German–English peace; all he could do was to bring the younger man greetings from his English friends.

Hess therefore knew at the end of April 1941 that the chances of peace were extremely slight. But he had not heard that Albrecht's last letter to the Duke of Hamilton had been intercepted by the Secret Service; for all he knew, an answer might be in the pipeline. The process of sending messages through neutral countries was inevitably uncertain and slow, and indeed at that moment steps were under way to arrange a secret meeting in Madrid with Sir Samuel Hoare. There is thus no discernible reason why Hess should have rushed off – as history says he did – on May 10th, in a desperate attempt to meet Hamilton in Scotland. *On the contrary, many considerations make it most unlikely that he planned to go to Scotland at all.*

One is the fact that the aim, all through, had been to meet Hamilton or some other emissary *on neutral ground*, in Lisbon, Madrid, Geneva, or Stockholm. In his letter to Karl Haushofer of September 10th, Hess himself was clearly thinking of a particular representative or country when he remarked, "As for the neutral I have in mind, I would like to speak to you orally about it some time."[19] And then he went straight on, "That isn't very urgent as yet, *since first an answer must be received from the other side*" (my italics). In other words, he was in no hurry.

Yet to do what Hess apparently did – to fly a single fighter into the heart of the enemy's territory and crash it there – was an enterprise both precipitate and suicidal. Apart from any other drawback, the pilot would have no means of getting home, to bring back any proposals the enemy might have made.

Another difficulty was the fact that Hess had never met Hamilton; nor did he have any idea where the Duke might be posted at that moment. For all Hess knew, he could have been sent abroad. Further, May 1941 was a particularly bad moment for any member of the German Secret Cabinet Council to deliver himself into British hands. Like his colleagues, Hess carried in his head the outline, if not every detail, of Operation Barbarossa, planned to take place in about

six weeks' time. The Germans fully expected the British to extort
information from their prisoners by torture, and if Hess had voluntarily given himself up to the enemy, he would have risked spilling the
secrets of the imminent invasion of Russia. The mission would have
been not only high treason but also sheer folly.

There was also a more bizarre and personal reason for Hess not to
undertake his mission in May. Karl Haushofer, whose prophetic gifts
he greatly respected, had had several dreams in which he had seen
Hess piloting an aircraft to a foreign country and walking in the halls
of a castle hung with tartan. These visions are supposed to have
influenced the Deputy Führer's decision to seek out the Duke of
Hamilton. The point about them, however, was that they were set in
the autumn, and suggested that August or September would have
been more propitious months for the project.

After Hess's sudden exit, Hitler quickly put it about that Hess had
gone mad, and his former colleagues, friends as well as enemies,
began to discern that in fact he had been cracking up all along. Yet it is
important to distinguish between what actually happened before May
10th and what people said afterwards.

To reiterate the facts: up to the moment of his flight Hess showed
no sign whatever of faltering. There is not one shred of contemporary
evidence to suggest that his grip slackened or that his mental attitude
changed in any way. The German press, during the first four months
of 1941, sang his praises continually, calling him "our Father", and
"our Father in conscience". Nauseating though it now seems, the
sheer volume of the propaganda-cum-news reflects the amount of
work that he was doing. In a typical effusion the *Nationale Zeitung* of
April 27th, 1941 – only a fortnight before his disappearance –
announced:

Rudolf Hess was once called the "Conscience of the Party". If we
ask why the Führer's Deputy was given this undoubtedly honourable title, the reason for this is plain to see. There is no phenom-
enon of our public life which is not the concern of the Führer's
Deputy. So enormously many-sided and diverse is his work and
sphere of duty that it cannot be outlined in a few words: and it lies in
the nature of the obligation laid on the Führer's Deputy that the
public at large hears little of the activity of Rudolf Hess. Few know
that many of the Government measures taken, especially in the
sphere of war economy and the Party, which meet with such hearty
approbation when they are notified publicly, can be traced back to
the direct initiation of the Führer's Deputy.[20]

Only in one respect is Hess known to have been disappointed as regards his own position, and that is in the fact that after the fall of France Hitler had created Goering his principal deputy, relegating Hess to third position in the hierarchy. The move seems to have exacerbated the old jealousy between the two men and made relations between them even edgier than before.

Apart from this, however, there is no contemporary suggestion that Hess felt his own standing, or his relationship with Hitler, to have deteriorated. After his flight, when the official campaign of vilification began, everyone began looking backwards through retrospectoscopes and seeing the Deputy Führer in a different light. He had felt himself losing prestige (they said); he had been relegated to the role of administrator only; he was desperate to re-establish himself by a grand gesture. Such arguments overlooked the fact that Hess always *had* been an administrator, and that grand gestures were very much alien to his character.

After his departure, his critics implied that he had become desperate and unbalanced. This again is not borne out by the facts. There was, for instance, nothing desperate about the way he handled Ribbentrop, the Foreign Minister, with whom he had a row in early 1941 over various factions' attempts to dominate the Foreign Office. According to Ulrich von Hassell (later a member of the resistance against Hitler),

> Hess received an incredibly rude letter from Ribbentrop, to which he replied – as one active Reichsminister to another – that Ribbentrop's letter revealed such a state of mind, the result of nervous exhaustion, that he preferred to resume the correspondence only when Ribbentrop had recovered his senses.[21]

So cool a rebuff hardly suggests a man going off his head. There is, on the other hand, some evidence that he was upset by the indiscriminate slaughter to which the war had given rise. One need not entirely believe Kersten's remark that once when the German headquarters was in Belgium Hess was moved to tears by the sight of shattered towns and villages. Yet a similar theme appears also in the memoirs of Count Lutz Schwerin-Krosigk, Hitler's Finance Minister, who had tea in Hess's Berlin flat a few weeks before his flight. "No one else was present," the Count recalled, "and he didn't conceal his desperation about the two great 'Germanic' nations destroying rather than supporting each other. If only one could talk to influential Englishmen personally, reminding them of the danger to Occidental civilisation and convincing them that Germany and quite certainly Hitler had no desire to wrest anything from Britain."[22]

Much argument has raged as to whether or not Hitler knew that Hess was trying to put out peace feelers. Here, I think, two separate issues have often been confused. There is no doubt that Hitler knew about Hess's general attitude towards peace with England, and of his dealings with the Haushofers. The *Stellvertreter*'s ideas on the subject were much the same as the Führer's. Yet at the same time it is equally clear that Hitler did *not* know of any specific plan by Hess to fly to Scotland that night.

It is certain that the two men remained on the closest terms until the last. They had a protracted meeting in Berlin on May 5th, less than a week before Hess disappeared. Their conversation lasted more than two hours; when they emerged, Hitler was in jovial mood and said jocularly to Hess, "You always *were* very stubborn in your ideas and opinions!"[23]

It is possible that they had again discussed peace initiatives. But when on May 11th, the day after Hess's flight, the news was brought to Hitler at the Berghof, he was deeply shocked and taken aback.[24] His reaction is not surprising. The ground had been only half-prepared for the putting-out of peace proposals. It seemed that instead of going to a neutral country, whence it would have been possible for him to return, Hess had flown down the enemy's throat, from which there was obviously no chance of escape. Besides, as I have already indicated, the moment was utterly inappropriate: the whole of Operation Barbarossa might be prejudiced. It is small wonder that Hitler decided his deputy had taken leave of his senses.

Doubts also persist about whether or not Hitler knew how much flying Hess had done in the months before his departure. Just as the aircraft which Hess took is persistently (and falsely) said to have been a secret one, so he himself is frequently (and wrongly) described as an amateurish, inexperienced pilot.

He was amateur only in the strict verbal sense that he was a lover of flying, not a full-time professional. His flying skill was of the highest order. He had sometimes flown as a test pilot for Messerschmitt, and had represented the firm at air-shows. On one memorable occasion between the wars – according to Willi Messerschmitt – he gave such a breathtaking display of aerobatics in an Me 109 that when he landed cracks were found in the aircraft's wings. Nor was he only a stunt-pilot: he won a round-the-houses race in Italy, and the annual race round the Zugspitze, Germany's highest mountain, in 1934. He is

Three forty-five p.m., May 10th, 1941. Hess's plane takes off. Note absence of auxiliary fuel-tanks. Photograph by his adjutant, Pintsch.

An Me 110D in flight, one of its two underwing tanks clearly showing.

With the long evening shadows falling at his side, Hess confers on the tarmac at Augsburg before take-off.

Below left: Hess has his helmet buttoned up before his last flight.

Below right: The whole serial number of Hess's plane – 3526/52.

said to have taken lessons in navigation and dead-reckoning from Hitler's personal pilot, "Father" Hans Baur, becoming so proficient that he was chosen to represent Germany in a "counter-Lindbergh" solo flight across the Atlantic, east to west. In the end he dropped out of the project, but he certainly did not lack flying experience, even if he was short of recent practice when hostilities broke out.

The idea of flying to make peace may have been inspired originally by Goering, who told Hitler just after England had declared war on Germany, "We must fly to Britain, and I'll try to explain the position." Hitler told him that such a move would be useless, but that he could try it if he wanted, and for some time it was rumoured that Goering would indeed make the attempt.[25] Hess is thought to have been influenced also by the fact that the Duke of Hamilton had been a dashing amateur pilot after his own heart, and the first man to fly over Mount Everest, an exploit recounted in the *Pilot's Book of Everest*, by the Duke and Group-Captain D. F. McIntyre.

In any case, when war broke out Hess was keen to get back into the air in some capacity, and in September 1939 he asked Hitler if he might join the Luftwaffe. Permission was refused, and Hess promised his leader that he would not fly at all for a year. He seems to have kept his undertaking; but as soon as the twelve months had run out, in the autumn of 1940, he began the series of training-flights that led up to his final sortie on May 10th.

According to Willi Messerschmitt, he made twenty training-flights between October and May; according to Pintsch, Hess's adjutant, the number was thirty. Whatever the precise figure, Hess was obviously not just joy-riding, but training for a particular long-range mission. Had the sorties not been flown with a serious end in view, they would surely not have been sanctioned. Nor would a Messerschmitt 110D have been kept available, distinguished though the pilot was. Aircraft of this type (as I have already shown) were desperately needed in Scandinavia. The factory could not produce them fast enough. In view of these factors, it is hard to believe that Hitler was not fully conversant with Hess's training programme.

As to the nature of the eventual mission, the details will probably never be known. According to Frau Hess, at one stage, early in 1941, she conceived the idea that her husband was planning a visit to Marshal Pétain, to cement a long-term peace with France.[26] A stronger possibility is that he meant to fly to Stockholm, Madrid or even Lisbon, neutral capitals in which he might meet an emissary from England. The least likely plan of all would have been for him to fly deep into enemy territory and drop by parachute (something he had never done before), hoping vaguely to find a man whom he had never met, and not even bothering to arm himself with a letter of introduction from one of the man's German friends.

5

Destination – where?

IT IS NOW time to examine in detail the circumstances immediately preceding and following Hess's flight. The fullest account so far given appears in Leasor's book *The Uninvited Envoy*: as has been said, the author was fortunate enough to interview one of Hess's adjutants, Karlheinz Pintsch, who supplied him with material and photographs. Yet the more closely one scrutinises Pintsch's version of the story, the less satisfactory it seems. It contains so many obvious red herrings that one has the impression of a man trying to divert attention from what really happened. Pintsch is now dead, so that his facts cannot be challenged directly, but left on their own, they smell fishy.

The first curiosity is the large number of training-flights that Hess is reported to have made. Willi Messerschmitt said it was twenty, Pintsch thirty. If in fact it was somewhere between the two, it means that Hess, who trained from October 1940 to the end of April 1941, must have flown on average just over once a week. Yet no record of his training-programme survives. Records must have been made: every time the Deputy Führer's aircraft passed the control tower on the Messerschmitt airfield at Augsburg its number must have been logged, along with its time out and time back. Who removed the records, and why?

As for the aircraft itself, Leasor, basing his account on the testimony of Pintsch, repeats the fallacy that the plane was a secret model. Except that during the war *all* military equipment was secret as far as the enemy was concerned, there was nothing special about a Messerschmitt 110D in the spring of 1941. In fact the production line was already running down to make way for the E type.

Next, Pintsch told Leasor that in response to requests from Hess, Willi Messerschmitt reluctantly increased the range of the Deputy Führer's aircraft by building two 700-litre fuel-tanks into the wings.[1] Not only does the company have no record of any such conversion being carried out: there is no record of Messerschmitt using or building 700-litre tanks at all. As I outlined in Chapter 3, the normal

110Ds *did* have provision for extra fuel-tanks, but these were carried *beneath* the wings, and were of either 300-litre or 900-litre capacity.

Had it been possible to accommodate further fuel inside the wings, Messerschmitt would undoubtedly have done so before resorting to the expedient of hanging tanks underneath, where they increased drag and detracted from the plane's performance. Every effort had been made to increase the range of the 110, irrespective of anything that Hess might be doing, and the fact is that there was no more room for fuel within the air frame. The idea that Hess had special extra tanks fitted in the wings thus does not bear examination.

In a further muddle – or as a further red herring – Pintsch told Leasor that Hess's plane was capable of flying 850 miles.[2] A 110D was capable of this distance without *any* extra fuel-tanks; with two extra 700-litre tanks (had such things existed) it could have done just over 1,000 miles, so that Pintsch's figure was nonsense. But even a 1,000-mile range would not have brought it to Scotland by the route which the pilot said he had flown.

Another mystery shrouds the earlier attempts at the flight which Hess is alleged to have made. Pintsch said there were two, but both the man who reached Scotland and Kaden, assistant to Piehl, the airfield manager, said there had been three. Kaden told the Hess family that the first had taken place early in November 1940, before the visit to Berlin of the Soviet Foreign Minister Molotov, which began on November 12th. According to Pintsch an attempt in January 1941 failed because one of the ailerons jammed and the plane could not gain enough height "to cross the mountains". The third attempt, said by Kaden to have been made on January 29th, had to be abandoned because of bad weather.[3]

The first January failure (Pintsch related) was particularly unfortunate, for just before Hess took off he handed over two letters, one addressed to Pintsch and the other to Hitler. If he did not return in four hours, Hess said, Pintsch was to open his own letter and take the other personally to the Führer as fast as possible. Four-and-a-quarter hours after take-off, with the plane still not back, Pintsch duly opened his own envelope and to his consternation read that his boss was flying to Scotland to seek peace with the British. Scarcely had the faithful adjutant begun to take in this shattering news when the Messerschmitt reappeared, with Hess safe and sound. Pintsch, let into the plan but sworn to secrecy, handed back the letter for Hitler unopened.

There is one gaping hole in this story. Hess – said Pintsch – flew for four hours and a quarter. He returned, it is alleged, because the aircraft would not "cross the mountains". If he had flown for two hours in the direction of Scotland, before turning back, he would have had no mountains left to cross. In two hours after take-off he would have been seventy or eighty miles out over the North Sea, with no further land between him and the coast of Northumberland.

The story of the second January failure is no more convincing. Why should Hess have abandoned the attempt, after flying for a relatively short time, *because of bad weather*? The weather at take-off cannot have been too bad, or he would never have set out. He may have hit a bad patch, but all the same he should have been confident of getting through it and into better conditions later on, for he had been furnished with a forecast of the weather at his destination.

According to Pintsch, Hess always took great trouble to get good weather forecasts. They were telephoned to him daily by some meteorological office, and typed out either by one of the secretaries or by Pintsch himself. They generally gave the weather at two different places, signified only as X and Y, but sometimes also at a third place, Z. Once, according to Frau Ilse Hess, she accidentally intercepted one of the messages. Answering the telephone in her husband's study, she found herself talking to a strange man who assumed she was the secretary and asked her in a matter-of-fact voice to take down the weather states for X and Y.[4] Later she often took down such messages. At the time, she thought one of the places referred to was in the Baltic, but after Hess had gone she came to assume that the two letters must have stood for Augsburg and Dungavel.

If one accepts Pintsch's account, one has to believe that the weather in late 1940 and early 1941 was so bad as to prevent Hess achieving his objective for more than six months on end. After the supposed attempt in November he was presumably all set to go at the first favourable opportunity. Yet none, apparently, presented itself until May 10th. Surely this is incredible. For one thing, the records of the Meteorological Office in London show that the weather that year was not exceptionally bad; and for another, it certainly did not prevent German bombers flying many hundred successful sorties against London, Birmingham, Coventry and other targets during that period.

Nor does the weather forecast for the actual day of the flight in any way add credibility to the general story. Pintsch himself typed out the prognostication for May 10th and gave it to Hess. The Deputy Führer glanced through it on his way to the airfield and handed the slip of paper back. After the war Pintsch gave it to Leasor. Translated, the forecast read:

X.   Thick multiple-strata cloud, some drizzle. Lower cloud breaking up on the South and East side of the mountains.

Z.   Clouds in several strata, deeply piled and solid to the North. Some drizzle. Lower cloud breaking up towards the South.

Y.   Cloudy, covered to the North, and some drizzle.

Pintsch implied that it was the state of the weather in Augsburg on the morning of May 10th, coupled with this forecast, which made Hess decide to go that day.[5] It was, apparently, fine and sunny – so much so that Hess got his driver to stop the car on the way to the airfield and spent some time strolling in the woods. This being so, it is hard to see how the forecast (reproduced below) can have had anything to do with a flight to Scotland. If X represented Augsburg, the forecast must have seemed totally inaccurate, with its promise of heavy cloud and drizzle. If Y was the area of Glasgow, that part of the forecast also was absolutely wrong, for over Scotland the evening of May 10th proved brilliantly fine – so clear, in fact, as to be an embarrassment to the pilot of the incoming Messerschmitt, who found no shred of cloud to give him cover. It also seems curious, to say the least, that the forecast made no mention of wind, which would

10. Mai 1941   11ʰ

x stärkere mehrschichtige Bewölkung, etwas Niederschlag. Untere Bewölkung an den Süd- und Ostseiten der Gebirge aufgelockert.

z Bewölkung in mehreren Schichten, im Norden tief heratreichend und geschlossen, etwas Niederschlag, untere Bewölkung nach Süden hin aufleckernd.

y wolkig, Norden bedeckt und etwas Niederschlag.

The weather report Hess received before making his flight on May 10th, 1941.

have been all-important to a pilot attempting a flight at the extreme range of his aircraft.

Further obscurity surrounds the question of Hess's *Fliegekarte*, or flight map. Hitler's pilot, Hans Baur, recorded in his memoirs that Hess came and asked him for a "map of the forbidden air zones", which was marked "Reich Top Secret" and showed the zones over which "even German planes were not allowed to fly, or only at certain definite heights".[6] Eventually Baur let Hess have a map, and he implied that without it the Deputy Führer would not have been able to escape from wartime Germany.

This, again, is a fanciful account of an everyday circumstance. During the war every square kilometre of German air-space – as already explained – was watched and controlled and divided into zones. Every pilot who took off had to be equipped with a map brought up to date that day, showing the times and heights which obtained in the various zones, and also any areas to which entry was forbidden. Without such a map, Hess could never have flown any distance from Augsburg, no matter where he was heading. Piehl, the airfield manager, must have furnished him with one every time he took off. There was no need for Hess to go to Baur on this score.

Even the question of how he obtained an aircraft in the first place needs further examination. At the Nuremberg trial, and also in letters to Frau Hess, the pilot claimed that he had first approached Air-General Udet, in Berlin; that Udet had told him no aircraft could be spared, and that this was the cause of a temporary cooling-off in relations between them (by the time of Nuremberg Udet was dead).[7]

Surely it is most improbable that Hess, who worked mainly in Munich, only a short distance from the Messerschmitt factory and airfield, and was in any case senior to Udet, would apply to the General in Berlin? The plane Hess wanted was a 110D. There were no 110Ds in Berlin, so that the request would anyway have had to be passed on to Willi Messerschmitt, whom Hess already knew and liked. Again, the story does not ring true.

Nor does the account of the radio. According to Leasor, Hess ordered the Messerschmitt factory to fit his plane with a special set "so adapted that he could use it as he flew".[8] There was no need whatever for such an additional piece of equipment: by that stage of the war, the *X-gerät*, or apparatus which enabled pilots to follow directional beams, was a standard fitting in bombers and other long-distance aircraft. There seems no doubt that Hess was training to fly along directional beams, or at any rate was interested in them, for on May 2nd, 1941, Messerschmitt noted in a memorandum that

Hess had asked him technical questions about how his plane would fly with the auto-pilot "switched right over", and "how accurate this radius will be and what influence winds may have on it".[9]

Wherever one puts a finger on the generally accepted story of Hess's preparations, it seems to fall apart. Nor does the standard chronicle of the departure-day carry any greater conviction.

Describing that day twenty years later, in the introduction to *Prisoner of Peace*, Ilse Hess recalled how she had been feeling ill, and had not joined her husband for lunch, at which he had entertained Alfred Rosenberg, Hitler's chief ideological adviser.[10] But after lunch, at two thirty p.m., Hess joined her as usual for a cup of tea, and she was surprised to see that he had changed into blue-grey breeches, airman's boots, a light-blue shirt and a dark-blue tie – "a colour combination I had so often advocated without the slightest effect!" He had put on the coloured shirt instead of his usual white one, he said, to give her "a pleasant surprise". He had been "summoned" to headquarters in Berlin, and intended to get in a couple of hours' flying from Augsburg on the way. (Who had "summoned" him is not clear. Hitler, the only person with the authority to demand his presence, was in the Alps.) Frau Hess asked when he would be back, and he said he was not sure. "Perhaps tomorrow; but I should certainly be home by Monday evening." (It was then Saturday.)[11]

Hess went for a quick last look at his four-year-old son (by then nicknamed Buz) with whom, Frau Hess noticed, he had spent an exceptional amount of time during the past few weeks.

He was then met by Pintsch in the official Mercedes and driven the forty-odd miles to the airfield at Augsburg. Pintsch is said to have shown him the weather report on the way. At some stage of the journey Hess supposedly handed over the letter for Hitler, saying that if he was not back in four hours Pintsch was to proceed with its delivery. At the airfield Hess changed into his blue Luftwaffe jacket, which he had brought with him in a briefcase, and over the top of his uniform he pulled on a leather flying-suit. This, unfortunately, he was obliged to borrow, since someone had removed his own, and he took the substitute suit off a hook in the changing room. (The owner was Piehl's assistant Helmut Kaden. He never saw his fine leather outfit again. Nor did Hess's own suit ever reappear in Augsburg. See also p. 85).

Piehl supervised the preparation of the plane. According to him, Hess entered the flight in the log as a training sortie over a bombing range. Piehl certainly expected him back later that evening (he hung about the airfield for several hours, waiting to see the plane safe home).[12] At first one of the Messerschmitt's engines would not start, but after some tinkering the mechanics got it going. Helping hands strapped Hess into his parachute harness and leather helmet, and at five forty-five p.m. the Deputy Führer took off on his last solo flight. Pintsch himself, evidently aware that this was no ordinary occasion, photographed the preparations, the technicians grappling with the reluctant engine, and Hess's actual take-off.

Pintsch later told Leasor that his instructions were to wait on the airfield until ten p.m.; then he was to return to Munich and catch the overnight train to Berchtesgaden.[13] But at nine p.m. – three-and-a-quarter hours after take-off – he went across to the green two-storey administration block and made a mysterious telephone call. By his own account the call was to the Air Ministry in Berlin, and its purpose was to ask for a directional radio signal to be beamed from Augsburg to Dungavel Castle, just south of Glasgow, so that Hess could pick it up for the final stages of his journey.[14]

There are two very odd facts about this telephone call. First, no call was received by the Air Ministry from Augsburg at that time on that evening. Normally, every call was logged meticulously; the log for that evening survives, yet no call from Augsburg is entered.

The second strange fact is that no equipment existed in Augsburg capable of sending out a directional beam strong enough to help a pilot trying to reach Dungavel. Nor is there any record of a beam being put out. Besides, one glance at a map is enough to show that even if such a beam had been technically feasible, its path would have lain dangerously close to the east coast of England. A plane following it would have passed within a few miles of the top of Norfolk, and would then have come in over Hull, leaving the pilot with a long, diagonal crossing of the north of England, during which he would have been prone to attack by fighters and anti-aircraft batteries. The main navigational ambition of the man who reached Scotland was, he said, to keep as far from the English coast as possible until his final run-in.

The way a pilot normally acquired a directional beam was to approach its expected path at right-angles. As he came near the beam his radio would start to pick up a pattern of short and long pulses, or dots and dashes, which changed into a continuous tone as he came on to the beam itself. He could then tell, from the varying pattern of the pulses, whether he was on the beam, or to its left or right. At long range the beam fanned out into an arc extending several degrees on either side of its centre line, so that a pilot could pick up the signal even if he was some way off. But even allowing for this kind of spread, a beam sent from Augsburg to Dungavel would have been perfectly useless to Hess if by then he had been pottering back and forth on the C–D leg of the North Sea rectangle. In any case, the night of May 10th brought the heaviest bombing raids that England had suffered to date, and by the time Pintsch made his call every available beam was directing the German bombers to their targets in the Midlands and South of England, or being held ready to do so. According to Pintsch, he was told that a beam could be transmitted until 10 p.m., but no later.

I suspect that the whole story of the beam was yet another red herring. But whom did Pintsch call, if not the Air Ministry? Was there any connection between this call and Goering's urgent telephone order to Galland, demanding that the Deputy Führer be shot down, and made at about the same time?

In any event, Pintsch had some difficulty reassuring Piehl, who naturally grew more and more worried when Hess failed to return, especially as the mist began to close in on the airfield towards dark. But Pintsch told him he felt certain that the Deputy Führer must have landed somewhere else for the night and would return in the morning.

At 10.30 p.m. he set out for Berchtesgaden. Having driven back to Munich he ordered Hess's private railway coach to be hitched to the train that left at midnight. After walking up and down the platform for some time, he boarded the train just before it left and spent the rest of the night in one of the compartments. By seven a.m. he was in Berchtesgaden, and from the station he telephoned Hitler's secretary Albert Bormann (Martin's brother) asking for an immediate appointment with the Führer. When he eventually saw Hitler, later in the morning, he handed over the letter left by Hess.

According to the author David Irving, in his book *Hitler's War*, a "bulky packet" from Hess had been delivered to the Berghof on the evening of May 10th. (How it had travelled is not clear.) But Hitler, thinking that it contained "more of the minister's interminable memoranda", had not even bothered to open the envelope. (Later inspection showed that it contained Hess's general peace plan, but without reference to his own trip.) Now, however, when Hitler read the much shorter, two-page letter brought by Pintsch, he "suddenly slumped in his chair and bellowed in a voice that could be heard all over the house: 'Oh my God! Oh my God! He has flown to Britain!'" Almost at once, Pintsch was arrested.[15]

Albert Speer, then Hitler's chief architect, was waiting to show the Führer some drawings, and also remembered the shouts:

While I began leafing through my sketches once more I suddenly heard an inarticulate, almost animal outcry. Hitler roared: "Bormann at once! Where is Bormann?" Bormann was told to get in touch with Goering, Ribbentrop, Goebbels and Himmler by the fastest possible means.[16]

Goering was at his castle outside Nuremberg, Ribbentrop in Fuschl. Both reached the Berghof that evening, and the scenes that followed on May 11th and 12th were never forgotten by those present. Paul Schmidt, Hitler's interpreter, remembered that the Führer was "as appalled as though a bomb had struck the Berghof".[17] Jodl, the Chief of the Headquarters Operations Staff, recalled that never in his life had he seen "a man in such a fury as when Hitler heard that Hess had flown to England. He was in such a rage he was fit to burst . . . He was afraid the Italians would think he was negotiating peace behind their backs and leaving them in the lurch."[18]

Keitel, Hitler's Chief of Staff, remembered the Führer's distress no less clearly. "Hitler was walking back and forth with me in his big study . . . and he was touching his forehead and he said: 'Hess must have had a mental derangement . . . I can't recognise Hess. It is a different person.'"[19] To Julius Schaub, the Führer's intimate factotum, he gave a glimpse of his real fear:

If Hess really gets there, just imagine. Churchill has Hess in his grasp! What lunacy on Hess's part! They will give Hess some drug or other to make him stand before a microphone and broadcast whatever Churchill wants. I cannot challenge it, because it's Hess's voice and everybody knows it.[20]

Only two of the senior officers present in the Berghof during those fraught days showed no surprise at the turn of events. One was Goering, who (if Galland's account is to be believed) had known about Hess's flight the night before, if not earlier, yet now dissimulated. The other was Martin Bormann, Hess's ambitious deputy. According to Dr Robert Ley, the Party Organiser, Bormann remained completely indifferent to Hitler's deep emotion. He was "ice-cold, as though it did not affect him in the least; indeed, some seemed to detect signs of pleasure in him".[21]

Bormann's reaction is easy to interpret. He was nakedly ambitious: he had long been trying to usurp some of Hess's functions and now, at the age of only forty, he saw the road to far greater power suddenly and miraculously opened to him. Goering's motivation is more complex, and will be discussed later.

Meanwhile, Hitler's immediate problem was to decide how to break the news to the German nation. All he knew for certain was that Hess had disappeared. The British so far had said nothing. There was a chance that Hess had failed to reach his destination and had crashed into the North Sea. General Udet (also summoned to the Berghof) and Goering both said they doubted very much if Hess would manage the flight (again one wonders about Goering's special knowledge). The distance and navigational problems were too great, they said. According to Speer, Udet thought that because of the prevailing winds from the west Hess would probably "fly past England and into empty space".[22]

Goaded by fear that the British would make an announcement before the Germans did, Hitler dictated draft after draft of a press release to his press chief Otto Dietrich, and a statement was eventually broadcast on May 12th. This, the official Party communiqué, claimed that Hess had been strictly forbidden to fly by the Führer "on account of a progressive illness" from which he had suffered for some years, but that he had nevertheless "managed to get possession of an aircraft again". "Towards six p.m. on Saturday, May 10th," the release continued,

> Hess took off from Augsburg on a flight from which he has not returned. A letter he left behind is so incoherent as to give evidence of a mental derangement, which gives rise to fears that he is the victim of hallucinations . . . Under the circumstances it is to be feared that Party Member Hess has crashed or met with an accident somewhere.

(It is worth repeating here that Hess had never shown the slightest sign of mental derangement, and had certainly never been treated for any progressive illness.)

At ten p.m. the same evening (May 12th) the British Broadcasting Corporation put out the German communiqué in English. An hour later, the message was broadcast again with added comments, among them that Hess had been "bumped off by the Gestapo". Not until the following morning did the B.B.C. announce that Hess was in Great Britain: "the only country in which Hess felt safe from the Gestapo".

In Germany Hitler quickly developed the idea that Hess had gone mad. According to Frau Hess, her husband had himself suggested – at the end of the letter he left for Hitler – that the Führer should use this ploy. According to her, the letter finished, "And if this project . . . ends in failure . . . simply say that I was *crazy*."[23] No one else who saw the letter, or heard it read out, remembers any such remark, and all copies of the letter have now perished. But Hitler did not wait to find out whether the project was going to succeed or fail. He immediately seized on the lunacy theme and played it for all it was worth.

Goebbels, the propaganda specialist, was furious, considering quite rightly that any such admission would infuriate the German people: if Hess had been insane, why had he been allowed to continue in office? Goebbels's intuition proved sound: though he took up the lunacy theme in official releases, it was greeted with widespread incredulity. As the Secret Police organ *Aussenstelle Bunde* on May 13th put it, "People simply do not believe that mental aberration can in fact have been the reason." If the Secret Police's own news sheet admitted that people did not believe the propaganda line, what more need be said?

Returning to Berlin, Paul Schmidt, Hitler's interpreter, found himself sarcastically asked by an old man who helped with the garden, "Did *you* know that we were ruled by lunatics?"[24] As Ulrich von Hassell remarked in his diary, "Hess's sporting and technical performance alone showed that he could not be called crazy,"[25] and Baron Ernst von Weizsäcker, Secretary of State at the Foreign Office, later put his finger on the reason why the Hess episode seemed so fantastic. "Yesterday he had been a demigod, and today he was nothing but a pitiful idiot."[26]

The clearest feature of the whole business is that it gave Hitler a terrible shock. Hans Frank, his legal adviser, considered that he "never recovered from the personal injury which Hess's departure meant for him".[27] Many other senior Nazi officials were scarcely less amazed and dismayed. To Goebbels, for instance, the incident seemed "more serious than the desertion of an Army Corps".[28] In other words, Hess's former colleagues were astonished by what seemed entirely uncharacteristic behaviour. The Führer's most faithful friend and admirer, his lifelong confidant, his *spaniel*, some said, had dealt his master a stunning blow. That is the central point: to have flown off to Scotland would have been totally unlike the careful, painstaking, dogged and above all loyal Deputy.

As I have tried to show, there is no evidence from the German end, apart from the testimony of Pintsch, that Hess did try to fly to Scotland. It is extremely unfortunate that the letter which caused Hitler such distress has not survived. It is doubly unfortunate that

Frau Hess lost the copy which (she said) her husband left for her. Only in this lost document was the idea of flying ever mentioned.

It may be as well, at this stage, to recapitulate such facts as there are. Hess *was* training for some long-range flight. He *had* discussed the possibilities of an English peace with the Haushofers. Albrecht Haushofer *had* written to the Duke of Hamilton, but his letter of late 1940 had been intercepted by the British Intelligence Services. (It is said that Hess also wrote to Hamilton in January 1941, but there is no record of his letter having reached England.)[29] The idea all along had been that Hess might meet some intermediary on neutral soil.

In the absence of anything more solid, one has to rely on human memory, and even Frau Hess herself, when writing in *Prisoner of Peace* twenty years later, appears to have seen some aspects of the affair through a retrospectoscope of her own. She mentions, for instance, that her husband's adjutants spent much time packing and unpacking boxes. Yet Hess took no boxes with him when he left. Indeed, he took no luggage aboard the Messerschmitt; and the man who arrived in Scotland carried no papers except some handwritten notes, a few photographs and some visiting cards.

Frau Hess also recorded how, at the last moment, her husband suddenly began to lavish affection on his four-year-old son Buz. According to her, he spent far more time than usual with the child, taking him to the zoo, playing games, and so on. Perhaps he did: yet no such increase in parental concern had apparently preceded Hess's earlier attempts to reach Scotland.

Then there is the business of the Kalundborg radio signals. Kalundborg was a station in Denmark which broadcast classical music, and at set intervals sent out directional beams to help German bomber pilots reorientate themselves after raids on England. In Frau Hess's version – part of which came from Messerschmitt's colleague Theo Croneiss – her husband suddenly acquired a new radio set, and one day she found the dial adjusted to Kalundborg. She also heard that he had arranged with the station "to broadcast a favourite melody" at set intervals.

This can only be nonsense. To have broadcast a particular tune at fixed intervals would have given a pilot no special information, except that Kalundborg was the station to which he was listening. Passages of Wagner or the Moonlight Sonata could not be broadcast in a precise direction, like a beam of pulses. Moreover, the directional beam which Kalundborg did send out was of use only to pilots already well to the north over the North Sea; having peeled out of raids over the Midlands and North of England, they would acquire the beam and, having got their bearings, turn south for home. Because the station lay on almost exactly the same latitude as Holy Island (the point on the Northumbrian coast at which the Messerschmitt that crashed in Scotland made its landfall) it would have been possible, in theory, for Hess to use the beam in the final stages of his sea-crossing – yet the man who landed never mentioned the beam at all. Once again, the whole story has an air of unreality.

As for Frau Hess's claim that her husband, a careful and even obsessive man, left the key of the safe inside one of their child's toys, so that at some later date she would open the safe and find in it a copy of the letter he had written to the Führer – this seems equally far-fetched. There were a dozen safer ways in which he could have made sure that she eventually got a copy of the letter. Supposing the child had found the key, and, having played with it, dropped it in some out-of-the-way place – in the garden, for instance?

It is unsatisfactory, I know, to leave so many questions in the air. Yet even though they cannot now be answered, I still feel it is essential that they should be asked.

The most important unanswered question concerns the motives of Hess himself. Was he trying to reach Scotland on May 10th? If not, what was he trying to achieve? Did he merely set off for another training-flight, after which he planned to go on to Berlin, as he had told his wife? His ultimate aim – the reason for all his training sorties – is still obscure. Because he had maps of the Baltic at home, the most likely explanation is that he was hoping to meet some intermediary in the one neutral country in that area – Sweden. But, as he had said in his letter to Albrecht Haushofer, he was waiting until he got some positive response from the other side.

By a strange irony, a reply *did* come on the very evening of his flight, when Albrecht received a prearranged message from Herr Stahmer of the German Embassy in Madrid indicating that Sir Samuel Hoare, the British Ambassador, had agreed to an exploratory meeting. Albrecht was furious with Hess for wrecking the whole, carefully prepared peace plan, and sarcastically described his flight as the exploit of a "motorised Parsifal", likening him to the eponymous hero of Wagner's opera, following his hopeless solitary quest.

Still stranger, on the morning of the flight the Duke of Hamilton had set in motion an attempt to answer Haushofer's long-delayed letter. On May 10th Hamilton wrote to the Air Ministry saying that he would, if necessary, be prepared to go to Lisbon to meet an emissary of the German peace group, and suggesting that first he should write back to Haushofer, asking if the meeting was still possible.[30] But the

project was killed in infancy by the mysterious arrival of the Messerschmitt 110 off Lindisfarne at ten p.m. the same evening.

In the past few years more and more scraps of evidence have come
to light showing that the British Secret Service had wind of Hess's
plans, and were hoping to ensnare him. In 1940, for instance, M.I.5
sent the Americans a report saying that high-level intelligence was
being passed from an unidentified source in Britain to "*Abteilung
Pfeffer of Hess's office*", and Frau Hess has admitted privately that,
immediately after her husband had gone, she found a file called
"Pfeffer" which was in his safe and destroyed it before Bormann
could get hold of it.

In Moscow, Stalin certainly believed that Hess was lured by the
British (see page 102); but in 1981, Sir Maurice Oldfield, Director
General of M.I.6 after the war, told Phillip Knightley of the *Sunday
Times* that the head of Hess's Intelligence Service was working for the
Russians. If this is true, Hess's mission was in some degree manipu-
lated by the K.G.B.

Again, there are indications to show that the British were certainly
expecting some top-level German visitor in the first half of 1941. For
weeks staff on the airfield at Lympne stood by to receive some Nazi
luminary, and some people even hoped it would be Hitler, kidnapped
by his personal pilot, Hans Baur. But far more precise expectations
were revealed in the story told by Albert James Heal, a former
Yorkshire Area Secretary of the Transport and General Workers'
Union.[31]

On May 9th, 1941, Heal was asked to translate a cipher message
from Germany which had just reached Ernest Bevin (then Minister of
Labour) in London. Bevin rushed north with it to Leeds because Heal
was the only man who could interpret it, the sender being an English
girl whom he had known in South Wales before the war, and with
whom he had worked out a private code. Heal met Bevin in the
Queen's Hotel in Leeds, and translated the message sitting in a
bedroom. It said simply that Hess was on the point of launching his
peace initiative, and would fly at any moment. According to Heal,
Bevin, in a state of great excitement, at once telephoned Churchill in
his hearing and passed on the news.

M.I.6 was particularly active in Scandinavia, and it may or may not
be a coincidence that on the night the Messerschmitt arrived in
Scotland, all telecommunication links between Stockholm and Berlin
were cut, without explanation, for ten hours. Again, it may have been
a coincidence that on May 20th – the day the prisoner was moved out
of the Tower of London – a Luftwaffe aircrew with well-established

M.I.6 connections, Heinrich Schmidt and Paul Rosenberger, flew a Dornier 217 on a night sortie from Aalborg to Lincoln, where, by arrangement, they unloaded a package before taking off again.

These few straws in the wind show, if nothing else, that a great deal more clandestine contact existed between Germany and Britain than is suggested by official accounts.

6

The British Reaction

THE PILOT WHO came to Scotland first gave his name as Hauptmann Alfred Horn, but soon dropped this pretence and claimed that he was Rudolf Hess. Since I do not know this man's real name, I propose to refer to him as "the prisoner", "the patient", "Jonathan" (his code-name) or "Prisoner No. 7" – the title by which he became known after he had been condemned to life imprisonment in Spandau Gaol.

To the English doctors in charge of him, and in letters to Frau Hess, he himself gave a highly coloured description of his own arrival.[1] His first difficulty was the brilliance of the weather. The small clouds far below him "looked like pieces of ice floating on the sea, clear as crystal . . . There was not a trace of the 'dense carpet of clouds at about five hundred metres' predicted in the weather report." (Who had given him this report, he did not say – certainly not Pintsch in Augsburg, whose forecast – see page 70 – contained no such phrase.)

So clear was the evening that for a moment the pilot "even thought of turning back". What deterred him was the fear that his aircraft might be damaged by a night landing, and that after any such accident the "cat could be out of the bag". Apparently he was not in the least deterred by the chance that he might run out of fuel. Had he come from Augsburg, as he claimed, he could not possibly have got back there without refuelling. Yet he seems to have made no effort to conserve fuel, for by his own account he was flying at 2,000 metres, or about 6,000 feet, which was only half the economical altitude for a Messerschmitt 110.

In any case, he had a stroke of luck as he approached the English coast, for he found the land covered by a veil of mist, and he dived into it, coming down "at a truly terrific speed" and roaring across country "at some 750 kilometres per hour [470 m.p.h.] with my two-thousand horsepower engines at full-throttle". The visibility, he found, was "surprisingly good" – and just as well, for he flew over the

Border Country "at not more than five metres from the ground, even less at times". On he went, enjoying every minute of this hedge-hopping, and waving greetings to men still working in the fields on that soft, warm evening.

At ten forty he passed over Dungavel, the Duke of Hamilton's home, but "to avoid all possibility of error" he flew on to the west coast of Scotland, turned south until he saw a "towering rock" which rose out of the water just off the mainland "magnificently illumin-ated, a pale reddish colour". Using this as a landmark, he continued down the coast until he saw another natural marker, and then turned inland again.

Again, one is struck by the pilot's lack of concern about his fuel. If he had come from Augsburg, he would have been at the extreme limit of his range when he made his first pass over Dungavel, and would surely have parachuted or tried to land as soon as he saw the castle. (He had, he claimed, memorised every detail of the route and knew it backwards.) Yet instead of doing that, he flew on for another half hour – and more than another hundred miles.

The account of how he finally extricated himself from his machine is so breathless as to be scarcely intelligible, but certain points are clear. Having sighted the environs of Dungavel again, he said, he took the plane back up to 2,000 metres, switched off the engines and tried to stop the propellers. One engine was so hot that it continued to run for a few moments, but then it, too, ceased firing.

When the pilot tried to bale out, however, he was overtaken by severe difficulties: "In spite of all the care I had taken to find out about *everything* from my good friends at Messerschmitts, there was just *one* thing I had overlooked. I had never asked about how to jump; I thought it was too simple." When he opened the canopy and tried to climb out, he was trapped by the pressure of the air-stream, which held him against the back partition of the cockpit as if he "were screwed to it". As he struggled, the aircraft gradually lost height. He seemed to have come down almost to ground level, made a loop (while hanging half out of the cockpit), lost consciousness, re-started the engines without noticing that he did so, climbed back to an altitude safe for parachuting, and then, just as the aircraft ceased climbing and went into a vertical stall, flung himself away from it.

The account bristles with anomalies, but only one is important. Did the pilot really risk parachuting for the first time, at the age of forty-eight, in the half-dark? And why had he not been briefed on the essentials of emergency escape from the aircraft – always the first thing a pilot is taught, before he has even climbed into the machine?

Normally, no pilot is allowed to take off unless he has mastered the procedure for baling out.

Hess had been flying the Me 110 for six months, and had had plenty of time to plan his return to earth, wherever it was he was intending to land. When NJ + OQ reached Scotland there was still enough light for the pilot to land in a field, on a stretch of road, or (most obviously) on the Duke of Hamilton's private airstrip at Dungavel, and it seems that in spite of his hectic account of his parachute-jump, this is what he tried to do, mistaking Eaglesham House for Dungavel at the last moment.

Whether or not he performed all the death-defying manoeuvres he described hardly matters now. Whatever else he had done, he landed safely, except that he cracked a bone in one ankle and also chipped one vertebra.

His last-minute navigation had been none too successful, for he came to earth near the village of Eaglesham, some thirty miles from Dungavel, and before he could even start hobbling towards his objective on his injured ankle he was arrested, in a relaxed manner, by a local farmer named David McLean. When the Scotsman challenged him and asked if he was German, the man replied, "Yes. I am Hauptmann Alfred Horn," and said that he wanted to go to Dungavel House, as he had an important message for the Duke of Hamilton. (Aircraft experts agree that if he *did* crash-land, and was thrown clear, he would almost certainly have been in shock.)

The Duke was then a Wing-Commander in the R.A.F., and as it happened was on duty that night at Turnhouse Airport, outside Edinburgh, whence he had already despatched an aircraft in an attempt to intercept the incoming Messerschmitt as it was tracked across Scotland by eye, ear, and radar. News of the mysterious visitor soon reached him, and he arranged to see him in the morning.

The prisoner, meanwhile, was taken to a Home Guard hut at Busby, on the southern outskirts of Glasgow, where he astonished all present by lying flat out on the floor in a yoga-type posture of relaxation. When Army and R.A.F. officers arrived to search him, they found that he carried *no identification documents of any kind*. Apart from a sheaf of handwritten notes, he had no papers except several photographs, most of which (he said) were of himself as a child, and two visiting cards, one from Albrecht Haushofer and one from Karl Haushofer. For some reason he carried these separately, one in the pocket of his jacket and the other in his trousers. He also had a Leica camera and an extraordinary assortment of drugs, including vitamins, sedatives, and an elixir from a Tibetan lamasery for the relief of gall-bladder trouble. But why did he have no identity disc or card, no Party membership card, no driving licence, or anything with Rudolf Hess's name on it? When asked why he had no papers, he said at first that he had "left them all in Germany". Then, when pressed for documents, he produced from his tunic pocket an envelope stamped with a Munich postmark and addressed merely to Hauptmann Alfred Horn, München 9.[2]

Over his Luftwaffe uniform the man wore a leather flying-suit; and this – though the British could not know it at the time – bore a give-away defect. The suit in which Hess took off from Augsburg belonged (as I have shown) to Helmut Kaden, who had written his name in full on the inside pocket. The suit worn by the man who came to Scotland bore no name at all (for many years the garment hung in Spandau Gaol where I myself inspected it; but in 1987 it was stolen). In 1941 the British could not of course appreciate the significance of the fact that the name was missing.

The first serious attempt to interrogate the pilot was made by Major Graham Donald, a member of the Royal Observer Corps who had been on duty in Glasgow. As soon as he saw the man, Donald felt sure he was Hess and began to question him in German. But before he could get very far he was interrupted by the arrival of the police who, like everyone else, told him he was an idiot to believe that "Alfred Horn" was the Deputy Führer of Germany.[3]

In the early hours of Sunday the man was moved to Maryhill Barracks in Glasgow, where he spent the rest of the night in the sick bay, frequently demanding to be taken to the Duke. An Army officer who came in during the night, and who had several times seen the real Hess in Munich before the war, was confident that he recognised the pilot as Hitler's Deputy; and when Hamilton arrived at ten o'clock in the morning, the pilot lost no time in claiming to be Hess. As the Duke recorded in his official report:[4]

I entered the room of the prisoner accompanied by the Interrogating Officer and the Military Officer on guard.

The prisoner, who I had no recollection of ever having seen before, at once requested that I should speak to him alone. I then asked the other officers to withdraw, which they did.

The German opened by saying that he had seen me in Berlin at the Olympic Games in 1936 and that I had lunched in his house.[5] He said: "I do not know if you recognise me, but I am Rudolf Hess." He went on to say that he was on a mission of humanity and that the Führer did not want to defeat England and wished to stop fighting. His friend Albrecht Haushofer told him that I was an Englishman who, he thought, would understand his (Hess's) point of view. He had consequently tried to arrange a meeting with me in Lisbon (see Haushofer's letter to me dated 23 September 1940).

Hess went on to say that he had tried to fly to Dungavel and this was the fourth time he had set out, the first time being in December. On the three previous occasions he had turned back owing to bad weather. He had not attempted to make this journey during the time when Britain was gaining victories in Libya, as he thought his mission then might be interpreted as weakness, but now that Germany had gained success in North Africa and Greece, he was glad to come . . .

He then went on to say that the Führer was convinced that Germany would win the war, possibly soon, but certainly in one, two, or three years. He wanted to stop the unnecessary slaughter that would otherwise inevitably take place.

He asked me if I could get together leading members of my party to talk things over with a view to making peace proposals. I replied that there was now only one party in this country. He then said he could tell me what Hitler's peace terms would be. First, he would insist on an arrangement whereby our two countries would never go to war again.

I questioned him as to how that arrangement could be brought about, and he replied that one of the conditions, of course, was that Britain would give up her traditional policy of always opposing the strongest power in Europe. I then told him that if we made peace now, we would be at war again certainly within two years. He asked why, to which I replied that if a peace agreement was possible, the arrangement could have been made before the war started, but since Germany chose war in preference to peace at a time when we were most anxious to preserve peace, I could put forward no hope of a peace agreement now.

He requested me to ask the King to give him "parole", as he had come unarmed and of his own free will.

He further asked me if I could inform his family that he was safe by sending a telegram to Rothacker, Herzog Strasse 17, Zürich, stating that Alfred Horn was in good health.[6] He also asked that his identity should not be disclosed to the press . . .

From press photographs and Albrecht Haushofer's description of Hess, I believed that the prisoner was indeed Hess himself . . .

I have quoted the report at some length to show the political naivety of the proposals which the prisoner put forward. Indeed, the ideas mentioned are so vague that they can hardly be called proposals at all. How could the Deputy Führer of a country locked in mortal combat with Britain blandly suggest an "arrangement whereby our two countries would never go to war again"?

Probably Hamilton thought that some of the woolliness was due to linguistic difficulties. The prisoner had spoken in English, fairly well, but did not understand the questions put to him. One has the impression that the initial speech had been more or less learnt by heart. In any case, Hamilton felt sure the man *was* Hess, and for extra security had him transferred to the military hospital in Buchanan Castle at Drymen, near the southern end of Loch Lomond.

Because of the obvious importance of what had happened, he himself arranged to fly south as soon as possible and report to the Prime Minister. On Sunday afternoon he piloted a Hurricane fighter to Northolt, and there found a message ordering him to continue to Ditchley Park, the country house in Oxfordshire which Churchill used as his secret headquarters at weekends. As Albrecht Haushofer had promised, Hamilton did indeed have access to Churchill.

When he arrived, the Prime Minister's party was just finishing dinner, and although Hamilton broke his news almost at once, Churchill refused to discuss it until he had seen his film of the evening, the Marx Brothers in *Go West*. The Duke, worn out by the strain of being on duty for the past four nights, fell asleep in a chair. He woke just as the film had finished, and found himself, for the next three hours, going over every detail of the episode with a much-refreshed Prime Minister.

Whether or not Churchill had been expecting Hess, he seems to have been immediately suspicious that the man in Scotland might be an impersonator, sent for some ulterior motive. Next morning in London he conferred with the Foreign Secretary, Anthony Eden. Casting about for someone who had known pre-war Germany well and would be able to tell for certain whether the prisoner was Hess or not, Eden suggested Ivone Kirkpatrick, who was then Controller of European Services at the B.B.C. but before the war had been First Secretary at the British Embassy in Berlin, from 1933 to 1938. Kirkpatrick was ordered to return to Scotland with Hamilton and identify the prisoner positively. He too had "one horrid moment of misgiving at the possibility of being hoaxed by an expert impersonator",[7] but all the same felt confident of knowing Hess if he saw him.

The journey north was slow and uncomfortable, and its timing was particularly unfortunate. With some difficulty an ancient and ill-named Rapide aircraft had been recruited, and they took off in it from Hendon on the evening of Monday, May 12th. Headwinds forced the plane to land and refuel at Catterick, and after some delay there they did not reach Edinburgh until after nine thirty p.m. They had missed lunch, and just as they were about to have some supper an urgent telephone call came through from the Foreign Secretary, saying that German radio had just announced that Hess was missing. Eden therefore instructed the two envoys to proceed with their identification as soon as possible.

They went on by car, but because the driver did not know the road, and all the signposts had been removed or swivelled to baffle invaders, they lost their way and did not reach Buchanan Castle until midnight. They thus arrived in the worst possible condition to make an impartial assessment: cold, hungry, exhausted, and alerted by the report of the German broadcast to the fact that Hess was missing. The bizarre scene which followed in an attic room was described by Kirkpatrick himself in his memoirs, *The Inner Circle*:

A door was opened, and there, fast asleep on an iron bedstead, I saw Hess. He was dressed in grey flannel pyjamas issued to soldiers in hospital and the familiar brown army blanket covered his recumbent form. Lighting the room was a naked bulb with a white enamel shade. In order to diminish the glare an old newspaper had been wrapped around the whole contraption.

Accustomed as I was to the pomp and splendour in which the Nazi nabobs lived, I surveyed the scene in silence. Then we woke the prisoner up and after a moment of dazed uncertainty he recognised me and gave me a warm welcome.[8]

How long the "moment of dazed uncertainty" lasted is a matter of some doubt. But there is a significant difference between the account which Kirkpatrick gave in his complacent memoirs and the version presented in his official report. A note preserved in the Prime Minister's file on the incident records:

Hess did not recognise Mr K at once but the latter was able to draw him on various incidents of which they had been witness in Germany together and immediately it became plain that there could be no doubt whatever about his identity.[9]

This identification has always struck me as extremely suspect. Kirkpatrick was widely regarded as a second-rate diplomat, and it is as if someone just senior enough to carry weight had been sent with orders to make a formal identification that would pass muster in official reports. Far more significant is the fact that men who really *had* known Hess were not allowed anywhere near the prisoner (see page 96).

Next the German seized "a large packet of manuscript notes" and launched into a long-winded and fearfully boring discourse on Anglo-German relations. This harangue, as out of place as it was futile, lasted *four hours*.

After an hour and a half, with the prisoner still not having come to the point, the monologue was interrupted by another telephone call from the Foreign Secretary, who wanted to know how things were going. Kirkpatrick told him that he had already identified the prisoner as Hess "without any doubt whatsoever". Returning to the bedroom, he "found Hamilton comatose and Hess itching to get on with his speech".

By three a.m. the bundle of notes had almost all been used and he was evidently reaching the end of his peroration. But my patience was exhausted. I cut him short and summarily demanded that he should define the object of his visit. He replied that it was to convince the British Government of the inevitability of a German victory, and to bring about a peace by negotiation.[10]

The prisoner then outlined, with childish simplicity, the way in which German bombs would reduce the whole of England "to rubble" if Hitler was thwarted. But then, when Kirkpatrick asked whether the Führer still intended to invade England, the man "looked rather sheepish and said he really did not know". Hardly were those words out of his mouth when he claimed to be "in the Führer's closest confidence", and therefore "in a position to speak with complete authority".

He spoke, in fact, with almost complete vacuity, explaining how Germany would rule Europe and Britain her empire, the two joining forces to "see the Americans off". The only small difficulty was that Hitler would not negotiate a peace with Churchill, but this could be resolved if Kirkpatrick would open negotiations himself.

As Kirkpatrick afterwards remarked, "Except to correct some of Hess's wilder deviations from the truth, I did not interrupt his speech, which lasted until nearly four a.m." By then Hamilton, who had not understood much of the prisoner's German, was three-quarters asleep. Both envoys were desperately hungry, so they withdrew and got the night sister to cook them some scrambled eggs.

Feeling slightly better, they drove back to Edinburgh, where they arrived at six a.m. and got a couple of hours' sleep. At eight thirty Kirkpatrick telephoned the Foreign Office in London and gave a résumé of what the prisoner had said, only to be told that "the Government were embarrassed by the whole affair and did not know exactly how to handle it".[11]

In retrospect the prisoner's behaviour seems grotesquely inappropriate. He showed no sign of normal civility or manners, and no sensitivity whatever. He asked no useful questions. He made no sensible proposals. Instead, he bludgeoned his audience, in the middle of the night, with four hours of half-baked history and political claptrap. It seems incredible that Kirkpatrick really thought the prisoner boring him so interminably was the Deputy Führer of Germany – a man of wide political experience, of natural good manners, and of proven skill in handling negotiations. Was it conceivable that a man of Hess's background and career should behave in this way? As Kirkpatrick himself put it, the prisoner "seemed to have little grasp, for a leader" of what was going on in Germany. Why did he need so many handwritten notes to remind himself of the generalisations that he poured out? Why had he not brought properly typed notes or proposals with him?

Yet from that first "positive" identification made in the dimly lit attic of Buchanan Castle flowed most of the decisions taken afterwards about the prisoner. It must be borne in mind that the identification was made in the most unsatisfactory circumstances possible. First, Kirkpatrick already knew that the man claimed to be Hess; second, he heard on the radio that the real Hess was missing, just before he saw him; and third, the prisoner *looked* exactly like Hess.

Behind the scenes in London a lively debate broke out as to how the Government should handle the strange arrival. On the evening of May 12th, when German radio announced that Hess had disappeared, Churchill telephoned Eden "immensely excited" by the news and wanting to make an immediate statement.[12] The B.B.C. therefore put out their brief announcement about Hess being in Britain, and Churchill and Eden together began to concoct a suitable longer statement.

For various reasons, however, no statement was ever given. Like Churchill, Duff Cooper, the Minister of Information, felt that a statement should certainly be made, but the view was opposed by both Eden and Lord Beaverbrook, the Minister of State in charge of Air Production, and the last two won the argument. "Now this is bad," wrote Harold Nicolson, Parliamentary Secretary to the Ministry of Information, in his diary. "The belief will get around that we are hiding something . . . The real fact is that we cannot get maximum propaganda value out of this incident both at home and abroad. I feel a terrible lack of central authority in all this."[13]

Largely through the energetic initiative taken by the *Glasgow Daily Record*, the full story of events in Scotland broke in the press, and for the next few days it dominated newspaper headlines. So much for the prisoner's request that his identity should be kept secret. The huge press coverage added further conviction to the theory that the prisoner *was* Hess: with every newspaper in the world shouting out that Rudolf Hess was in Scotland, the Deputy Führer's arrival on British soil became more than ever a *fait accompli*.

As Nicolson feared, the Government's silence made speculation rage, and the wild range of ideas propounded was neatly satirised in A. P. Herbert's poem, "Hess":

> He is insane. He is the Dove of Peace.
> He is Messiah. He is Hitler's niece.
> He is the one clean honest man they've got.
> He is the worst assassin of the lot.
> He has a mission to preserve mankind.
> He's non-alcoholic. He was a "blind".
> He has been dotty since the age of ten,
> But all the time was top of Hitler's men . . .[14]

While rumours seethed in public, Churchill gave Eden instructions about how the prisoner should be handled:

1. On the whole it will be more convenient to treat him as a prisoner of war, under the War Office and not the Home Office; but also as one against whom grave political charges may be preferred. This man, like other Nazi leaders, is potentially a war criminal, and he and his confederates may well be declared outlaws at the close of the war. In this case his repentance would stand him in good stead.
2. In the meanwhile he should be strictly isolated in a convenient house not too far from London, and every endeavour should be made to study his mentality and get anything worthwhile out of him.

3. His health and comfort should be ensured, food, books, writing materials, and recreation being provided for him. He should not have any contacts with the outside world or visitors except as prescribed by the Foreign Office. Special guardians should be appointed. He should see no newspapers and hear no wireless. He should be treated with dignity, as if he were an important general who had fallen into our hands.[15]

The Government's dilemma was not eased by the existence of *The Flying Visit*, a short satirical novel by Peter Fleming, published the year before. With his strange penchant for anticipating future events, Fleming had inexplicably foreshadowed the Hess affair. In *The Flying Visit* it is Hitler himself, rather than his Deputy, who parachutes into England at night, but the consternation of the British Government, who do not in the least want him, and have no idea what to do with him, is uncannily like that which gripped Whitehall in May 1941.

On May 14th Kirkpatrick was instructed to interview the prisoner again, so he returned to Buchanan Castle with the Duke of Hamilton; but neither on that day, nor on the next, when he saw the prisoner for the third time, did Kirkpatrick get the least bit of sense out of him. Indeed, when he asked whether there was any chance that Hitler might invade Russia, and "pressed him again and again" on the subject, the prisoner's answers were so vague that Kirkpatrick got the impression he "was so much out of things that he really did not know".[16] Such evasiveness could, it is true, have been that of a man still deeply loyal to Hitler, covering up his knowledge of the imminent Operation Barbarossa; but, taken with the rest of the prisoner's political inadequacy, it looks far more like the reaction of a man who really did know nothing of Hitler's intentions, towards Russia or anywhere else. (When he was told that Germany *had* invaded Russia on June 22nd, he merely made the ambiguous remark, "So they have started after all.")

Almost at once the prisoner began to exhibit a weakness of character in no way corresponding to the dogged determination which had always been the hallmark of the real Hess. In running the huge Nazi Party machine and resisting the challenge of ambitious colleagues such as Goering and Martin Bormann, Hess had always shown exceptional resilience and tenacity: yet now, after only *four days* in captivity, the prisoner had become totally demoralised by his lack of progress and had begun to show signs of the persecution complex which haunted him for most of his time in Britain. The sentries guarding his door, he told Kirkpatrick, had been issued with exceptionally heavy boots, so that they could annoy him the more with their stamping. His food was being systematically poisoned.

On the evening of May 16th he was secretly taken south on the overnight train from Glasgow to London, and he spent the next four days in the Tower of London. The idea that he should go to the Tower had come from the War Office, and there on May 19th he was interrogated for the first time by a professional – Major Frank Foley of M.I.6, who from 1920 to 1939 had worked in Berlin, ostensibly as Passport Control Officer in the British Consulate, but also as controller of the Secret Service in the German capital. Married to a German wife, speaking German perfectly, familiar with German affairs, he was ideally equipped to ferret out the prisoner's secrets.

And what did he discover? Nothing. After ninety minutes in the Tower he gave up in disgust and reported that the man was not worth talking to, since he knew nothing at all.[17]

Foley's first report is not available for public scrutiny; but it clearly raised in some British minds the most acute doubts about the prisoner's identity. Why should Eden have sent urgently to the British Embassy in Cairo asking for copies of letters written by Hess, unless he wanted to compare the handwriting on them with that of the man in custody? On June 6th the Embassy duly obliged, sending letters written by Hess to his parents in Alexandria during 1935, 1937 and 1938, *together with copies of the envelopes*. And how had such correspondence come to be in British hands anyway, unless it had been intercepted by the Secret Services? After the war, Eden professed the blandest ignorance about what lay behind the lone aviator's arrival – but clearly he knew more than he ever let on.

So, I feel certain, did Churchill – even though, on the surface, he was as puzzled as anybody. On May 17th he sent the President of the United States a summary of the situation in a long telegram headed "Former Naval Person to President Roosevelt", to which he added a note of his own:

Hess seems in good health and not excited, and no ordinary signs of insanity can be detected. He declares that this escapade is his own idea and that Hitler was unaware of it beforehand. If he is to be believed, he expected to contact members of a "peace movement" in England, which he would help to oust the present Government. If he is honest and if he is sane, this is an encouraging sign of the ineptitude of German Intelligence Service. He will not be ill-treated, but it is desirable that the Press should not romanticise him and his adventure. We must not forget that he shares responsibility for all Hitler's crimes and is a potential war criminal whose fate must ultimately depend upon the decision of the Allied Governments.

Mr President, all the above is for your own information. Here we think it best to let the Press have a good run for a bit and keep the Germans guessing. The German officer prisoners of war here were greatly perturbed by the news, and I cannot doubt there will be deep misgivings in the German armed forces about what he may say.[18]

In anticipating "deep misgivings in the German armed forces", the Prime Minister was perfectly right. Not only members of the German services but (as we have seen) the highest officials of the Nazi State were thrown into confusion by Hess's disappearance. Goebbels, the propaganda chief, was so shattered by the incident that he retired to bed for three days, pretending to be ill. Thereafter he became more and more amazed that the British made no propaganda use of their star captive: that they failed to make any capital out of him was, in Hitler's view also, the greatest political mistake of the entire war. Even if they could not administer the mind-bending drug feared by Hitler and force the prisoner to broadcast live to the German people (as a superior answer to Lord Haw-Haw), they could surely at least have wrought havoc on German morale by sending out damaging statements which the Deputy Führer was supposed to have made.[19]

Why did the British never do any such thing? Why did they fail to use such a potentially powerful propaganda weapon? Why, moreover, did they refuse to allow any photograph of the prisoner to be taken during his entire four years in England? Why was Harold Nicolson, on behalf of the Ministry of Information, obliged to make the fatuous statement in the House of Commons that "such ignominity should not be put on this fundamentally decent man"?[20] *Ignominity?* How could it have been ignominious for *any* member of the enemy forces to be photographed in the middle of a bloody war, when hundreds of people were being killed or left homeless by nightly air-raids? The statement is so absurd that even now it makes one angry. On May 15th, Duff Cooper wrote to the Prime Minister asking permission to send a photographer to take pictures of the prisoner. Even if the photographs were not released at once, he suggested, it would do no harm for the Government to have pictures in its possession:

I would send a photography expert to take a series of photographs which would not present the subject in too flattering a light, which I believe a photographer can very easily arrange. These, if it were approved later, would be for publication in this country. At the same time he might take other pictures in which the subject could be made to look his best, and these might be useful for distribution over Germany . . . Incidentally, if he were to escape, an unlikely but not impossible occurrence, recent pictures of him might be of great value.

The press at present only have photographs taken before the war in Germany and published with official approval.

I cannot think that the prisoner can possibly object to being photographed, [and even] if he did object, is there the slightest reason why we should pay any attention whatever?

On this memorandum Churchill noted, in handwriting, "Wait a few days. He is on the move."[21]

So he was, but only for the next week – and the prohibition on photography was never lifted. There is only one explanation of the Government's attitude which seems to make sense: that the British did realise, or anyway suspect, that they were victims of an elaborate deception. The refusal to allow *any* photograph strongly suggests that they were not confident they had the right man, that they were afraid to publish a photograph for fear that it would not correspond to the appearance of the real Hess. The failure to use the prisoner for propaganda purposes seems in general to indicate a lack of confidence; it is as if the British feared that the real Hess might suddenly reappear in Germany and so ridicule any claims they had made.

It has been argued that Churchill wanted to play down the Hess affair because he was afraid that any serious talk of peace with Germany might undermine British morale: a nation fighting for its life might well be softened by the idea that a chance of peace existed. For this reason, it is said, Churchill consigned the prisoner to psychiatric care and put about the idea that Hess was dotty.

No doubt the Prime Minister was anxious to conceal from the public the strength and social standing of the British peace group, which included some of the highest in the land. Among those named by Albrecht Haushofer as being in favour of an Anglo-German agreement were Lord Halifax, Foreign Secretary from 1938 to 1940, and his deputy R. A. Butler, Lord Dunglass (the Prime Minister's Parliamentary Private Secretary), the Duke of Hamilton, Owen O'Malley (British Minister to Hungary), William Strang (Assistant

Under-Secretary of State at the Foreign Office), Lord Lothian (British Ambassador in Washington), Oliver Stanley (Secretary of State for War) and Sir Samuel Hoare (Ambassador in Madrid). The German peace-makers hoped that the Royal Family itself could be – or perhaps already had been – drawn into their intrigues, for the Duke of Windsor had made ill-judged contacts with the Nazis in Lisbon during 1940. According to one report, he had even met Hess there, although this story is poorly corroborated.

Clearly it would have been damaging for the power of the Halifax clique to be made public in 1941. Equally, it might have given a dangerous boost to the group's aspirations if word got out that a serious peace initiative had arrived from Germany. Yet such considerations scarcely account for the Prime Minister's extreme caution. As Harold Nicolson remarked, Churchill was uncharacteristically indecisive over the issue. He could have handled it in a far more positive way. He could have ridiculed Hess and his mission, saying with truth that the envoy appeared to represent no one but himself. He could easily have gone further than that: here (he could have said) was clear evidence of the incipient disintegration of the Nazi hierarchy. Clearly the Reich was cracking up under the strain of war. This was England's great chance to smash Nazism once and for ever. Instead of being seen as something sinister and dangerous to Britain, Hess's apparent defection could have been seized upon as a great new incentive.

In the event, Churchill made no announcement at all; and in the background great care was taken to ensure that no one who had known Hess at all well could gain access to the prisoner. Immediately after Foley's first abortive interview, another M.I.6 officer with a thorough knowledge of Germany did his best to find out what was really going on. Sir Roger Chance had also worked in Berlin, nominally as Press Attaché at the British Embassy, before the war, and he had got to know Hess well enough to stay with him several times. Yet now, when he sought permission to see the prisoner, it was immediately refused.[22] Other men who had known the Deputy Führer and tried, but were not allowed, to meet the captive included M. J. Lipski, the former Polish Ambassador in Berlin, the journalist Sefton Delmer and Wing-Commander Frederick Winterbotham, the Secret Services' Chief of Air Intelligence.

A particularly curious incident occurred during the prisoner's few days in the Tower. One night the authorities summoned Charles Fraser-Smith, who supplied M.I.5, M.I.9 and other secret departments with special equipment such as compasses made into buttons.

Hess in his heyday.

After the crash – the main fuselage
section showing the markings NJ+OQ.

The twisted remains of the guns from
Hess's aircraft. Why were they packed
with grease?

The wreckage under guard in Scotland.

Arriving at the Tower, he saw a figure lying asleep (or drugged) at one side of the room, and he was asked if he could make an exact replica of the man's Luftwaffe uniform. In his book *The Secret War of Charles Fraser-Smith*, published in 1981, he described how he went away, made and delivered a copy within four hours – but what the replica was wanted for, he never knew. Later he admitted privately that he always assumed that the man who flew to Scotland was a double.

Yet another suspicious feature of the prisoner's first few days in England was the alleged rescue mission said to have been mounted on the night of Sunday, May 18th.[23] That afternoon, it is said, some secret agency monitoring German radio had intercepted "by unusual means" a message apparently intended for 11 Group, R.A.F. The message warned that a bomb attack would be made on Luton Hoo, in Bedfordshire, at one a.m. next morning, as a diversion to cover the descent of German parachutists, whose mission was to rescue Hess from the nearby R.A.F. Interrogation Centre at Cockfosters, to which most German prisoners of war were taken.

According to Major John McCowen, an R.A.F. intelligence officer who took part in the defensive action, all available searchlights and anti-aircraft guns were rushed into the area. The Home Guard was deployed around the spot where the landing was expected, and "with a supreme effort by all concerned the trap was set with minutes rather than hours to spare".

After a long wait the action proceeded exactly as forecast. A few bombs fell, and although the searchlights failed to pick up the aircraft which were audible overhead, their beams did "flick over . . . one or more falling parachutes". The intensive activity which followed was "suddenly called off" at breakfast-time, but McCowen later heard that two parachutists, with German labels only half torn out of their plain clothes, had been arrested by the Special Branch. Later, it was said, the men were executed.

To James Leasor, the author who gave McCowen's account of the night's events, the incident "bore the stamp of poor preparation that had characterised Hess's own flight". To me it bears the stamp of total unreality. For one thing, Hitler had already disowned Hess and did not want him back. For a second the alleged rescuers had no means of extricating him from the country. For a third, the Germans were not so incompetent as to be unable to tear labels out of clothes efficiently. For a fourth, they were not such fools as to think that two men could break into the heavily guarded, maximum-security centre at Cock-fosters – to which, in any case, the man they were supposed to be after had never been taken. Even if their mission had been to *kill* the Deputy Führer, rather than rescue him, they would never have got anywhere near him.

The entire incident sounds to me like a hastily staged mock-up. But to what end, and to fool whom, was the episode arranged? I should very much like to know the nature of the "unusual means" whereby the warning message was intercepted: whether it came from Germany, or emanated from some British Intelligence source intent on creating a diversion. Was the whole raid engineered by Himmler, or by Admiral Canaris, head of the German Secret Service, who used this method of a parachute-drop heralded by a prior warning on other occasions? Or was the incident laid on *by the British* to add credibility to the claim that Hess had reached British soil? At this distance of time the mystery is not likely to be solved. It remains yet one more unsatisfactory element in a tangle of untidy loose ends.

On Churchill's initiative the prisoner was soon delivered into the hands of the psychiatrists. As one of them later wrote, their task was threefold: to keep the man safe from escape, safe from himself, and safe from attack. The authority who guided them throughout was Churchill himself.

On May 21st "Jonathan" was transferred from London to Mytchett Place, a gloomy and run-down Victorian red-brick mansion near Aldershot, which was hastily fortified with barbed-wire entanglements and slit trenches to make a secure but comfortable open gaol. Inside, the house was equipped with hidden microphones, and a team of personable young officers from the Brigade of Guards was recruited, both to provide security and to furnish the prisoner with agreeable company. Into the mess, also, came three officers of the Political Intelligence Service – but needless to say, neither the men nor the microphones picked up the slightest scrap of worthwhile information. For security cover, the place became known as "Camp Z".

Whatever his real thoughts about the prisoner, Churchill still reckoned it worthwhile to humour his constant requests for an interview with a representative of the Cabinet. Hoping it might yet prove possible to discover something of Hitler's secret intentions, the Prime Minister arranged for the prisoner to be visited by the Lord Chancellor, Lord Simon, together with Ivone Kirkpatrick. Because the decision had already been taken to minimise interest in the captive, it was essential that the public should not know that a high-level official visit was being paid to him. For the occasion Simon therefore became a distinguished psychiatrist, "Dr Guthrie", and Kirkpatrick a colleague of his, "Dr Mackenzie". In preparing the arrangements, the prisoner was referred to simply as "J" or "Jonathan".

He himself knew that the alleged doctors would in fact be politicians and he was told the date of their visit – June 10th. Yet as the day approached he became extraordinarily nervous. The real Hess would surely have welcomed an interview with Simon, for here at last was a chance to state his case to a man close to the centre of power: this was what he said he had wanted all along. "Jonathan", by contrast, became so agitated as to be almost *hors de combat*.

In the words of one of the doctors looking after him, the announcement of the official visit "coincided with a remarkable increase in the prisoner's restlessness and anxiety". The many "cultured and highly intelligent officers" surrounding him got the impression that he had an inferiority complex and "cut a very poor figure by comparison with the average member of the intellectual classes. He himself made quite pathetic pleas from time to time that he felt at a disadvantage and that he was no negotiator."[24]

Considering that the prisoner probably never *had* been involved in political negotiations, his apprehension is hardly surprising. It is clear, now, that he was afraid the fraudulent nature of his mission might be exposed by discussion with a politician of superior intelligence and perception.

Did it not seem extraordinary at the time, to the men in charge of him, that an officer who had run the entire Nazi Party organisation, who had made countless political speeches before immense audiences, and who had outwitted formidable opponents at the negotiation table, should behave in so craven a fashion at the prospect of merely meeting a member of the British Government? How could it be that he turned to jelly at the idea of an encounter he had continually requested? Fortunately for the prisoner, Hitler and Goebbels had been pumping out statements which developed the theme of Hess's mental illness of long-standing, so the British naturally believed that their captive was to some degree psychotic.

In the event, the three-hour meeting with Kirkpatrick and Simon, which took place on June 10th, proved no less of a fiasco than the previous official encounters. On the morning the prisoner declined to get up, so that his visitors were obliged to have lunch without knowing whether or not they were going to be able to see him. At the last moment, however, he pulled out of his funk, "dressed with great care in his Air Force uniform, and was in a very confident and almost arrogant mood".[25]

Again he bombarded his visitors with a mixture of threats, history and cajolery which proved absolutely futile. Yet the fact that nothing useful emerged from the discussion was due at least in part to the ineptitude of the interrogators: not once did either of them cross-question the prisoner sharply or press him hard for details about his own background, his relationship with Hitler, or his ability to do something practical about the woolly proposals he had brought with him. Instead, they merely made a few gentle attempts to bring him down to earth, and answered his more menacing remarks with bland, self-satisfied generalisations such as, "I do not think that that particular argument will be very good for the British Cabinet, because, you know, there is a good deal of courage in this country, and we are not very fond of threats!"[26]

One extract from the official transcript will show the futility of the proceedings. Dr Guthrie (Lord Simon) spoke mainly in English, Dr Mackenzie (Kirkpatrick) mainly in German, and an interpreter was present to resolve any linguistic problems. Having established that the prisoner had come without Hitler's knowledge or authority, the interrogators tried to discover whether any other members of the Nazi hierarchy subscribed to his ideas about peace.

DR GUTHRIE: Are there other important people in Germany who share the views you want me to listen to?
JONATHAN: The ideas are the ideas of the Führer – and they are what will decide the issue, once and for all.
DR MACKENZIE: And you know nothing of the other people's ideas?
JONATHAN: They agree with the Führer as a matter of course. It is an absolute matter of course. If the Führer says to them, "My ideas are so-and-so", they say, "*Jawohl!*"
DR MACKENZIE: Yes, but are the other people in the picture?
JONATHAN: That I don't know. I don't know if some of them are in the picture, or how far the Führer has talked with some of them.
DR MACKENZIE: You really can't be certain whether your ideas tally with the ideas of the leading personalities? You can only say that if the ideas are those of the Führer, they will be approved by the others. But you can't be sure whether the leading personalities already hold these views?
JONATHAN: I don't know. But anyway, it's meaningless.[27]

Even though the conversation remained on this superficial level throughout, the interview left the prisoner in "a state of virtual collapse". The doctors imagined that his exhaustion was due to the "overwhelming mental superiority of his British antagonist". Doubtless this was even truer than they suspected; doubtless also, the strain had been enormously increased by fear of exposure.

For the interrogators, the three-hour conversation served no purpose whatever, unless to secure some sort of official record of an attempt at drawing the prisoner out. It is no longer clear precisely what brief Simon and Kirkpatrick had been given, but the banality of the exchanges suggests that the interview was conducted as much as anything for the record, so that there would be something, at least, in Government files.

Not surprisingly, Kirkpatrick afterwards described the session as a "Mad Hatter's tea party", and an "unequal struggle", in spite of Lord Simon's efforts to lift the conversation on to a reasonable plane.[28] For Kirkpatrick, the prisoner had become something of a *bête noire*. Before their first encounter in Scotland he had been forced to abandon a much-needed steak uneaten because of the haste demanded by the Foreign Secretary. To arrange for the prisoner to be moved to London he had had to call off a proposed round of golf; and for the third interview he had had to return suddenly from a private trip to Ireland.

That was almost the end of Churchill's attempts to extract useful information from the prisoner – although in September 1941 he did send Lord Beaverbrook, then a member of the War Cabinet, to see him and get a seasoned sceptic's opinion as to whether or not he was sane. Once again the news of an impending visit by a highly placed politician threw "Jonathan" into confusion: he said he was too ill to undertake an important interview, and, according to the doctor, "indulged in dramatic gestures".[29] But then, when Beaverbrook arrived under the alias "Dr Livingstone", he talked to him for an hour, and said afterwards that he had enjoyed the conversation. Beaverbrook decided that the man was of perfectly sound mind, but once again nothing emerged from the meeting except banalities, and thereafter the prisoner was left to moulder in the hands of the psychiatrists.

One is forced to conclude that the British acted either with great naivety and incompetence, or with great deviousness. I now feel certain that they realised their prisoner was an impostor, but for some reason decided to cover the fact up.

To this day members of the Foreign Office are shifty and evasive when asked about the Hess affair. Several times in the course of my enquiries I put questions, either directly or through intermediaries, about whether there was any suspicion in the Foreign Office that the last prisoner in Spandau might not be Hess at all. On every occasion the enquiry produced a sudden silence, a marked fall in temperature, an offhand remark such as "I shouldn't be surprised", or some equally inadequate response. It may or may not be significant that two Foreign Office files on Hess were removed from the Public Record Office in July 1978 by the Foreign Office itself and not returned for six months. They both show every sign of having had all contentious material carefully removed.

Nor is the behaviour of the Ministry of Defence any more re-assuring. In 1941 the wreck of the Messerschmitt was brought from Scotland to England, and on May 16th the *Daily Telegraph* announced that it would be exhibited in London next day. On the newspaper cutting Churchill scrawled in his own hand, "See that this is stopped and report forthwith."[30] His order was carried out, and the aircraft, having spent some time locked up in Oxford, passed into the care of the Imperial War Museum. Today the remains are at the Museum's depot near Duxford, outside Cambridge.

It is a well-known fact that the Ministry of Defence keeps a dossier on every plane crash in the United Kingdom which involves a military aircraft. Yet no records are available of the crash of the Me 110. Herr Ebert, head of the historical department at Messerschmitt, has repeatedly written to the Ministry asking for records of the crash to be made available to him, but far from collecting any information, he has not even been favoured with the civility of a reply. One is hardly surprised to find that in the Public Record Office, although one War Office file on the Hess affair is now open for inspection, another is closed for seventy years.

Why, if Churchill himself was aware of the deception, did he keep up the pretence? The Deputy Führer's supposed presence in Britain proved a severe embarrassment in the Government's relations with Russia. When Beaverbrook went to Moscow in September 1941, as head of a delegation to discuss arms supplies to the Soviet Union, Stalin accused England of using Hess as a line of communication with Hitler and of planning to abandon Russia to fight Germany alone. When Churchill saw Stalin in 1944, the Soviet dictator's line was much the same. As Churchill himself wrote later:

He asked me at the dinner table what was the truth about the Hess mission . . . I had the feeling that he believed there had been some deep negotiation or plot for Germany and Britain to act together in the invasion of Russia which had miscarried. Remembering what a wise man he is, I was surprised to find him silly on this point. When the interpreter made it plain that he did not believe what I said, I replied through my interpreter, "When I make a statement of facts within my knowledge I expect it to be accepted."

Stalin received this somewhat abrupt response with a genial grin. "There are lots of things that happen even here in Russia which our Secret Service do not necessarily tell me about."

I let it go at that.[31]

Even at the end of the war Churchill was still extremely sensitive about the issue. In April 1945 the Duke of Hamilton, who was going to a conference in America, wanted to take with him a letter from the Prime Minister explaining the part he had played in the affair. Churchill refused to give him one, remarking in a minute:

Surely it is not for the Duke of Hamilton to undertake this particular task . . . I have never been asked to do such a thing before. The Russians are very suspicious of the Hess episode, and I have had a lengthy argument with Marshal Stalin about it in Moscow in October, he steadfastly maintained that Hess had been invited over by our Secret Service. It is not in the public interest that the whole of this affair should be stirred at the present moment.[32]

Throughout the war the Government's handling of the affair was ambiguous, to say the least. Years afterwards the American psychiatrist Maurice Walsh recorded that during 1950 he met in Mexico a British psychiatrist who, "as a medical officer in the British Army", had examined the man known as Hess in 1941. According to Walsh, this doctor had "actually considered Hess to be schizophrenic", but he "was requested not to report this by a very high official of the British Government, because this would have an adverse effect on the conduct of the war and would influence the Nazi War Crimes Trial".[33]

In conversation with the present author,[34] Walsh revealed that the psychiatrist in question was Brigadier Rees, and that the report which he was asked to modify was one submitted shortly before the Nuremberg trials in 1945. The story exposes the fact that the British wanted to have it all ways as far as their prisoner was concerned: in 1941 they wanted him thought mad enough to justify his being kept in psychiatric care, and yet in 1945 they wanted him declared sane enough to stand trial at Nuremberg, where (the chances were) he would be sentenced either to death or to life imprisonment.

As Ivone Kirkpatrick remarked in his memoirs, the Hess affair was "one of the oddest in history, and the oddest thing about it was that it was not in character".[35] That was precisely the point. If any of the other Nazi ministers had flown to Scotland, it would have been surprising, but afterwards understandable. The Hess affair *never* became understandable, for the Deputy Führer was the one man close to Hitler whose loyalty was such that he would never have flown off to the enemy territory without his leader's consent.

The most tantalising questions of all are those about the prisoner's own state of mind. What did *he* suppose his position was? Did he believe that he had carried off his bluff, or did he realise that his posturing had been seen through? Why – whatever he thought – did he maintain silence, not only during the war, but at Nuremberg and throughout his life sentence in Spandau?

The only plausible answer is that he *did* know that his cover had been blown, but that someone – probably one of the Secret Service officers – quietly made it clear to him that if he did not go through with his charade, he would be killed. If this was indeed what happened, it would make sense of his persecution mania: his fear of being poisoned was not irrational, but based on the very real possibility his captors might decide at any moment that his usefulness had come to an end. Repatriation during the war would have been equally disastrous: he would certainly have been executed for treason, whoever he was. For the wretched prisoner, there was no way out. He was trapped.

7

A Case for Treatment

"HE IS A VERY difficult and uncooperative patient indeed," said one doctor's report,[1] and the remark was an accurate summing-up of the prisoner during his four-year stay in Britain. The doctors in charge of him were constantly puzzled by the oddity of his behaviour: they were never certain whether the ills of which he complained without ceasing were real or imaginary, whether the persecution feelings from which he appeared to suffer were genuine or simulated, whether he was mentally unsound or perfectly sane.

Their difficulty in assessing his true state of health, mental and physical, was bad enough during the war, but it became even greater during the Nuremberg trial, when he suddenly revealed to the court that the loss of memory which had appeared to plague him intermittently for the past four years had in fact been simulated "for tactical reasons". If he had never really lost his memory, had he ever really experienced the various ailments and feelings of persecution about which he had made such a fuss? Or had he been acting all the time?

From the start the psychiatrists who looked after him at Mytchett Place noticed some odd features. Hess, they knew, had been a vegetarian, with fastidious eating habits. But "Jonathan", though often intensely suspicious that he was about to be poisoned, ate enormous quantities of all kinds of indifferent food, including beef and chicken curry, at a positively alarming rate. Besides, his table-manners were hardly those of a strictly brought-up German of the upper middle class. He sat slumped at meals with his elbows splayed out sideways on the table; he tore bread into great chunks, drained his soup by raising the plate to his lips, and shovelled solid food into his mouth like a boy racing for a second helping.

A third strange fact was that he did not know the rules of tennis, and said he had never played,[2] even though tennis had always been a popular game among the expatriate colony in Alexandria, where the real Hess had been brought up. (Frau Hess confirms that her husband in fact played tennis well and with enthusiasm.[3]) A fourth oddity was that the prisoner did not know the names of common flowers in the garden at Mytchett, even though the Hess family had had large gardens in Alexandria and in Munich, where well-to-do people filled their houses with cut flowers and pot plants as a matter of course.[4] (These two last peculiarities came to light well before the prisoner began to suffer from – or feign – amnesia.)

Nor did the prisoner exhibit any of the personal mannerisms which had so irritated the real Hess's colleagues. Never in Britain, at Nuremberg or in Spandau was he known to whistle or fool around with his chair in the manner described by Hanfstaengl.

Another anomaly would have come home to the doctors more clearly if they had been able to study recent photographs of the real Hess. Frau Hess insists that her husband was in good physical shape when he left Germany, and had not lost weight recently. The man who reached Scotland was, by contrast, spectacularly thin, even cadaverous. A vivid impression of him was drawn by Major H. V. Dicks, the psychiatrist who took charge of him towards the end of May:

> The contrast between photographs previously seen in the illustrated papers and the man as he now appeared was prodigious. He was gaunt, hollow-cheeked, pale and lined; whereas the full face produced an impression of baleful strength, the profile disclosed a receding forehead, exaggerated supra-orbital ridges covered with thick, bushy eyebrows, deeply sunken eyes, irregular teeth which tended to be permanently bared over the lower lip in the manner of "buck teeth", a very weak chin and receding lower jaw . . . The whole man produced the impression of a caged great ape, and "oozed" hostility and suspicion.[5]

Even given that the man was under considerable stress, it is medically impossible that in little over two weeks he could have lost enough weight to produce this kind of difference, especially as he was eating plenty and taking little exercise.

Another curiosity was that although the prisoner had brought with him an amazing selection of esoteric medicines, he never made any serious effort to recover them from the authorities, and appeared to exist perfectly well without them. A survey of the elixirs was made by the Medical Research Council, whose report rather tartly remarked:

> It seems clear from the remarkable collection of drugs that Captain H. [Horn] was intent on protecting himself against all assaults of

the devil so far as his flesh was concerned, and, if he knew the action of all the drugs he carried, he has obviously missed his vocation and ought to have made a very handy general practitioner.[6]

The report went on to outline some of the remedies that the pilot had carried, and pointed out that his "reliance upon allopathy for real bodily ailments and his further belief in homoeopathy for other discomforts seem to represent a curious outlook on medical science".

In retrospect it looks very much as if the drugs – which he never used again – had been assembled as part of the pilot's cover. Just as the photographs of Hess in infancy and the Haushofer visiting cards had been given him in an attempt to furnish proof of his identity, so the drugs provided were apparently designed to add verisimilitude. The same is true of the Leica camera belonging to Frau Hess, which the pilot carried round his neck when he arrived. (The camera, along with a pair of gloves, was eventually returned to Frau Hess by the Duke of Hamilton, but the half-used film that had been in the Leica vanished for ever.[7])

The more one studies the behaviour of the prisoner during his time in Britain, the more it looks as though he was playing a part – and playing it for most of the time rather badly, like a ham actor out of his depth. There would be no point at this stage in going through every detail of his physical and mental ups and downs; all the same, it is instructive to examine various incidents once again. (The quotations which follow are mostly from The Case of Rudolf Hess, the symposium compiled by the doctors in charge, and edited in book form by Brigadier J. R. Rees, the Consultant Psychiatrist to the Army, who took over the case in 1941.)

The first doctor to examine the pilot closely was Lieutenant-Colonel Gibson Graham, the physician (not psychiatrist) who saw him at Drymen, in Scotland, when he arrived there with the broken ankle and the chipped vertebra. Graham accompanied him south to London and then to Mytchett, but soon, because the prisoner's behaviour became so peculiar, he felt he should get a psychiatrist's opinion.

Rees saw him for the first time on May 30th, and on June 19th, less than three weeks later, reported that he had "deteriorated markedly" since his first visit: "Hess's mental condition, which was somewhat masked before, has now declared itself as a true psychosis (insanity)." Rees suggested that although continuous sleep treatment or electro-convulsive therapy might both be tried, neither was likely to produce a cure, and he concluded: "Hess may therefore be a mental patient on our hands permanently."[8]

The patient's chief obsession was that he was surrounded by Secret Service agents who were trying to bring about his death, principally by poisoning or, failing that, by driving him to suicide. From the start he was intensely suspicious about food, and even when he ate with the other officers, and the food was served from a communal dish, he would carefully choose a portion (like a chop) "but never the one which happened to be nearest him". On some occasions, even though selecting his food suspiciously, he had to be restrained from over-eating. He seems never to have asked for purely vegetarian dishes.

On May 28th he said that a "devilish scheme" had been initiated during the past few days to prevent him resting, either by day or by night:

> Noises were made continuously and deliberately to prevent him sleeping – doors were opened and shut loudly, and people ran up and down uncarpeted stairs, the guard kept clicking his heels; motor-cycles were kept running up and down in front of the house to prey on his nerves, and aeroplanes were flown over the house to disturb him. It was all a plot.[9]

The man's complaints were not as irrational as this brief summary makes them sound. Mytchett was by no means a quiet place, and the stairs, which were mainly uncarpeted, did echo loudly. Outside, motor-cycles came and went in abundance. To a man under stress, the noises were no doubt a genuine irritation. According to the nursing staff, he felt that the racket was being deliberately augmented in order to annoy him.

Besides (as I have already suggested) if the man was a secret agent, and suspected that the British knew it, he had good reason to expect that they might try to poison him: poison would, after all, be the quietest and easiest way of getting rid of him. His fears on this front were therefore not entirely irrational either.

In fact, far from trying to kill him, the British doctors were extremely anxious that he should remain alive. Whatever the feelings and motives of the Government, the psychiatrists were charged with the straightforward task of maintaining the prisoner in good condition. Besides, as Rees himself pointed out, there were other political implications to consider:

Had any harm come to him, either from outside or at his own hands, there would have been serious risk that this would have been attributed to a deliberate policy of the British Government and would have had its repercussions on Allied prisoners in German hands.[10]

In his summary of the patient's condition, Colonel Graham wrote that although he had seen no signs of mental instability when he first came across the man, "as time went on his behaviour and reactions led me to form the opinion that one dealt with a psychopathic personality".[11] Simple incidents, the doctor reported, were "misinterpreted and given a sinister meaning", and besides delusions of persecution the man showed "marked hypochondriacal, paranoid tendencies".* In general, "he showed a lack of sane grasp of affairs, and his motives were vague and incoherent."

* *Paranoia* is essentially an irrational fear of persecution. A patient afflicted may feel that people are against him in his job or socially: if he is severely afflicted, he feels that people are out to kill him. The German prisoner's main fear was of being poisoned. The British doctors, knowing nothing of his real background, assumed the fear to be irrational. If in fact the man was a secret agent, the fear was perfectly rational: it was quite on the cards that the British would try to get rid of him quietly.

Similarly, his apparently irrational obsessions about international Jewry using hypnosis, and the doctors being glassy-eyed as a result of it, were based on standard Nazi doctrines of the 1920s and 1930s, when such ideas were widely touted all over Germany.

His other obsession – about noise being made deliberately to annoy him – can now be seen as a typical reaction to long-term imprisonment: a form of imprisonment neurosis which is now understood but had not been diagnosed in the 1940s.

In general there was a much more solid foundation for his strange behaviour than anyone realised at the time.

Schizophrenia is a disease, or psychosis, which normally starts during the patient's teens. In the worst type, *paranoid schizophrenia*, the patient not only shows paranoid symptoms but also hears voices guiding or threatening him. He is usually completely irrational and unable to take part in a normal conversation, since he is continually going off at tangents. Another symptom of acute schizophrenia is withdrawal from the world: the patient often refuses to speak for hours or days on end.

Because schizophrenia is associated with childish, aggressive, or almost any kind of odd behaviour, a person suspected of having the disease is said to have *schizoid traits*. If a patient is normal when examined, but has a past history that includes episodes of such odd behaviour, he is classed as a *latent schizophrenic*.

In the case of the German prisoner, because of his apparent paranoia, the psychiatrists expected to find obvious schizophrenia. When they did not, they were puzzled. They did, however, have plenty of evidence of juvenile behaviour and peculiar attitudes, and they concluded that the man displayed schizoid traits and was a latent schizophrenic.

When Brigadier Rees first saw him, he thought the prisoner had "excellent intelligence", but was "childish in his outlook and consequently unstable and with bad judgment". He thought him a "man of unstable mentality", who had "almost certainly been like that since adolescence".[12] (The real Hess, as we have seen, had no history whatever of mental disturbance: if his mental condition *had* deteriorated to the state exhibited by the prisoner, the disintegration would have had to occur in little more than a fortnight.)

On Rees's recommendation, an Army psychiatrist fluent in German – Major Dicks – moved into Mytchett, and from then on the prisoner had continual psychiatric supervision – even though, at first, no mental nurses were employed. His symptoms, though varying in degree and intensity, remained broadly the same throughout the war.

To the officers obliged to live with him, he proved an exceedingly tiresome companion, not least because of his capriciousness. At one moment he would attempt to be haughty and arrogant; at the next he would behave like a child. One day, for instance, when troops paraded in the garden, he was out on the terrace and "gave the most curious display by doing what was practically a goose step down the path in front of them as though to demonstrate his own military status and techniques".[13]

At meals his behaviour was often equally puerile. If the first course was soup, he would wait till everyone had been served and then suddenly exchange his plate with that of the Mess President of the day. Sometimes he would refuse one course, or take only a few vegetables; but then, when "sufficiently urged by other people in the manner in which a child might be cajoled, he would . . . heap an enormous portion on his plate and eat ravenously".[14]

Again, one gets the impression that he was acting – on these occasions the part of someone diet-conscious. The trouble was that at heart he was very greedy. Never again during his captivity did the prisoner show any inclination towards yoga exercises or postures: evidently, after his first night in Scotland, he abandoned this facet of the real Hess's behaviour.

The aim of the British was still to extract useful information from him if possible, but all attempts to draw him on political issues proved useless. Nor would he even talk much about his own background. By pure chance Major Dicks had known Rudolf Hess's brother Alfred before the war, but even he found he could get little response when trying to chat about the prisoner's former life. Although the man would give a brief outline of his past, it was, Rees recorded, peculiarly frustrating to each of us who tried to take a full history, as we did on a number of occasions, that we always came up against a suspicious attitude and a refusal to communicate the facts of his past life in any adequate way.[15]

To Rees and his colleagues, the refusals were part of the man's generally uncooperative attitude. But if the prisoner really had been Hess, would he not have been all too eager to bore his captive audience to tears with endless accounts of his career – his exploits in the First World War, his early political struggles, his multifarious dealings with Hitler, the Nazis' triumphant rise to power, his stunt-flying for Messerschmitt, and a thousand other details? As it was, the double could give only the vaguest outline of these events, and in retrospect it is all too obvious why he consistently refused to supply details. He *could* not: he had none to give.

He never talked of his own military service, and never spoke of his war wounds. Nor did he ever mention that he had been decorated. (Hess had been.) Instead he stuck to generalisations and harped on the achievement of his flight to Scotland, before which, he said (as if to magnify the achievement still further), he had done very little flying. Yet even here – as I showed in Chapter 3 – he must have come perilously close to being exposed, for the map of his route which he proudly drew was manifestly absurd, and anyone with a technical turn of mind would have seen through it at once.

When he did discuss members of the Nazi hierarchy, he made some curious judgments. He was, of course, a supporter of the Party and a fan of Hitler, but he also said he liked and respected Goering, whom the real Hess had despised and hated. Goering, said the prisoner, was a good chap. Himmler, on the other hand, he did not like at all. Although in letters Frau Hess told him how much Himmler was helping the family, he did not care for him in the least, and indeed struck the British orderlies as being definitely afraid of him.

He also made some obvious mistakes. In Scotland he got his age wrong, claiming to be forty-seven, whereas Hess had been forty-eight, and tried to laugh off the error by pretending it had been part of his deception while he was posing as Alfred Horn. Later he said he had been born in 1896, two years after the real man. Further, he said he was one of four children – two girls and two boys – whereas Hess had only one brother (Alfred) and one sister (Margarete, or Gretl, who married an army officer). Rees was so much misled that in his book he credited the prisoner with a non-existent extra sister married to an opera-singer.

On June 15th, 1941, "Jonathan" made what has always been called his first attempt at suicide by throwing himself down the stair-well at Mytchett in the middle of the night. To anyone who has visited the house, it is clear that the incident was not a real suicide dive but rather an hysterical attempt to attract attention.

The prisoner's suite of bedroom, bathroom, and sitting-room was on the first floor of the house. On the night of June 15th he complained that he could not sleep, and just as Major Dicks was about to go into his room, he rushed out past the guard, through the open door, fully dressed in his flying uniform and boots, with a wild, distraught look in his eyes, and vaulted over the banisters. He hit the stone floor of the hall with a thump, and lay there groaning melodramatically. Those present rushed to his rescue, and it was soon found that he had fractured his left thigh. He therefore had to spend the next few weeks in bed, with his leg under traction. According to Dicks, the prisoner "claimed he had taken a header", but in fact the officer had seen him clear the banister feet first, like a hurdler.

During his recovery his morale fluctuated sharply. At times he was calm and rational, at others the victim of wild persecutory fears of poisoning. Though he never accused the men in charge of him of bad faith, he said he believed them all to be "under the influence of some rare poison or mesmerism" which was forcing them to torture and poison him. He began to hide glucose and sleeping-draught tablets under the carpet and in the lining of his flying boots: these, he said, contained poison, and he intended to give them to the Swiss minister (who visited him from time to time) for analysis.

He also began to complain of severe stomach aches and cramps, but because no clinical cause could be diagnosed, the staff concluded that the pains were imaginary. According to Captain Johnston (who succeeded Major Dicks as the psychiatrist in residence), by early 1942

> he was complaining almost daily of severe abdominal cramps which he dramatised by striding up and down the room, writhing and groaning in a ridiculous manner. The object of this behaviour was apparently to demonstrate to us the terrible effects of the poisons we were supposed to be administering to him.[16]

It is clear that the prisoner's complaints seemed histrionic at the time. Yet it is also clear that he should have been examined more thoroughly by a competent general physician, and that a serious attempt should have been made to get him to have a barium meal, so that his stomach and intestines could be properly X-rayed. As it was, the wretched man was caught in an impossible situation: once he had been labelled psychiatric, no one took his complaints of physical discomfort seriously, and because he had been cleared physically by Lieutenant-Colonel Graham when he first arrived, the psychiatrists assumed that his physical ailments existed only in his mind. Any surgeon or general physician seeing cramps as severe as those from which he constantly suffered should have suspected immediately that he might have a duodenal ulcer.

In June 1942 he was moved to Maindiff Court Hospital, near Abergavenny, an area quieter and more suitable for a long stay. By then the British evidently considered him only a minor security risk, for he travelled from Mytchett in an Army estate car, with no outriders, accompanied only by the driver, together with Captain Johnston and one other officer.

Maindiff had been the admission centre of the Monmouthshire County Mental Hospital's Board. By 1942 it was being used not for mental cases but for the treatment of patients from the Services, and most of the building continued in the same role, only one single-storey wing being set aside for the special prisoner.

In spite of attempts to keep the matter dark, news of his coming preceded him, and the domestic staff were lined up to witness his arrival. Before long his presence was an open secret in the town of Abergavenny. An officer on the staff sold the story to the *Daily Mirror*, went off on leave and never returned. (He later received a two-year gaol sentence.) Thereafter newspaper reporters had to be driven out of the town in herds, and people in the neighbourhood became jumpy. One guard, Taffy Richards, was accidentally shot and wounded by a colleague, and a local farmer was arrested while trimming his hedges.

Considering the apparent importance of the prisoner, the security arrangements at Maindiff were remarkably slack. "Jonathan" was allowed to move freely around his wing of the building, even at night, and also to go out into the garden, which was surrounded by a high fence. Once a week he would go out for walks into the nearby countryside, accompanied by only one or two officers, who walked with him, and two orderlies who followed a hundred yards behind, none of them armed. Whitecastle was one favourite rendezvous, and the Sugar Loaf Mountain another. Although the climb up the Sugar Loaf was fairly steep, the prisoner almost always outwalked his escorts, and never once complained of being short of breath.

In general the atmosphere at Maindiff was easy-going. But there was one curious exception: the strictly enforced rule that no member of the staff was to photograph the prisoner, and that if any photograph of him was discovered to have been taken it was to be destroyed immediately. Clearly this was a direct extension of the Government's official ban on photographs of any kind. (The ban was evidently upheld with good effect, for not a single picture taken during the war has survived.)

Life at Maindiff was relatively comfortable. The prisoner had newspapers, books, writing materials and a radio, and at first he showed such a marked improvement that Dr Ellis Jones, his new mentor, recorded, "His condition was such that the account given of his mental state at Mytchett was almost incredible."[17]

In these new and pleasant surroundings the prisoner began to display a surprising range of intellectual interests. He read widely, often studying Shakespeare plays as well as his more familiar German authors, and showed a deep attachment to the music of Mozart, Brahms, and others. He also revealed an altogether exceptional ability as a draughtsman. He drew mainly still-lifes – flowers, bowls of fruit and so on – but the sketches were done with such skill and originality that two of the staff at Maindiff who were themselves amateur artists reckoned his gift outstanding. Unfortunately the sketches all disappeared, along with many other papers, in a thick blue file which vanished when the prisoner was moved to Spandau. (According to Frau Hess, her husband *could* draw, and would sometimes make sketches to illustrate particular points in a discussion, but never sat down deliberately to create a picture.)

At the end of September 1942 the prisoner's supposed delusions returned in such force that the staff began to consider the possibility of transferring him to a mental hospital. Fortunately another improvement made this unnecessary.

Then, in October, he began to complain that he was losing his memory. During the war and afterwards, the doctors argued endlessly and with no definite conclusion about whether this amnesia was real or faked. At times it seemed to cause the prisoner genuine distress that he could not remember anything about his past life. But then he would undermine the impression by suddenly admitting that the memory loss had been deliberately simulated, only for another bout of apparent amnesia to begin soon afterwards.

So puzzling was the whole syndrome that in May 1944 the doctors obtained permission from the War Office to "elicit the complete psychological setting of the symptom" by injecting the patient with an anaesthetic and seeing what he would reveal of his true state of mind during the post-narcotic stage. Dr Dicks was brought back into action for the attempt (which took place on May 7th) mainly because his German was so fluent.

The anaesthetic Evipan was administered at nine p.m., and Dicks waited until the patient was suitably drowsy before he entered the room, in case his sudden reappearance should provoke an unfavourable reaction. At the appropriate moment he and Major Jones began a long series of questions designed to stimulate the patient's memory; but all they got in return was a series of groans and complaints – *until* one of them mentioned the surgeon Sauerbruch and the prisoner's war wound, whereupon the session was soon brought to an end by "Jonathan" recovering consciousness. Unproductive though the experiment proved, it is worth reprinting part of the transcript:

DICKS: Remember your little son's name?
PATIENT: (Whispers) I don't know.
DICKS: Your wife's. Ilse, it is.
PATIENT: I don't know.
DICKS: You remember your good friends, Haushofer . . .
PATIENT: No.
DICKS: Willi Messerschmitt.
PATIENT: No. (Groans) Bellyache! Oh God!
DICKS: Why this pain?
PATIENT: (Groans.)
DICKS: And how you lived in Alexandria as a little boy.
PATIENT: No.
DICKS: And all the stirring times with Adolf Hitler in Munich.
PATIENT: No.
DICKS: You were with him in the fortress at Landsberg.
PATIENT: No . . .
   (Then, after many questions answered only by groans or calls for water)
JONES: Now tell us what was your wife's name, and your boy's.
PATIENT: (In English) Wife's name and your boy's . . .
JONES: You were in Alex as a little boy, remember? And how you told me that father took you to school, your trips to Sicily, etc., your visits to the circus.
PATIENT responds only by echolalia of the last words in each of many English sentences.
JONES: And your army service in Rumania.
PATIENT: (In English) I don't know.
JONES: Haushofer – he was your dear friend. And Sauerbruch,

the great surgeon, who operated on your wound. Remember your
wound?
PATIENT: (No reply, but Phillips and Jones notice a quick gleam
of recognition at these two stimuli.)
JONES: But at least, who are you? And your wife?
PATIENT: (Confidently repeats his name.) And your wife.[18]

These exchanges, the report continued, were followed "by repeated exhortations that here were all his old doctors eager to help
him", but the patient sat up and called for water and food. The
session had lasted an hour and a quarter. Several years later the
prisoner boasted in a letter to Frau Hess that he had tricked
the doctors throughout: that "by calling up every scrap of will-
power" he had managed "not to lose consciousness while pretending
to be unconscious", and he had deliberately given his negative
answers "speaking softly in a flat, absent-minded voice".

After a long time I was able to recall my own name, which I
breathed in the same flat manner. Finally I thought it time to return
to consciousness and woke up, eyes full of astonishment, to return
slowly to life. It was a real drama. Add: a *complete* success! They
were now utterly convinced that my memory was quite gone.[19]

To prove the success of his deception, the prisoner added, he had
later repeated to the doctors all the questions they had asked him
during the time he was supposed to have been unconscious. He
thought himself tremendously clever to have brought off such "a
terrific 'leg-pull' ".

At the time, the psychiatrists did not particularly notice that it was
the mention of Sauerbruch and the war wound that brought the
patient's pretence sharply to an end. But now, with the advantage of
hindsight, it is fascinating to see how this one subject made him
abruptly abandon the game he had been playing. The evidence
bearing on all the other questions was far away, safely buried in the
past and in enemy territory; but the evidence that he had never been
wounded in the chest or operated on by Sauerbruch was right there
with him, in the form of his unscarred torso. Further questions on the
subject might have become extremely awkward. No wonder he
terminated the proceedings so swiftly.

His reasons for feigning memory-loss cannot now be established
with certainty. He may have done it in the hope of being absolved
from responsibility for what was happening in the war. But whatever

his motivation, the fact remains that amnesia was an extremely useful disability for a double to suffer: it gave him the perfect excuse for not remembering details of his past, and so greatly strengthened his protective armour.

Even while his memory was allegedly out of action, the doctors noticed that every now and then he inadvertently recognised some name, face, or person, and this made them suspicious; but it was not until February 4th, 1945, that he himself announced his memory had returned. That morning he got up earlier than usual, in a state of great agitation, and declared "that he had something important to tell the world, and asked that the information he was about to give should be forwarded to the Prime Minister". He then produced a list of names, including those of Winston Churchill, Rudolf Hess, Anthony Eden, Brigadier Rees, and the Bulgarian Government, and explained that all these people had been driven to various misdeeds by the malign hypnotism of the Jews – Churchill to change his attitude from being anti-Bolshevik to pro-Russian, Eden to insult Goering at a pre-war banquet,[20] and so on.

That afternoon he came down to the kitchen and borrowed a knife with a slim blade some eight inches long. He wanted it, he said, to impale slices of bread, so that he could make toast. The duty nurse, Private James Reigate, noticed that he was wearing his Luftwaffe uniform. The prisoner gave Reigate a Nazi salute before returning to his room on the ground floor.

Ten minutes later, he rang his bell for assistance. Answering it, Reigate found him sitting back in his armchair, in his shirt, having taken off his jacket. In the front of the shirt was a bloody hole, with bloodstains spreading all round it. The knife, with the blade also covered in blood, lay on the arm of the chair. The prisoner said, "I tried to reach my heart, but I don't think I did." Later he claimed to have pushed the knife eight inches into his chest.[21]

In fact, as it soon transpired, he had done no such thing. Reigate quickly fetched Dr Jones and the two senior nurses on duty, and the doctor, finding that the wound was superficial, sewed it up with a couple of stitches, not even bothering to use a local anaesthetic. The nature of the two parallel cuts – one an inch long, the other three-quarters of an inch – showed that what the prisoner had done was to pull a fold of skin away from his chest with his left hand, twist it to a vertical position, and then push the blade of the knife through it with his right hand. When the fold was released, it of course reverted to its normal position, so that the twin cuts lay horizontally. Once again, as with his jump over the banisters at Mytchett, he had faked an attempt

at suicide. Dr Jones himself remarked that the episode was "theatrical" rather than dangerous. (It need hardly be added that the
prisoner's uniform, which a German officer traditionally donned for a
suicide attempt, emerged unscathed, since he carefully took off the
jacket beforehand. I myself saw it in Spandau, and it showed no sign
of ever having had a knife thrust through it.)

This incident was completely misunderstood – through lack of
medical knowledge – by the historian David Irving, who, in his book
Hess: The Missing Years, 1941–45, credited the prisoner with a
genuine attempt at suicide. What Irving did not realise was that if the
knife *had* penetrated the pleural cavity at all, it would have punctured
the vacuum and collapsed the left lung. The prisoner would at once
have become a hospital case, and in need of life-support. As it was, he
remained sitting up in bed, none the worse.

Next day "Jonathan" said he had stabbed himself because he could
see he was never going to be allowed to leave England, and because
Germany was so obviously losing the war. The country would be
overrun by Russians: it was only a matter of time before they reached
the Channel and Bolshevised England too. His delusions appeared
worse than ever. The knife, he said, had been put in his way by the
Jews, because he alone had recognised their secret power of hypnosis.

He began a hunger-strike and for eight days took nothing except
water. But then, as the doctors proposed to force-feed him, he began
eating normally again. After the incident with the knife he was never
left alone. A medical orderly was in the room with him all the time,
and as a means of isolating himself from the presence of the nurse he
read a great deal.

In July 1945 he again complained that his memory had gone, but
this time the doctors were far more sceptical, noticing several slips
that gave his pretence away. Even so, he maintained it right to the end
of his time in England.

During his stay at Abergavenny the prisoner compiled an enormously long statement about his treatment at the hands of the British
– nearly 15,000 words about how he had been systematically poisoned
by powerful chemicals added to his food, how the doctors had taken a
fiendish delight in each new form of suffering that they had managed
to inflict on him, and how everyone concerned had participated in the
general endeavour to cause his nerves "to collapse".

His departure left the British doctors groping uneasily for terms in
which to describe his condition. He had admitted deceiving them for
so much of the time that they inevitably wondered whether he had

deceived them *all* the time. Summing up the case, Rees remarked that the patient was "undoubtedly a constitutionally unstable man", who had "probably for many years had a paranoid or delusional tendency".[22] Notwithstanding the eccentricity of his behaviour in England, Rees wrote, he thought him responsible for his own actions and "certainly able to plead in a court of law",[23] an opinion soon seconded by an international panel of doctors at Nuremberg.

At this stage it would be unreasonable to blame the psychiatrists for seeing things largely in terms of the Freudian theories which were then in vogue. To Rees, not only the patient but also a large proportion of the German nation suffered from father-fixation and similar stigmata.

In this particular case it made little difference that the British doctors viewed the prisoner in such a light: their job was not to cure him, but to preserve him intact until such time as he could be brought to trial, and in this they manifestly succeeded. Through more than four years of captivity they handled a difficult patient as well as they knew how, and they delivered him safely to Nuremberg.

Even so, the level of purely medical care which the prisoner received is frankly disturbing. Believing his stomach pains to be greatly exaggerated, or even entirely the product of his delusions and imagination, the doctors at Mytchett and Maindiff gave him no medication whatever.

Thirty years later, in Spandau, Prisoner No. 7 suffered a perforated duodenal ulcer, and it seems highly probable that it was this same ulcer that plagued him during his years in Britain. Had it been diagnosed and dealt with in the 1940s, he could have been spared an incalculable amount of discomfort.

The failure to diagnose the ulcer was by no means the only bad result of the Government's decision to make the prisoner spend the whole war in psychiatric care. A far more serious consequence was that the man's real identity remained undetected.

If he had stayed in the care of general physicians, or if at any stage he had been examined by a surgeon who already had some knowledge of the real Hess's background, the truth would inevitably have come out. Yet, by a series of flukes, the man never *was* seen by any doctor with the requisite combination of surgical and historical knowledge.

On the night he arrived in Scotland he was examined by Colonel Graham, a competent physician who found no chest scars or signs of earlier damage to a lung: a chest X-ray, he reported, showed "clear lung fields, save for a small calcified area in the upper right zone"[24] (the result of tuberculosis). Graham, however, did not know much about the real Hess's past history.

Major Dicks, who knew from Alfred Hess that the prisoner was supposed to have been wounded in the chest, seems never to have looked closely at his torso. Nor apparently did Brigadier Rees. After the prisoner had jumped down the stair-well at Mytchett, he was examined by a surgeon, Major J. B. Murray; yet he, too, while confirming "the absence of thoracic or abdominal injury", failed to remark on the lack of wound-scars, almost certainly because he had little knowledge of Hess's military career. It was not until I myself saw the prisoner in 1973 that, by pure chance, the necessary conditions were fulfilled for realising the true state of affairs.

Early in his captivity the prisoner began writing letters to Frau Hess, to Frau Rothacker (Hess's aunt in Zürich), to other members of the family, and to friends of Hess like Karl Haushofer. Many of these letters have been published in three volumes printed in Germany, and a selection has appeared in the English translation called *Prisoner of Peace* (various editions of the book have sold over 100,000 copies in Germany).

At first sight the numerous references to family affairs and friends seem to constitute obvious proof that the writer of the letters was Hess himself. Yet if the correspondence is studied in chronological order, a striking pattern soon emerges. A very high proportion of the events and people mentioned occur first in earlier letters which the prisoner had received from Germany: almost everything he says about his former life is an echo of something already written by another correspondent. It would take a computer analysis to work out precisely what proportion he himself initiated, but even without going into that amount of detail it is clear that his modest amount of original material could easily have been mastered by an intelligent double.

The pattern becomes even more curious when considered in the light of his methods of receiving and answering mail. As several of the men who looked after him in Mytchett and Maindiff still testify, he showed absolutely no enthusiasm or emotion when a letter came from Frau Hess, but would often leave it lying about unopened for several days. When he did rouse himself to reply, he would spread out numerous earlier letters on a large table, together with many small scraps of paper on which he had made notes, and thus, furnished with several dozen reminders, he would write his answer.[25]

The use of the *Lachlinie*, or laughter-line – a characteristic squiggle which Hess had employed to denote amusement – might again be taken as a sign of authenticity. But this, too, was a detail which an impostor would immediately have been taught. The *Lachlinie* had originally been a purely family sign, in use for several decades, but Hess had employed it so freely that it had become a positive irritation to his secretaries and other staff: everyone who had dealings with him knew about it.

During his long periods of alleged amnesia, the prisoner of course had an ideal excuse for making no effort at all to remember pre-war events and people. But all the time, with each letter that came from Germany, he was naturally building up a store of knowledge and extending his repertoire. Gradually, during the war and after it, he must have grown into the personality and background of the man he was pretending to be.

Early in 1944 he told Frau Hess that he had lost his memory, and when he wrote again six weeks later he remarked, "When you do not write, I can't write either, for I need stimulus. Without a letter of yours I truly do not know what I can say to you . . . At the very least, tell me how the boy likes going to school."[26]

The text would have served well for a description of his letter-writing as a whole. Not merely during the periods of apparent memory-loss, but all the time, he scarcely knew what to write unless given suitable cues. As Rees himself remarked, "During all his time in this country he showed little interest in his wife, and when her letters failed to come to him, he would not bother to write to her."[27] But the boy Wolf Rüdiger and his progress offered one infallible subject: it was always natural and easy to ask how the little fellow was getting on.

The prisoner's correspondence is riddled with omissions. He never, for instance, asked Frau Hess whether or not she had found the copy of the letter for Hitler which was said to have been left behind in the safe, with the key hidden in Wolf Rüdiger's toy tank. He never enquired whether the top copy of the letter had reached the Führer – surely the first thing that the real Hess would have wanted to know. He never asked Frau Hess how she was getting on, and even granted that the Hesses' relationship had been cool, this argues an incredible lack of simple curiosity. Though he wrote to old Karl Haushofer, in terms more affectionate than the real Hess had used, he never apologised for having wrecked the carefully planned peace initiative. He never wrote to either of the secretaries – Hildegard Fath and Ingeborg Sperr – who had worked for Hess daily in Munich and Berlin before and during the war.

Most of his letters contained only generalisations when they referred to past experience. A description of Egypt, for example, sounds as if it came straight from some travel brochure. There is a marked dearth of particular incident. But at the same time, oddly enough, there is also a wealth of dates. In his conversation, too, the man spouted dates all the time – so much so that when at Nuremberg he met Walter Funk, formerly Hitler's chief cashier, Funk derisively labelled him "the Date Machine" (an excellent name for a man anxious to establish that his memory has gone). Knowledge of dates might again be taken as a sign of authenticity; but when dates are poured out senselessly, parrot-wise, they at once sound like somebody trying to establish his *bona fides*. Who normally greets an old acquaintance by announcing, "I last saw you on March 10th, 1940" – or whenever it was?

It was not as if censorship deprived the prisoner of the chance of saying what he wanted. His letters *were* censored, he knew; the authorities had at first been alarmed by the *Lachlinie*, which they imagined was a secret sign alerting the reader to a cryptic message buried elsewhere in the text. But the prisoner was quite sane enough to invent a method of outwitting the security system.

The censorship was so slack, he found, that with each new letter he would include a copy of the last one. The staff, glancing through the copy and recognising it as a duplicate of the letter from the week before, assumed it was identical with what they had already blue-pencilled, and let it go unscathed. In fact it was a copy of the original, uncensored version. It was thus that the prisoner managed to convey to Frau Hess enough information about his surroundings – mainly the red earth and the mountains in the distance – for Karl Haushofer to deduce that his place of confinement was in or near Abergavenny.

And yet, although most of the contents of the letters can be traced to some incoming stimulus, there are passages which defy explanation. For instance, in June 1943 the prisoner remarked that he had learnt to play chess when he and his brother Alfred had scarlet fever, and then added, "When I was in the hospital at St Quentin during the First World War I was the only one to defeat the Berlin crack player Cohn, who took on twelve opponents at once."[28]

How could a double possibly know about the scarlet fever – unless it was perhaps some important part of family lore? Or did the prisoner simply invent the episode, relying on the fact that Alfred, who was three years younger than he was, would not remember? As for being in hospital at St Quentin, there is no mention of this on Rudolf Hess's service record, detailed though it is. He was in several other hospitals from time to time, but never one at St Quentin. One is left wondering whether the *double* was in hospital there, and wove this element of his own background into the story of Hess.

As for the prisoner's handwriting, Frau Hess insists not only that it was the same as her husband's, but that it never varied since he was a young man, except for one short period when it became shaky because he was seriously ill. This is a striking fact but not, in my view, a conclusive one. Given practice, it is relatively simple to imitate someone else's hand; and if there were slight differences at first, they could be accounted for by the stress of the writer's new environment.

In an attempt to satisfy my own doubts, I sent copies of the real Hess's handwriting, together with copies of the prisoner's, to eight professional graphologists. Five of them considered that both sets of writing had been done by the same person, three that they had not.

It might have been safer for the prisoner not to write at all. Yet a total failure to communicate with home would in itself have been suspicious and, in any case, the incoming letters were all the time furnishing him with more information.

All the time, in letters and reported conversation, one gets the impression of an impersonator who has half learnt his lines but has not got the full picture. Thus in talking to the British doctors about Karl Haushofer, he remarked that he had great respect for the old man's clairvoyant powers, as several times during the First World War the General had declined to board a train because he foresaw that it would be bombed – and he had always been right. What the prisoner never described, however, were Haushofer's dreams of Hess flying to a foreign destination and walking through a tartan-hung castle. It is as if the prisoner had grasped the well-known, general background, but not the particular fact. (Later, in Spandau, he told Speer that his flight had been provoked by "supernatural forces" in a dream that he himself had had – another variation on the original theme.)[29]

His final exit from Maindiff was ignominious. Knowing that he would raise all kinds of objections if he heard about their plans too early, the doctors did not tell him he was leaving until the morning of his departure, October 10th, 1945. He thus had to pack in a hurry, and, according to Brigadier Rees, by the time he was bundled out he had "lost all of his former haughty manner". He was driven to Madley, in Herefordshire, and from there flown via Brussels to Nuremberg.

8

Nuremberg

MANY VIVID DESCRIPTIONS have already been written of the Nazi war
criminals' trial that took place in the shattered city of Nuremberg
between November 1945 and October 1946. One of the clearest is
that of Airey Neave who, as a twenty-nine-year-old major, was called
upon to serve the 24,000-word indictment on each of the accused. His
book, *Nuremberg*, gives a sharp impression of the tension, squalor,
pathos, horror and sheer boredom of the Nazi leaders' final appearance in public.

Yet of the many bizarre features which Mr Neave described, none
exceeded in its strangeness the behaviour of Convict No. 125, the
prisoner known as Rudolf Hess. As during his years in Britain, he
changed his line so often, so abruptly and so completely that doctors
and lawyers alike were left mystified as to his true state of mind.

The legal aspects of the trial are already history. The constitution of
the International Military Tribunal, the arguments used by prosecution and defence, the sentences given – all these are a matter of
record. But the medical aspects of the trial of this particular prisoner
are still very much alive, for the question that must be answered is
this: how was it that all the doctors who looked after him failed to
realise that he was an impostor? The prolonged arguments about
what crimes the real Hess had or had not committed were totally
irrelevant. The man in the dock clearly had little knowledge of the
actions with which he was being charged.

He arrived in Nuremberg on the evening of October 10th. Dr Ellis
Jones, who had accompanied him from Wales, left him in the care of
Major Douglas Kelley, the American psychiatrist to the prison. His
appearance startled young Major Neave when he came to his cell to
deliver the indictment:

Hess stared straight through me with his burning eyes. His glance at
my British uniform was unfriendly . . . Then he lifted up one

manacled hand in an odd gesture of derision. He bared his teeth in
a mischievous grin.

"Rudolf Hess?"

I was calm but disturbed by his wild appearance. There was no
answer, and I put the indictment in his left hand which had now
been freed. His wrists were dreadfully thin . . . Whether Hess was
mad or not, he certainly looked it.[1]

Mr Neave's descriptions of the defendants tend to be theatrical; but
his picture of "Hess" is backed by the record of the experienced
psychiatric observer Major Kelley, both in his own book *Twenty-two
Cells in Nuremberg*, and in his contribution to Rees's symposium.
There can be no doubt that when the prisoner reached Nuremberg he
was under severe stress, the most immediate cause being that he
feared his identity would be revealed.

The man's true mental condition became the subject of intensive
research and speculation. During the next few weeks he was repeatedly examined by doctors and psychiatrists trying to determine
whether or not he was sane. From their reports, and from the records
of the trial itself, it is clear – now – that for much of the time he was
deliberately pretending to have lost his memory when in fact he had
not.

Until now it has always been assumed that this was the real Hess
simulating amnesia intermittently. But why he did it – to what end –
has never been made clear. The prisoner seems never to have hoped
that loss of memory would save him from retribution: indeed, he
expected to receive the death penalty. He never tried to use amnesia
as an excuse for past deeds. It would have been a different matter if he
had been trying to convince the specialists that he was unfit to plead.
But he did not do this. On the contrary, just as his counsel was calling
for further medical examinations, he himself amazed the court by
declaring that his memory-loss had been faked, and that he was fit to
conduct his own defence. Evidently he had not been malingering in
the normal sense of the term.

At the time, the prisoner's behaviour made so little sense that
everybody concerned assumed unofficially that he *was* slightly mad.
But the official view, taken by the international tribunal, was that he
was *not* insane, and the sentence passed was based on this assumption. The many obvious contradictions between public and private
opinion have never been resolved.

If the man in question really had been Hess, his behaviour would
have been inexplicable; yet if, as I believe, it was not Hess who

stood in the dock but his double, his attitude is far more compre-
hensible.

For reasons which I shall explain presently, the most important fact
of the double's life was that his true identity should not be exposed.
The pretence that he was Hess had to be maintained at all costs.
When he came to Nuremberg he knew that he would be confronted
by "colleagues" whom he had never met and past situations in which
he was supposed to have participated but of which in fact he knew
nothing. It was essential, therefore, that he should keep his amnesia
at hand as an insurance against any *faux pas* he might make. If he
failed to recognise someone whom Hess had known, or failed to
remember something notorious that Hess had done, his excuse and
explanation were ready-made. Without that invaluable loss of recall,
he would very soon have been exposed. Even with it he felt vulner-
able – witness, for instance, his refusal to speak to the other defendants before the trial began, even though conversation was officially
allowed when they all met at meal-times (otherwise they lived in
separate cells).

Once again, it seems extraordinary that although repeated physical
examinations were made, none of the doctors involved noticed the
tell-tale absence of wound-scars. The prisoner was examined on his
arrival at Nuremberg, and then at monthly intervals. That at least one
of the examinations was done carefully and in detail is shown by the
report prepared by Captain Ben Hurewitz, the U.S. Army surgeon to
the prison at Nuremberg, who saw the prisoner on November 10th.[2]
The patient, he wrote, appeared to have suffered "an appreciable
weight-loss, as evidenced by the sunken eyes, drawn face and the
prominence of the bony structures of the chest". Apart from being
thin, however, the man was in reasonable shape and showed no
abnormality. His scalp, Hurewitz reported, was "essentially normal". (The surgeon saw no trace of the scar on the head which the real
Hess was said to have got when hit by the beer glass thrown at Hitler
in 1921.) The prisoner's chest was also "within normal limits",
although the doctor immediately saw the result of the so-called
attempt at suicide with the kitchen-knife:

Two well-healed linear scars one-eighth of an inch apart are
present over the sixth rib two inches from the lateral margin of the
sternum. The superior one is ¾" in length and the inferior one is 1" in
length. A papilloma [wart] ¼" in diameter is present over the right
costal margin slightly anterior to the right axillary line.[3]

A surgeon thorough enough to record the presence of a wart a quarter of an inch across would surely have noticed major scars caused by a rifle bullet. Yet Hurewitz saw none, and he confirmed this to the present author verbally, more than thirty years after the event.

The official international examination of the prisoner – supposedly carried out by the delegates of four nations – was lamentably inferior to this careful single-handed survey. Had it been done properly, it might at last have revealed the truth; but like much of the other business at Nuremberg, it was made in a great hurry and under hopelessly unsatisfactory conditions.

On November 8th, in London, Brigadier Rees was summoned by the War Crimes Executive and told that he had been nominated to go out to Nuremberg. Because the Russian delegation was known to include a leading physician and an eminent neurologist, besides a psychiatrist, the British quickly recruited counterparts in the form of Dr George Riddoch and Lord Moran. The party left on November 12th, but bad weather made their journey slow and tiresome, and the time available to them in Nuremberg turned out to be less than twenty-four hours altogether. Only one of the three American delegates arrived in time to take part, and the French representative, Professor Jean Delay, reached Nuremberg just as all the others were leaving.

The ill-balanced panel of three Englishmen, three Russians and one American met on November 14th. Dr Rees's first task was to brief his colleagues as thoroughly as possible with the background of the prisoner's four-and-a-half years in Britain, a formidable task when conducted against the clock and through interpreters.

An extraordinary group interview followed. Because of his previous suicide attempts, the prisoner was kept handcuffed to an American guard throughout. Fettered by his right wrist, he sat at one side of a large table, with the members of the commission round the other three sides. Dr Rees – the only one whom the prisoner had met before – arranged to come in last, so that the others could observe closely whether his arrival produced any flicker of recognition.[4]

It did not. He approached from behind, so as to appear suddenly, but "a courteous greeting and handshake" produced not the slightest sign of recognition. The prisoner's manner, Rees recorded, "while slightly anxious, was apparently exactly what would be expected with a total stranger". Questions about the defendant's recent experience in England also "met with a blank expression of complete ignorance". The only suspicious feature of the meeting was that after a few exchanges in good English the prisoner said he could not understand properly unless questions were put to him through the interpreter. This, thought Rees, might have been a move designed to give him more time. Yet in spite of some penetrating enquiries from the Russians and the Americans, "little was found . . . to disprove or discredit the amnesia".[5]

According to Rees, the panel also made "a careful physical examination" – although how this can have been achieved with the patient continually handcuffed to his guard, is hard to make out. The survey certainly did not include a rectal examination, as it should have done. (Had one been made of Goering, it would have revealed one of the two cyanide capsules with which, at the last moment, he committed suicide, thus frustrating his executioners.[6]) It is hardly surprising that the examination of the prisoner thought to be Hess "revealed little of note in the way of disease or abnormality". Once again his secret passed straight through a filter which should have caught it.

In reaching their conclusions on his mental state, the international panel of course relied heavily on the case-history and opinion that Rees gave them. He, after all, had known the prisoner for more than four years, whereas the others had seen him for only a few hours. The British evidence was thus crucial, and contributed powerfully to the panel's decision that the prisoner was fit to stand trial.

The fact which my research has brought to light – that Rees, according to the American psychiatrist Walsh, really thought the prisoner schizophrenic, but suppressed his true opinion under political pressure – shows that the trial of Convict 125 was an even greater farce than it appeared at the time.[7] A schizophrenic is *not* fit to stand trial. If the man was thought to be schizophrenic, he should never have been sent into the dock.

Whether or not it would have made any difference if Rees had been allowed to state his honest opinion, it is impossible to say, for the Russians were also under strong political pressure, in their case to get the prisoner tried and executed. Very likely they would have overruled the British even if Rees had tried to hold out against them. All the same, it is a travesty of justice that the true medical opinion of the prisoner's mental state was never put forward.

In the event, the reports written by the different delegations varied slightly in detail, but their general tenor was that Convict No. 125 was fit to be tried. In due course the decision was disputed by Dr Günther Rohrscheidt, the prisoner's counsel, but his application to have the man properly examined in hospital was rejected.

Before the trial began numerous other attempts were made to

Above: The pilot in the cockpit had a gap between his two middle teeth, the prisoner at Nuremberg had none.

Below: Cameo at Nuremberg: Goering laughs at Convict No. 125.

The prisoner at Nuremberg.

determine whether the prisoner's amnesia was genuine or faked, but none of them produced a conclusive result. On October 9th, for instance, the Americans suddenly confronted him with Goering, who was incredulous when a former colleague – as he thought – had no idea who he was. The same happened when Karl Haushofer was brought in that afternoon. The aged professor – by then seventy-six – had known Hess for a quarter of a century, and now was not merely astounded, but acutely dismayed, to be met with a blank lack of recognition. The conversation, recorded by the Americans, was extremely bizarre:

Haushofer: "*Mein Gott!*"

Colonel Amen (to the prisoner): "Do you know this man?"

Prisoner: "Pardon me, but I really don't know who you are."

Haushofer: "Rudolf – don't you know me any more? I'm Haushofer."

Prisoner: "Are we on first-name terms?"

Haushofer: "We've called each other by first names for twenty years . . ."

The doctors were unable to decide whether the man genuinely could *not* remember events and people, or whether by then he had so perfected his technique of non-recognition that he was able to baffle observers with his acting.

A typical *impasse* was reached on October 30th, when a number of packages which he had brought with him from England were opened in his presence. Many of the parcels were packages within packages, sealed with red wax, some bearing the initials "R.H." Most of them contained pieces of chocolate, bread, sugar, lumps of jam, and so on, saved from the prisoner's meals and containing, he claimed, poisons that affected his brain, blocked his nose, weakened his heart, ruined his memory, and stopped up or loosened his bowels. On each parcel the prisoner had inscribed the effect of the particular poison. And yet, in the words of the American psychiatrist Dr Kelley:

When shown this bizarre collection, he smiled in his usual superficial fashion and denied any knowledge of them whatsoever. He readily admitted that the writing on each package was in his handwriting and identified various documents which were in the lot. He made no attempt to read these documents but seemed content merely to glance at them, identify his handwriting and hand them back. His only explanation for the time-consuming wrapping and sealing job which he had performed was: "It certainly seems a good way to pass the time." At this particular examination it

was impossible to determine whether or not he really recognised
any of the packages.[8]

The result was just as ambiguous when, a fortnight later, he was
confronted by Hess's two former secretaries. "This," reported
Kelley, "was a rather dramatic interview." The prisoner was seated
with his back to the door, and Hildegard Fath, who had worked with
Hess for seven years and knew the family very well, was brought in
without warning from behind him. He "appeared to recognise her,
but demonstrated little emotion and later denied ever knowing her".
She, in turn, was badly upset, and began to talk about the family,
producing pictures of Wolf Rüdiger. The prisoner, however,
"apparently was little interested" and told her he had lost his
memory.

When Inge Sperr came in, the man showed even less reaction, but
later in the interview there occurred an incident which seemed
significant to the American observers. The prisoner, when asked
something, once again replied, "I do not remember," whereupon one
of the girls picked up a photograph and said, "Here, maybe this will
help you remember." The reaction was surprising. He "immediately
waved his left hand at her hurriedly and said in a very low voice, 'I do
not want any help'." Later he denied even making the remark, but as
far as the Americans were concerned, "it was obvious to all present
that he did not want to run the risk of giving himself away".[9]

Giving himself away is the key phrase. To the Americans it meant
only that the prisoner might betray the fact that he was faking his
amnesia. But now it is clear that the man feared he was on the brink of
a far more fundamental revelation: he was afraid that close associa-
tion with the secretaries – one almost a member of the Hess family –
would reveal his almost total ignorance of the true background. No
wonder he muttered that he did not want any help; the more help the
girl had given him, the more awkward his predicament would have
become.

Later, he grew worried about the way he had upset Hilde Fath, who
had been perfectly convinced that he had not the faintest idea who she
was. Seeking to allay any doubts that she might have formed about his
behaviour (and perhaps even about his identity) he tried to make
amends by asking Frau Hess to apologise on his behalf. But he never –
so far as I can discover – wrote to Fräulein Fath herself.

He behaved in exactly the same way when confronted by Hess's
former colleagues. At one point, according to Colonel Burton
C. Andrus, the American Commandant of the prison, he passed

Goering in a corridor and, recognising him immediately, gave him a Nazi salute, a gesture for which he was promptly reprimanded.[10] But on the occasion when he was abruptly brought before Goering, Karl Haushofer and Ernst Wilhelm Bohle – three of Hess's closest colleagues – he greeted them "with a totally blank stare", so much so that all of them were convinced that he had lost his mind.

The Americans and Russians were not so certain. As Mr Justice Jackson, the U.S. prosecutor, remarked at one point, "He is in the volunteer class with his amnesia." And because of what another observer called "the spottiness of his reaction", which "indicated obvious malingering", it was proposed that a second attempt to unlock the doors of his memory should be made by hypnotism, carried out while the patient was sedated. This, however, he absolutely refused to allow. Dr Kelley afterwards reported that he talked to the prisoner at length about the technique. "He was at first willing to try it, stating that he was sure it would fail. When I told him that it always worked, he rapidly changed his mind."[11]

The attempt could have been forced on him, but, as Justice Jackson put it:

We did not dare to administer that, to be perfectly candid, against his objection, because we felt that however harmless – and in over a thousand cases observed by Major Kelley there has been no ill effect, although some cases are reported where there has – we felt that if he should be struck by lightning a month afterward, it would still be charged that something that we had done had caused his death.[12]

Colonel Andrus, the Commandant, expressed his opinion a good deal more robustly, and in his blunt way got nearer the truth than anyone else:

From the moment the man in the old coat and flying boots began talking about the chocolate [the parcels he had brought with him], I made up my mind that his madness was all a sham. He was – as I expressed at the time in verbal and written reports – a total fake.[13]

Nor were the Americans much impressed by the prisoner's constant complaints of stomach cramps. Often he would sit up in bed or on a chair and rock backwards and forwards, with his arms wrapped round his abdomen, grimacing violently. And yet, as Major Kelley pointed out, "in spite of the apparent extreme pain, he could break off in the middle of such a demonstration to discuss how horrible the pain actually was." The Americans found that "neglect was the best remedy for this illness, indeed the only remedy", as the prisoner refused to take medicine of any kind.[14] Every now and then he warned his fellow defendants that attempts were being made to poison them, and he himself used Ribbentrop as a poison-taster, getting him to sample food first.

During November the defendants were shown a long film made up of sequences shot by American cameramen in the Nazi concentration camps. The atrocity scenes reduced several of the prisoners to tears, but the defendant known as Hess only looked confused. One of the doctors heard him tell Goering he did not believe what he had seen, and afterwards in his cell kept muttering, "I don't understand." (The real Hess certainly would have understood, for he had toured early concentration camps with Himmler.)

The trial itself began on November 20th, but the case of Hess did not come up until ten days later, on November 30th. The question of whether the defendant was fit to stand trial was then brought before the tribunal, and the various physical and psychiatric reports were considered at length. The defendant's counsel, Dr Rohrscheidt, claimed that his client was *not* capable of pleading, and asked, as already mentioned, for more thorough examinations to be carried out in hospital, perhaps over a period of several weeks. But he undermined his own position by admitting that the defendant had expressed a wish to attend the trial, adding that "he does not feel himself unfit to plead".

The President, Lord Justice Lawrence, quickly took advantage of this opening and invited the defendant to speak. The brief statement which the prisoner then made was one of the most startling of the trial:

Mr President, I would like to say this . . . In order to anticipate any possibility of my being declared incapable of pleading – although I am willing to take part in the rest of the proceedings with the rest of them – I would like to give the Tribunal the following declaration, although I originally intended not to make it until a later point in the proceedings.

My memory is again in order. The reasons why I simulated loss of memory were tactical. In fact, it is only that my ability to concentrate is slightly reduced. But in consequence of that, my capacity to follow the trial, my capacity to defend myself, to put questions to witnesses or even to answer questions – these, my capacities, are not influenced.

I emphasise the fact that I bear the full responsibility for everything that I have done or signed as signatory or co-signatory. My attitude, in principle – that the Tribunal is not competent – is not affected by this statement. Hitherto in conversations with my official defence counsel I have maintained my loss of memory. He was, therefore, in good faith when he asserted I lost my memory.[15]

The immediate effect of these remarks – which could not possibly have been made by a schizophrenic – was all that the defendant had hoped. In his own words, "the faces of the judges and prosecutors were not very intelligent, and some of them sat with their mouths open. Laughter broke out from the press box, and then reporters dashed out through the door."[16]

The President adjourned the session at once. The news flew round the world, and afterwards the prisoner was as full of childish delight at his *coup* as he had been when he tricked the psychiatrists in Wales. According to Major Kelley, who interviewed him in his cell that evening, "he was elated over the impression he had created in the courtroom", and "very proud of his acting ability in fooling everyone".[17] And yet, although he admitted that in the past he had been shamming, and claimed that his memory was again in good order, he still seemed unable to recall many of the details about which he was questioned.

It would be fruitless at this distance of time to follow the snail-like progress of the tribunal in detail. The court sat for 217 days. The case for the prosecution alone extended over five months. Every word was translated simultaneously and relayed through headphones to everyone taking part.

Throughout these marathon proceedings the prisoner known as Hess thoroughly perplexed the other Nazi leaders in the dock. Physically he passed muster. His appearance was close enough to that of the real man to escape suspicion. No doubt all the Nazi leaders had changed a good deal since May 1941, and it was not surprising if four and a half years of captivity had changed Hess's double more than the rest. He had certainly lost weight, so that his cheeks were hollow and his facial bones more prominent than before. Yet one remark made in a letter to Frau Hess in January 1946 suggests that he himself was nervous about his appearance. "Do not let yourself be taken in by bad flashlight photographs or by tendentious reports," he wrote. "I am still exactly the same man, inwardly and outwardly, as my comrades have recognised with joy."[18]

This last remark was far from the truth. He was manifestly *not* the same man, in any sense of the phrase, and the other Nazi leaders received him with anything but joy; indeed, they were dumbfounded by the character and behaviour of the person whom everyone took for the former Deputy Führer. For example, when Ribbentrop heard about the statement he had just made in court, he was incredulous and "hardly able to speak. He just kept repeating: 'Hess? You mean *our* Hess? The Hess we have here? He said that?'" According to Major Kelley, "Ribbentrop became quite agitated and seemed to feel such action was not possible. He stated: 'But Hess did not know me. It is just not possible. Nobody could fool me like that.'"[19]

Several others – among them Schirach and Streicher – felt that the defendant had disgraced both himself and his country. As Streicher put it, "I think Hess's behaviour was a shame. It reflects on the dignity of the German people."[20]

Goering's reaction was much more ambiguous. It is important to remember that in May 1941 the Reichsmarschall knew far more about the disappearance of the real Hess than he had admitted to Hitler, and that he was somehow implicated in the plot which removed the Deputy Führer. Now, at Nuremberg, his attitude to the prisoner from England was thoroughly enigmatic.

First he was annoyed – or pretended to be – at the way the defendant had fooled the entire tribunal. But later, sitting next to the pseudo-Hess day after day, he treated him as an amusing freak, laughing at him in a condescending way as though he was an eccentric child. Behind his bantering exterior, however, lay some deeper and more sinister knowledge, for during one session he was overheard in the dock drawing up a motion that his neighbour should tell the court his "big secret". According to Dr G. M. Gilbert, the prison psychiatrist, Goering said, "By the way, Hess, when are you going to let us in on your great secret? . . . I make a motion: Hess tell us his big secret during the recess. How about it, Hess?"[21] The prisoner had been hinting that he was about to stun the court with some mighty revelation, and Goering was evidently trying to provoke him. Yet what the secret was, and whether Goering had prior knowledge of it, we shall never be sure.

The animosity that had always grated uncomfortably between Goering and the real Hess was markedly absent. Not only was Goering's attitude during the trial friendly if patronising; his neighbour, far from showing the disdain with which Hess had always treated Goering, seemed actually to like him.[22]

Outside the court Goering apparently shared his colleagues' general belief that the prisoner called Hess was crazy. During one conversation in his cell he remarked, "As far as Hess is concerned, I must admit you have me licked. His memory is definitely shot, and I don't believe any more that he was faking in the first place . . . God! What a farce it is going to be when he gets up to testify!"[23]

Before that happened, the defendant acquired a new advocate. He himself claimed that Rohrscheidt had broken faith and released confidential information. In fact the lawyer had broken a leg in an accident. In the event, the prisoner was defended by Dr Alfred Seidl, an outstanding young lawyer then still in his twenties.

When details of the prisoner's mission to England were revealed in court, the former Nazi leaders were appalled by the naivety of the whole operation. (This was the first time they had heard the British end of the story.) Goering kept turning to his neighbour and asking, "Did you really say that?" When the man replied, "Yes," Goering was beside himself with scorn, and at the end of the session he slapped the defendant on the back in mock congratulation. According to Dr Gilbert, several of the others "literally threw up their hands in expressions of disgust and desperation at 'such stupidity . . . such childish naivety'".[24] Both Goering and Papen pointed out that if there had been any real negotiating to do, either of them could have contacted the British through a neutral power "at a moment's notice".

While the case against him was heard, the defendant continued to behave as he had since the trial started, ostentatiously leaving his earphones off so that he could not follow the proceedings and looking around the courtroom with his inane grin. Often, to the great irritation of the other defendants, he buried himself in the pages of a novel. He did this on the day that the Russian prosecutor opened his case against him, and when at lunch one of the psychiatrists asked him why he did not pay attention to the accusations, he replied that he was not obliged to listen to foreigners slandering his country.

This "protective negativism", as the doctors called it, increased throughout the remainder of the trial. The defendant was supposed to go into the witness box on March 24th, but when the day came he changed his mind about doing so, and left his counsel to plead on his behalf. According to Dr Gilbert, the reason was that "he did not want to be subject to the embarrassment of not being able to answer questions the prosecution would ask".[25]

Dr Seidl certainly did his best. His case was vigorously and persuasively argued: he sought, in general, to show that Hess had not been associated with any of the more vicious forms of Nazi aggression, and claimed that with his flight to Britain the Deputy Führer "committed his entire person in an attempt which sprang from the desire to avoid further bloodshed at all costs". But the submission was hardly helped by his client's decision, on August 31st, to make a final statement himself.

The defendant first obtained permission to remain sitting down, because of his poor health, and although he knew that the final speeches were supposed to be short, launched into an immense, rambling oration. After twenty minutes the President interrupted him, whereupon he began suggesting that witnesses had been brainwashed into giving false evidence, and that the men who had run the Nazi extermination camps had been hypnotised into doing so by the same malign influences that had made the glassy-eyed doctors in England try so persistently to poison him. Positively ordered by the President to finish his statement, he went on:

> I was permitted to work for many years of my life under the greatest son whom my country had brought forth in its thousand-year history. Even if I could, I would not want to erase this period of time from my existence. I am happy to know that I have done my duty to my people, my duty as a German, as a National Socialist, as a loyal follower of my Führer. I do not regret anything.
>
> If I were to begin all over again, I would act just as I have acted, even if I knew that in the end I would meet a fiery death at the stake. No matter what human beings may do, I shall some day stand before the judgment seat of the Eternal, I shall answer to Him, and I know He will judge me innocent.[26]

With this embarrassingly vague finale, the prisoner retired to his cell. But his mind cannot have been nearly so confused and irrational as it appeared in court, for that same day he sent Frau Hess a perfectly logical letter, ending with the statement that he faced "the latest trick played upon me by the strange fate that guides me" with a "quiet and balanced mind and a smile, with the same imperturbability with which I shall receive the verdict".[27]

The judgments were given on September 30th, and the individual sentences on October 1st. Twelve men were sentenced to death and seven to various terms of imprisonment. The prisoner known as Hess received life – a sentence which the Soviet prosecutor, Major-

General I. T. Nikitchenko, considered inadequate, calling instead for death.[28]

The defendant himself, as he afterwards wrote in a letter to Frau Hess, had expected to be executed. But since he did not bother to put on the earphones when he went up into the dock, and paid no attention to the President speaking in English, he did not even hear what sentence had been passed on him. Afterwards, according to Dr Gilbert, he strutted back to his cell "laughing nervously, and said that he had not even been listening, so he did not know what the sentence was – and what was more, he didn't care".[29]

In a letter written next day, he described himself as being "in a state of most perfect calm", and certainly his correspondence of that time shows no signs of pressure. Yet to the men in charge of the gaol, he seemed "as strange as ever", and one day soon after the verdicts had been given he came as close as he ever had – or has since – to giving himself away. When an officer called his name, he stood to attention holding the broom with which he swept out his cell, and answered, "Sir, there is no such person as Hess here. But if you are looking for Convict Number 125, then I'm your man."[30] At the time the remark was dismissed as just another of the crazy prisoner's crazy utterances: now its simple truth is apparent.

The letters alone show that the prisoner was not nearly as mad as he made out, and his subsequent behaviour confirms the fact. What nobody at Nuremberg realised was that he was playing not one part but two. The doctors suspected, quite rightly, that he was playing the part of a crank in order to confuse his inquisitors; but they failed entirely to realise that he was also playing the part of Hess. His motive in feigning amnesia was not to escape justice; if this had been his object, he would never have gone into the witness box and admitted that he had been shamming. No. His aim in constantly losing his powers of recall was simply to preserve the secret of his identity.

Looking back, one can pick out various crisis points at which his cover was severely threatened. One was the meeting with the secretaries. Another was the proposed visit of Frau Hess. The other prisoners were granted permission to see their families, but the man known as Hess refused absolutely to receive Frau Hess or any other relative, giving only the specious reason that it would be beneath his dignity to have to talk to a member of the family through wire mesh in the presence of hostile witnesses.

At one stage he did provisionally agree to see Frau Hess, warning Dr Seidl in a memorandum that she might be "alarmed by my iciness in the event of a visit",[31] but later he changed his mind.

Another acute threat was the authorities' insistence on taking a blood sample so that his blood-group could be established. Obviously afraid that this would reveal a discrepancy with the records of the real Hess, he resisted the doctors to the utmost – so much so that Major Kelley remarked, "It nearly required a special act of the Tribunal before he would permit us to withdraw blood."[32] Luckily for the prisoner, blood-groupings were not classified during the First World War, and in any case the real Hess's records were not to hand. They were, as far as can be ascertained, somewhere among the hundreds of thousands of captured Nazi documents which the Americans were holding in Nuremberg, but as yet these were unsorted, so that individual dossiers could not be found quickly. If anyone had hit upon Hess's service record, with its details of his various woundings, the prisoner's pretence would have been shown up at once.

Yet another indication of his fear of exposure was his refusal – apparently idiotic, unless the real reason is appreciated – to supply the French psychiatrist Professor Delay with a specimen of his signature. When the doctor asked him to sign his name, he did so, but immediately scratched the signature out. After this had happened several times, Major Kelley asked him to write a short autobiographical study. This he refused, on the grounds that the study might be published "to his detriment". He did, however, eventually agree to write a brief description of his cell, so that his handwriting could be studied.

On another occasion one of the guards asked him to sign a dollar bill on which he had already collected several other prisoners' autographs, as a souvenir. In Major Kelley's words:

> Hess smiled, agreed to sign, took the bill and went to the back of his cell. He then faced the soldier, smiled again, bowed, and proceeded to tear the bill into little fragments which he threw out of the window. Hess smiled again to the soldier and said: "Our German signatures are precious."[33]

With the exception of Goering, who managed to commit suicide, the prisoners condemned to death were hanged on September 16th. Those sentenced to imprisonment remained in Nuremberg Gaol until July 1947. During the autumn of 1946, the man known as Hess called for a typewriter and hammered out the text of the address that he would have given the tribunal had the President not cut him short. The speech would hardly have done him much good, even if he had managed to deliver the whole of it. It covered forty-nine sheets of paper and developed at immense length the theme which he began in the dock – that responsibility for the atrocities perpetrated under the Nazi régime should be laid on the Jews, who had managed to bewitch large sections of the human race in their attempt at world domination. Not only the Allies, but the Nazis too, had become hypnotised, he claimed, and it was this mass-mesmerism that led to the gas chambers and concentration camps.

Another part of the manifesto was devoted to the prisoner's plan for setting up and taking control of a new régime in Germany, with himself as Führer of the Fourth Reich. To call this plan half-baked would be to damn it kindly: part-grandiose and part-puerile, it is an extraordinary combination of vagueness in large subjects and exactitude in small ones. "Reichsminister Speer", for instance, was "to be assigned the job of lessening the crisis in Germany", and he was to be given "all the help necessary to set up feeding stations and transportation, to issue blankets and field-kitchens. At every large railway station there should be a kitchen to give food to soldiers who are on their way home."

The author himself demanded offices in Nuremberg Gaol where he could "receive a great many long-distance telephone calls, telegrams and letters". His personal tailor was to make him a new uniform with adjustable seams, as he would "probably put on weight" when he was released. The new capital was to be in Munich. Many former Nazi leaders were to be released and given senior posts in the new administration. The former President of the Reichstag, Herman Esser, "who is now in a camp in Ludwigsburg, is to be released and given a car for fastest possible transport to Munich". The new Führer would also need a car for himself, and three other vehicles, in which the new leaders would drive to Munich. "If possible," wrote the prisoner, "I want German cars." All travellers on their way to see him in Munich were to be given free railway tickets.[34]

Whether the prisoner himself took all this seriously, or whether he disingenuously concocted the plan in a further attempt to convince the authorities that he was insane, it is impossible to tell. Certainly he devoted an enormous amount of energy to the task of putting his ideas on paper, and some psychiatrists have seen in his cultivation of the fantasy an attempt to escape from the ghastly realities of the Nazi régime.

Whatever his true feelings, there is an extraordinary contrast between the lunacy of his manifesto and the calm good sense of his letters to Frau Hess. In the summer of 1947 she was arrested by the Americans because of her past Nazi associations, and when the prisoner wrote to her during June his letters were perfectly rational and coherent, especially when he spoke of Wolf Rüdiger:

> Meanwhile, we may have to go through some more difficult times; but that, too, is part of what fate has in store for us. If in consequence the boy is separated from your influence for a few months, this must not be taken too tragically. He has such good stuff in him that this experience will not decisively influence his future. The grave early troubles that have fallen to his lot, also, in his early years will counteract other influences and tend to the good. This or that tendency which may not be quite what we would like will be ironed out as he grows older. I think I remember writing to you from England about a family I knew who, on principle, left their children to themselves, influencing them as little as possible – even taking little notice of real naughtiness – and the experiment turned out extraordinarily well.[35]

Occasionally in his letters the prisoner hinted that much of the evidence in "the great trial" had been "fiction", but he never once mentioned the mass-hypnotism and global Jewish plot on which, in court and in his manifesto, he blamed the entire Nazi *débâcle*. There seems to have been scarcely any connection between his public and private *personae*, and indeed he himself seemed scarcely aware of the unbridgeable gap between the two. In his letters he often wrote about his "conception of personal honour", and how he believed that

> the honour of an individual cannot be injured, or even touched, by any acts of expression on the part of another . . . Honour can suffer solely as a result of dishonourable conduct on the part of the individual himself. Accordingly, many things that might well get on the nerves of others pass me by.[36]

In other words, he was quite satisfied with his own past performance. From someone who had spent the past five years acting with the utmost childishness – lying, cheating, being constantly found out and humiliating himself in every conceivable way – such self-satisfaction comes oddly, to say the least. Yet the prisoner was apparently as little put out by the fiasco of his own behaviour as he was by the record of the Nazi administration.

In considering his demeanour in court, it is as well to bear in mind that much of what he said, especially about the Jews, was standard Nazi claptrap, such as one would have picked up in any German café during the 1920s and 1930s. There is no doubt that the man was a lifelong Nazi supporter, and that his ideas were based on the ramblings of Strasser and other Party prophets, who preached that the Jews used hypnotism and black magic in their efforts to establish world domination, that they exercised similar dark powers in seducing Aryan virgins, and so on. (Their ravings were so extreme that some Nazis – for instance the S.S. leader Ohlendorf – criticised them bitterly on the grounds that they damaged the party's credibility.) Convict No. 125 was not alone in trying to shelve the blame for what the Nazis had done by pinning it on the global Jewish conspiracy. Funk later made similar allegations in Spandau, and no one suggested that *he* was mad.

In the same way, pseudo-Hess was not alone in planning a Fourth Reich. Doenitz used to talk about *his* provisional government in much the same way. The creation of imaginary new régimes seems to have suited the mentality of defeated Germans particularly well. The act represented an escape into pleasanter circumstances. As such, it was not in itself an indication of mental instability.

Only if one believes that it was Hess who stood in the dock at Nuremberg does the man's behaviour seem incomprehensible. As soon as one realises that the prisoner was *not* Hess, but an ordinary man forced into the Deputy Führer's shoes, his demeanour is far easier to explain. He could not feel guilt for Hess's crimes, as he had not committed them. He did, however, feel the irony of his fate in being forced to accept the sentence, and he commented on this in letters to Frau Hess.

Perhaps the most pathetic feature of his whole record at Nuremberg was the way in which he tried to ape the leader he was representing. No leader himself, he had not the slightest idea of how a statesman should behave, and so made a fool of himself continually. Just as in Britain his efforts to negotiate with military and Government officials had ended in fiasco, so at Nuremberg his attempts to assume the mantle of Hess were absurdly inappropriate. By struggling all the time, in the depths of his own confusion, to behave as he imagined the Deputy Führer would conduct himself, he appeared even more eccentric than he really was.

9

Spandau

ON JULY 18TH, 1947, this strange and gloomy man was moved from Nuremberg to Spandau Gaol in Berlin, where he became Prisoner No. 7, having been numbered last, after his six companions. He remained in Spandau for the rest of his life, and the story of his confinement is as pathetic as the man himself.

His new surroundings were gaunt and grim. Originally built in the 1870s as a military stronghold, Spandau was an immense fortress of dirty red brick, with high walls surmounted by watch-towers. Before the war it had served as a civilian gaol, housing 600 prisoners: then the Nazis had used it as a clearing station for victims on their way to concentration camps. They had equipped it with excellent facilities both for hanging and for decapitation: eight prisoners could be hanged simultaneously, and in the guillotine room the floor sloped, so that the blood would run off easily. When the Allies prepared the place for its new inmates they removed the guillotine and converted the execution room into an operating theatre. They also surrounded the walls with a barrier of barbed wire, and a six-foot electric fence carrying a 4,000-volt charge.

Since there were only seven new prisoners, only one section of the huge gaol was needed to house them. Each man was allotted a small, freshly painted cell containing a bed, a table and a chair, and issued with prison uniform which had his number stamped on the back of the jacket and the knees of the trousers.

Spandau was chosen from several possible alternatives after much debate among the four Allied powers. The Americans had wanted to keep the seven prisoners at Nuremberg. The Russians wanted them in Plötzensee, another prison in Berlin, but in the Soviet sector of the city. Spandau lay in the British sector and its presence in Berlin, combined with the fact that the four Allied powers administered the gaol jointly, had a profound effect on the way the prisoners were handled.

The system was that each power ran the prison for a month at a time – Britain in January, May, and September; France in February, June, and October; Russia in March, July, and November; and America in April, August, and December. During each country's month of office, its senior representative automatically became chairman of the prison directors for that month; but because there were four powers involved, any important decision had to be taken by all four, so that the opportunities for bureaucratic obstruction and the use of the veto were endless.

Almost all the obstruction came from the Russians. From the start they did everything they could to make the prisoners' lives miserable, and in the tense political atmosphere of the late 1940s, when Berlin was a flashpoint which could have touched off another world war, sharp rows broke out in Spandau about the treatment of the inmates. During the Russian months the food was so bad that the inmates' weights all fell. The other Allies talked of unilateral action, of removing the prisoners to the West or at least changing their régime without consulting the Soviet representatives. But fear of Russian retaliation on a wider front always prevented any major innovation. Similarly, the Russians were to some extent inhibited by the fact that they were anxious to retain a foothold in Spandau – one of the few places in the West to which they had official access.

Political considerations thus influenced the treatment of all the prisoners, but they had a more damaging effect on Prisoner No. 7 than on any other, for to the Russians Hess was always the last living symbol of Operation Barbarossa, the Nazi invasion which ultimately cost the Soviet Union over twenty million lives. Just as at Nuremberg the Russians called for the death of the man who they supposed was the last surviving architect of Barbarossa, so they later blocked every Western attempt to bring about his release.[1]

From the start the behaviour of No. 7 was enigmatic, and in May 1948 the American pyschiatrist, Maurice Walsh examined him in response to an appeal from Colonel F. T. Chamberlin, the U.S. representative on the Allied Medical Board which was responsible for the health of the Spandau inmates. No. 7 had been acting tiresomely, refusing to obey the prison regulations, shouting out repeatedly at night about his stomach cramps, and so on. Chamberlin therefore decided to have a new psychiatric evaluation made.

Walsh's visit fell in a British month, and the Western Allies agreed to his request to interview No. 7 alone. The Russians however vetoed the idea, and the British and French withdrew their permission. The result was that the interview had to be performed before a typical

Spandau full house, complete with supporting cast, which was described by Walsh himself:[2]

> Colonel Chamberlin sat at the right-hand chair on the far side of the
> table. I sat next to Colonel Chamberlin. The English Medical
> Officer sat next to me, and the French Medical Officer next. At the
> end of the table sat the Russian Medical Officer, with the Russian
> Interpreter standing next to him. The American Interpreter sat
> near the end of the table on the opposite side of Colonel Chamber-
> lin. The French Governor of Spandau stood in the room away from
> the table with an interpreter. The French and Russian Governors
> of the prison were in the room at least part of the time . . .

For much of the time there were fifteen people present, and as
Walsh restrainedly remarked, the conditions "presented certain
difficulties", not least because he was allowed to talk to the prisoner
in German only for the first ten minutes. Thereafter he was obliged by
the Russians to speak to the interpreter in English, have the question
translated into German, and wait for the German answer, which he
understood anyway, to be translated into English, Russian, and
French by the interpreters.

Throughout this cumbersome procedure the prisoner remained
"affable and pleasant" to everyone's slight surprise, and answered
most questions "promptly and fully". The survey ranged over his
present health, his flight to England and the reasons for it, his role in
the Third Reich, his various losses of memory, his general state of
mind, and so on. To readers already familiar with the situation, the
results will seem entirely predictable: the prisoner answered questions about his own background with reasonable fluency, but clearly
knew nothing whatever about the background of Hess.

Before he came to England, he said, his health had been perfect,
and he had used homoeopathic medicines to prevent disease, rather
than to treat it. Asked whether "the great responsibility that he had
had as the second person in the Reich did not produce nervous
stress", he answered that he had never felt under pressure "except for
short periods when important events such as the declaration of war
were pending", and that even then he "noted only some difficulty in
sleeping".

When asked "whether he ever heard voices talking to him through
his mind" – a common symptom of schizophrenia – he "laughed and
answered with some gaiety that he had never heard voices talking that
did not come from people in his immediate environment".

About his flight to England, he said he had planned the mission entirely on his own, telling no one else; but when Walsh asked him how long he had had the idea beforehand, "it was impossible to secure a definite answer".

The prisoner's replies to questions about the balance of power in the former Nazi Government were exceedingly naive. He had never had the slightest suspicion, he said, that Goering or anyone else might be scheming to seize his place or diminish his influence. Asked whether he thought that in 1941 his influence had been waning, he answered emphatically that it had not.

Later Walsh again suggested that, as Deputy Führer, the prisoner must have been the target of much animosity and jealousy:

> He was asked if he did not believe that many others were jealous of him and were seeking to do him harm. He denied this, stating that he was aware of no animosity against him . . . He was asked whether in the German Reich officials were not in danger at times. He answered that if officials were faithful and did their duty, they were secure in their positions. He was asked whether dismissal from an official position in the former German Reich did not put the dismissed official in danger. He answered with a smile that this was not so, and that this impression had been created by foreign propaganda.

The total unreality of this reply was matched by that of several other answers. No. 7 felt no guilt about the Nazi concentration camps, he said, because the atrocities were "matters about which he knew nothing with certainty and over which he had no control". He "recalled nothing of his early life in Egypt except dim details of the family dwelling and his immediate family". When Captain Parkes, a British medical officer, said he believed that Rudolf Hess had consulted a German heart-specialist before the war, the prisoner was asked whether this was so, and "after brief thought he replied that he could not recall consulting a German cardiologist, and asked for the name of the German doctor in question, which Captain Parkes could not recall".

The inadequacy of these answers is now glaringly obvious. It seems incredible that nobody was suspicious of them at the time. The reason, however, was simple: the prisoner's amnesia was by then such a well-established fact that his inquisitors were not in the least surprised by his failure to remember details of Rudolf Hess's early life or political career. If he could not even recall that he had twice lost his

memory in England (which he said he could not), how could he be
expected to remember the pressure put on him by Goering, Bormann
and the rest?

It took him "a few moments" even to think of the age of his son,
which he correctly gave as nine, and "he expressed no emotion
whatever while discussing his wife and child". Yet in general Walsh
found that the prisoner made great efforts to impress him "with his
sincerity and normality. He was most courteous and responsive . . .
he did not give the impression of being grandiose or of over-
estimating his own importance, but rather an impression of some
humility and considerable quiet self-assurance was gained."

Walsh reported that in his opinion the prisoner was definitely "not
psychotic at the present time", even though in the file there was all the
evidence of his paranoid wartime behaviour. No. 7, he concluded,

> is an individual of superior intelligence with schizoid personality
> traits, and . . . he has no psychosis at the present time, but there
> would appear to be adequate evidence that he has experienced at
> least two episodes of hysterical amnesia and of depression, with
> suicidal attempts, both of which occurred only at a time when he
> was exposed to strong emotional stress.

Thus in 1948 Walsh gave the prisoner a fairly clean bill of mental
health. Eighteen years later, however, writing in a specialist journal,
he claimed that he had been obliged by political pressure to water
down his report.[3] The American surgeon of the Berlin garrison, he
said, had told him to omit all mention of mental disease, since the
Russians would not like it. They preferred to believe that Hess had
always been perfectly sane, that he was fully responsible for his
actions, and could therefore justifiably be kept in gaol for life.

In fact, Walsh wrote in 1964, his interview had made it possible to
"establish unequivocally" that the prisoner "had a latent schizophrenia": "There was no doubt about the basically psychotic nature of his
psychiatric illness, or that he had experienced recurrent psychotic
episodes for several years."

This, thought Walsh, "was indeed an astonishing situation". "The
former second highest officer of a modern state was found to have a
chronic and extremely severe psychiatric disorder which should have
incapacitated him from any post of responsibility for the lives and
health of human beings."[4]

How Walsh could tell that No. 7 had a "chronic and extremely
severe psychiatric disorder" is not clear. As the doctor reported after

his interview, the prisoner showed no sign of it during the meeting in 1948. It seems that the diagnosis must have been made mainly from a perusal of the patient's records, always a risky proceeding.

But, in any case, the inference which Walsh drew from his diagnosis was entirely false. Only because Hitler himself had been schizophrenic and subject to psychotic episodes, he concluded, had it been possible for someone with such a severe psychiatric illness as that suffered by the prisoner to become Deputy Führer.

The psychiatrist was completely misled – as many of his predecessors had been – by his natural belief that Prisoner No. 7 *was* Rudolf Hess. Although he called No. 7's disorder "chronic", Walsh seems to have ignored the fact that no sign of psychiatric disturbance had ever been noticed in the real Hess. Though often under great pressure, the Deputy Führer had always remained rock-solid, and only after his sudden disappearance had rumours of his insanity been put about.

No. 7, by contrast, clearly was a man of unstable temperament, to say the least, and quite incapable of ever having held high political office. Whatever the precise nature of his psychiatric disorder, he immediately went to pieces under the stress of captivity, and during the war repeatedly showed symptoms of paranoia. The very idea that he could have been Hitler's number two is patently absurd, and should have been so in 1948.

Yet Walsh's interview changed nothing, and the prisoner settled down to what one of his fellow inmates, Schirach, accurately described as a process of "oysterisation", deliberately enclosing himself in a thicker and thicker shell, into which he could retire if he wanted to avoid awkward questions. He himself was aware of the process, and in one of his letters mentioned "the protective skin" around his soul growing thicker and beginning "to develop the rings of years".[5] As time passed he shunned contact with the other prisoners more and more. At first he took a small part in the one communal activity they managed to arrange – gardening – but later he gave this up and withdrew increasingly into himself. It was typical of him that when further trials of former Nazis began at the end of the 1950s, and his colleagues eagerly discussed the evidence printed in the newspapers, No. 7 would refuse to read the reports, saying that he could not talk about that sort of thing and wanted nothing to do with it. Of course he could not talk about it – a matter which the real Hess would have known through and through, but about which *he* knew next to nothing.

On a purely intellectual level No. 7 was by no means outclassed by his fellow prisoners. In Britain he had amassed a library of more than a hundred books, and when these were sent over to Spandau he was delighted. Thereafter, even though his choice of book was censored, he added steadily to his collection, always reading and quoting Goethe, studying philosophy (particularly Nietzsche and Schopenhauer), history (Ranke's classic account of the Papacy was a great favourite) and drama, with a special interest in *Hamlet*. (How he could quote Goethe – or anyone else – if he had no memory, is not clear.) Once after Schirach had read aloud from a German translation of Dante's *Divine Comedy* he described the poem in a letter as "unbelievably beautiful, with the ring of purest music". In music itself, he delighted in Bach, Mozart and Schubert, which he listened to on the prison gramophone, and he keenly discussed the composition of Wagnerian operas, *Parsifal* especially. Later he took a close interest in the American and Russian space programmes, and when Wolf Rüdiger as a young man began to show flair as a designer of airports, he swapped ideas with him eagerly.

As the years went by Spandau's meagre population thinned out still further. Von Neurath was released in 1954, Raeder in 1955, Doenitz in 1956, Funk in 1957. Speer and Schirach went in 1966, leaving No. 7 the sole inhabitant of the huge fortress.

Perhaps the most striking feature of his incarceration was his steadfast refusal to see any member of his family. Some of his fellow prisoners, Speer especially, agreed that visits from the family caused severe emotional strain; nevertheless, he and the others went on seeing relatives at the permitted monthly meetings. No. 7 alone refused to meet any kith and kin. For twenty-two years in Spandau he received no visitor but his lawyer, Dr Seidl. His excuse was always that he did not want to subject himself or his relations to unnecessary emotional stress, yet his refusal worried both his fellow inmates and members of the staff, several of whom begged him to change his mind. It was not as if he was ashamed of his past record. In the court at Nuremberg he had said that he had no regrets, and he repeated the phrase in letters to Frau Hess: *Ich bedaure Nichts* – I regret nothing.

Speer and Schirach, particularly, used to press him to have visits, believing that if he behaved more normally, his chances of being released might improve. Under their pressure No. 7 at last agreed to have Wolf Rüdiger come and see him, only to change his mind, allegedly because the boy had not got a high enough mark in his latest examination.

After the departure of Speer and Schirach, only the prison staff were left to keep up the pressure. But then, at Christmas 1969, No. 7 did at last agree to see Frau Hess and her son.

One factor that tipped the balance was undoubtedly the urging of
Colonel Eugene Bird, who had first served at Spandau as a warder in
1947 and had now returned as the American director of the prison.
Determined to write a book about his eccentric charge, he cultivated
as close a relationship with No. 7 as he could, and frequently besought
him to receive members of his family.

Yet the most potent reason for the prisoner changing his mind was
the fact that he had been dangerously ill with a perforated ulcer. At
the beginning of December 1969 he became convinced he was dying,
and it was under this stress that he agreed to the visit. When it took
place on Christmas Eve, he was still recuperating in the British
Military Hospital.

By then he was seventy-six. It was twenty-eight years since Frau
Hess had seen her husband. More than a generation had passed since
the day he took off from Augsburg. As in any man of the prisoner's
age, his sinuses had begun to collapse, softening the outlines of his
face. Many of his teeth had been extracted, further altering his
appearance. The chance that Frau Hess would notice any real
discrepancy must by then have seemed remote.

And yet she did. Inevitably the meeting was charged with emotion.
It took place across a four-foot-square table, and one of the conditions
was that visitors and prisoner must not touch each other. According
to Colonel Bird, who was present, when Frau Hess and her son came
in, No. 7

shot up from his chair. He saluted, his hand to his brow, palm
inwards. "Hello! I kiss your hand, Ilse!" Hurriedly Wolf Hess,
smiling but cautious, put his hand on his mother's arm. "Mutti,
don't give him your hand."

Frau Hess, staring unbelievingly at the husband she had last seen
on May 10th 1941, said: "I kiss your hand, Father." Wolf Hess
smiled across the table at his father who was still on his feet. "We
don't dare shake hands, but how are you?"

Frau Hess changed the subject. "It's a long time since I have
flown – the last time was with you."

"Yes. Times have changed. And you have changed."

"And you too!" she smiled. "You have changed. Your voice is
much different now to how I remember it."

"How do you mean?" asked Hess, puzzled.

"Your voice is deeper, much deeper than before."

"Oh – you mean it is more *manly*?" They both laughed.[6]

Whether she realised it or not, Frau Hess had stumbled on a physical near-impossibility. Any normal man's voice *rises* with age, rather than deepens. Physical processes associated with ageing inevitably push the timbre up rather than down. Only if the man has a disease of the vocal cords called myxoedema, which causes a thickening of the tissues, can his voice drop in old age. Prisoner No. 7 had no such disease; it is physically impossible that his voice could have deepened with the passage of time.

At the interview, the prisoner turned the observation into a joke neatly enough, and after the half-hour meeting had finished he seemed thoroughly pleased with the way it had gone. He told Colonel Bird how happy he was to have seen the visitors, and that he was sorry he had held off for so long. Then he made a curiously enigmatic remark. "What a big man my son is!" he told Bird. "Of course he was a complete stranger to me. Like somebody I have never seen before."[7]

In due course No. 7 returned from the hospital to Spandau, and, with the ice broken, he was confident enough to receive regular visits not only from Frau Hess and Wolf Rüdiger, but also from Hess's sister, Gretl Rauch. By then he had not only exchanged countless letters with members of the family, he had also read at least two books about the whole episode – those by Rees and Leasor – so that his knowledge of the real Hess's background had become much more secure.

Even so, he refused absolutely to discuss anything that had happened before May 1941, and the way in which he pulled down a portcullis on the past emerges vividly from the conversations he had with Colonel Bird. Bird cultivated his friendship assiduously, collecting material for his book, and he repeatedly tried to tempt No. 7 into making revelations about Nazi history; but again and again the old man evaded his questions with answers of incredible banality. Armed with the knowledge that the prisoner was not Hess, one can see exactly why he was forced to answer in the way he did.

Bird frequently pressed him, for instance, to admit that, as a member of the Nazi Secret Cabinet Council, he must have known about the plans for Operation Barbarossa before he flew to England. Always he denied any knowledge, but only in the vaguest of terms. On one occasion the question brought a long silence and then the reply, "I'm sorry. I don't know. If I knew anything about this Barbarossa, I cannot remember. But in any case I did not fly to England for this reason. I only flew to make peace."[8]

In an attempt to forestall the American when he asked the question again, No. 7 wrote down his answer: "Before I flew to Scotland I did not know of Hitler's intention to attack Russia. I did know, however, that he was no friend of the Soviet Union."[9]

Not surprisingly, this did not satisfy Bird, and a few days later he returned to the attack with two spurs to galvanise the prisoner's memory. One was a copy of *Motive for a Mission*, an account of the Hess affair by James Douglas-Hamilton, second son of the Duke who was involved; the other was a recording taken from a British television film about Hess broadcast to mark the thirtieth anniversary of the flight. On the anniversary itself, Bird confronted the prisoner with both these *aides-mémoire*, but No. 7's reaction was just as clam-like as before.

When Bird pointed out that according to Hamilton's book Hess *had* known about Barbarossa, the prisoner was visibly shaken: "His face dropped and noticeably paled. His eyes sank even further under the brows, and he looked drawn and old. He said nothing."[10]

Yet, needless to say, the book and the film evoked no revelations about the past. It could conceivably be maintained that in denying knowledge of Barbarossa the prisoner was still trying to protect himself against the revenge of the Russians. Yet would the real Hess not have side-stepped the questions with ease, throwing out a mass of spurious and no-longer-checkable details about how he had never sat in on meetings of the Secret Cabinet Council after the outbreak of war, describing exactly who *did* sit in on them, and so on? He could have launched dozens of red herrings for the American to swim after.

The prisoner's almost total ignorance was again apparent when Bird brought up the question of the Reichstag fire – the burning of the parliament building in Berlin on February 27th, 1933, which had always been one of the most potent symbols of the Nazis' rise to power. Though much about the fire was still mysterious, it was no longer politically contentious, and there was no reason on earth why the real Hess – had he still been alive – should not have been glad to talk about it. But all the prisoner could do, evidently, was to steer clear of any conversation that might expose his lack of knowledge. So when the American told him, "It is believed by many that you are the only living person who really knows the truth behind the burning of the Reichstag," and asked him to glance through a new book about it to refresh his memory, the reaction was inevitable:

He was silent for a moment, then his eyes met mine. "I knew nothing. I know nothing now." His eyes dropped and his hands clenched tightly together. "Even if I did know something, I don't want to talk about it. I do not want you to leave that book in my cell."[11]

Quite rightly, Bird felt that the prisoner was not telling the truth, but the American never began to discern the reason for all the lies and evasions he was getting. Even when No. 7 at last agreed to talk about Hitler, Bird got only the blandest of generalisations which anybody could have picked up from reading books or articles in the press.

When he returned to the United States on leave, Bird went so far as to have photocopies made of the Haushofer–Hess correspondence in the Washington archives, but when he brought the copies back to Spandau and showed them to No. 7 they evoked no more than the usual half-baked recollections. They did, however, goad the prisoner into some kind of an analysis of Churchill, and the detail in which No. 7 discussed the former Prime Minister amazed Colonel Bird:

> "It seems astounding to me," I told him, "that you can recall important things like this . . . yet you cannot remember things that are vital to history: like whether or not you knew about Barbarossa before you took off. Sometimes you give the impression you really didn't know."
>
> "I do?" said Hess sharply. "I give you this impression? If you believe it is the truth *and you have proof*, write it down in your book. I do not really care now."[12]

By that stage Bird was submitting drafts of his book to the prisoner, for his approval, and in the end, after repeated changes of mind, No. 7 did allow him to include a paragraph implying that Hess had known about Barbarossa. But by then, one feels, he had become thoroughly fed up with the whole charade, and gave in purely from exhaustion. Zealous though they had been, Bird's enquiries had yielded precisely nothing in the way of new historical fact.

Equally futile were Bird's attempts to make the prisoner write his memoirs. Speer had managed to smuggle *his* reminiscences, mainly written on lavatory paper, out of the gaol with the help of a friendly warder; and, with the American Commandant's connivance, there would have been no physical difficulty in No. 7 doing the same. But for reasons which are now clear, he could not possibly write an autobiography. His lack of knowledge about the real Hess's political career was embarrassing and dangerous enough in everyday conversation; in an attempt at a memoir it would have been disastrous.[13]

One particularly unfortunate phrase which Bird used to describe No. 7 was "the most over-doctored patient in the world". If he had written "the most overlooked", he would have been nearer the truth, for the fact is that the medical treatment accorded the prisoner during much of his time in Spandau was of a lamentably low standard. He was, as Bird claimed, constantly attended by doctors, but neither their qualifications nor their expertise were generally of a high order. The main reason was that they were obliged to spend most of their time on administrative tasks, and so rarely had a chance to practise medicine. A further complication was that purely medical considerations were always liable to be clouded by the political pressures of Spandau's four-power control system.

By far the worst instance of this tendency – indifferent care being exacerbated by political considerations – was the case of the perforated (or burst) ulcer, which nearly killed No. 7 in 1969. Considering that the patient had been *in care* continuously, the episode was medically quite unacceptable. It is worth recounting in some detail, for it was as a direct result of the *débâcle* that I myself became involved with the prisoner three years later.

His history of stomach cramps and aches extended right back, as we have seen, to his earliest days in England. The pains continued on and off through his years at Spandau, but there, as elsewhere, the staff paid little attention to his complaints, considering them greatly exaggerated.

Then, in the middle of November 1969, he became really ill. Unfortunately it was a Russian month and for a few days the Soviet authorities took no action, even though No. 7 had stopped eating and stayed in bed all day, groaning loudly. On November 19th the Russians at last called in the senior British doctor, Lieutenant-Colonel Declan O'Brien, who found the prisoner's stomach so distended that his trousers would not do up. Altogether his appearance caused O'Brien great alarm.

Even so, it was several more days before he could persuade the Russians to grant official approval and allow the patient to be moved to the British Military Hospital. It was only the insistence of O'Brien that got him transferred. The Americans were surprisingly inert, and did not push as hard as they could have. Without the British intervention, the patient might well have died.

O'Brien – who alone of the senior doctors present had surgical experience – already suspected that No. 7 might be suffering from a perforated ulcer, and in due course various tests confirmed his suspicion. In the hospital the doctors attempted to administer a barium meal, but it was most unsatisfactory as the patient began vomiting, and everything had to be done in a hurry. But the test did at least give a negative result: because no barium leaked out of the stomach or small intestine, the doctors knew that there was no open perforation.

But they still did not know what was wrong, so they took an X-ray of the chest, which showed a pocket of air under the diaphragm. There was their diagnosis – and a particularly fortuitous one, too. The presence of the air, assessed along with the previous barium meal, showed that an ulcer *had* burst, but a few days before, and had now sealed itself again.

The patient was still extremely ill, being sustained by an intravenous saline drip and blood transfusions. To make sure that the perforation had not occurred in the large intestine, the doctors tried to administer a barium enema for an examination of the lower bowel. This nearly proved fatal, for the patient was tipped up, head downwards, while the barium was poured into his colon, and the extra pressure on his diaphragm combined with the distension of his small intestine to cause severe respiratory distress.

The attempted enema was quickly abandoned. O'Brien diagnosed temporary heart-failure and at once prescribed appropriate drugs. The patient's life was saved, but not by much.

This episode, as I say, was easily the worst that occurred. Yet No. 7's entire medical record shows all too clearly that the treatment he received through the 1950s and 1960s left a great deal to be desired. Not until 1970 was a consultant stationed in Berlin; it was thus twenty-three years before adequate professional care became available to Prisoner No. 7.

Ninety per cent of the entries in his records consisted of useless notes like "Better today" or "Still complaining of stomach-ache". At one time a trainee doctor studying to be a venereologist was considered enough of an expert to give the Commanding Officer of the British Military Hospital advice on how the prisoner's duodenal ulcer should be treated. At no stage does anyone seem to have thought of using a fibre-optroscope, through which a doctor can examine a patient's stomach and duodenum without giving an anaesthetic. The facility was certainly available in Berlin by the end of the 1960s and in the British Military Hospital by the beginning of the 1970s, but No. 7 was never afforded the luxury of such a modern system. The frequent German complaints about the standard of care he was receiving were absolutely justified.

Apart from his stomach troubles, the prisoner's health was surprisingly good, and it is particularly noticeable that he suffered very few respiratory problems – a record completely at odds with the history of the real Hess. A person who has sustained a severe lung injury is susceptible to attacks of bronchitis ever after. A bullet-wound in the lung is followed in a high percentage of cases by atalectasis, or patchy scarring and collapse of the surrounding lung-tissue. A person like the original Hess, who had a long convalescence and afterwards was always short of breath when walking up hills, could expect to suffer bronchial attacks almost every winter. The fact that No. 7 never had any such attack is on the face of it astounding – until one accepts that the prisoner never suffered a lung-wound anyway.

It was as a direct result of the 1969 crisis that I myself had a chance to examine No. 7 in 1973. As I explained in Chapter 1, he was brought to the British Military Hospital for precautionary barium tests, and it was while these were in progress that I saw his torso and its give-away lack of scars. Had I known his background as thoroughly as I do now, I might have challenged him more strongly about his real identity. But at the time, seeing how severely he had been shaken by my question about his war wounds, and being none too sure of the true state of affairs myself, I judged it best to leave him alone.

Even so, my question had given him an opportunity to declare the true facts. Yet once again he chose to say nothing, to withdraw behind the secret which he had preserved for so long. Already, at that stage, he had been in prison for more than thirty-two years. For thirty-two years he had maintained the fiction that he was Hess; for thirty-two years he had done everything he could to assume the character of the former Deputy Führer. Perhaps, by then, he really believed he *was* Hess. After half a lifetime behind bars, he could not abandon the disguise he had cultivated for so long; it was, as he himself told me, too late.

During those years many attempts to secure his release had been made on his behalf, first by his lawyer Dr Seidl, and then later by Wolf Rüdiger Hess. The first of Dr Seidl's appeals was made to the Allied Control Commission in 1947, the second to the United Nations Organisation in 1956, the third to the European Commission for Human Rights in 1957, and the fourth, in 1966, to the Queen of England, the Presidents of the United States and France, and the Chairman of the Soviet Government. All these attempts were frustrated by the Russians, to whom Hess was the prime enemy surviving from the Nazi régime.

In 1966, after the failure of his fourth petition, Dr Seidl tried at least to get some of the prisoner's conditions improved: he asked, for instance, that No. 7 should be allowed a watch (something denied him ever since his arrival in Spandau), that his choice of books should no longer be censored, that he might have the facilities for making himself a cup of tea or coffee in his cell, and that he should be allowed a bath every day, rather than once a week. So lacking were the Russians in any trace of normal humanity that only the last of these modest requests was granted.

From 1967 Wolf Rüdiger took an increasingly active part in campaigning for No. 7's release. That summer he visited England and Scotland, including the site of the parachute landing in 1941. Yet although public opinion was undoubtedly on his side, he noticed a curious echo of the British authorities' wartime ambivalence. He was taken to see Maindiff Court, near Abergavenny, but although he was anxious to have a private talk with Dr Ellis Jones, he was never allowed to be alone with him. An Army officer stuck to him like a shadow and made sure he was never on his own. In Wolf Rüdiger's own words, "The whole thing was distinctly odd. Without any doubt I was prevented from talking to Dr Jones privately. Also, I had the firm impression that he wanted to tell me something that he could not divulge publicly – but he too was prevented."[14]

More than twenty years after the end of the war, the British evidently still had something to hide.

In the autumn of the same year Wolf Rüdiger held a press conference in Berlin. In the years that followed, his cause was taken up by many prominent people in different countries, not least Lord Shawcross, who had been Chief British Prosecutor at Nuremberg, and Airey Neave, by then a distinguished Conservative Member of Parliament. In the press on both sides of the Atlantic numerous reasons were put forward for releasing the prisoner – that he was and always had been insane, that he was physically ill, that he had already served a long enough penance, and so on.

None of the appeals made any impression on the Russians, whose moral and intellectual sterility is best illustrated by an extract from the official newspaper *Pravda* published in January 1970. The campaign to release Hess, the article said, was a

cunning propaganda move by forces which would like to perpetuate racism, Nazism and apartheid, turn back the course of history, disarm the people morally and dissipate their watchfulness against the intrigues of the forces of aggression and war . . . Imperialism is merciful . . . to criminals, whether they are fascists or racists, because its own policy of international brigandage and aggression, neo-colonialism and racial intolerance is itself criminal.[15]

So bigoted were the Soviet authorities that even when No. 7 was lying ill in the British Military Hospital, and Spandau had no inmate at all, they insisted on maintaining the full paraphernalia of the prison guard, manning the watch-towers and patrolling the empty cells. This was what Airey Neave called "the great Spandau madness"; yet for the Russians it had a certain method, since they were determined to hold on for as long as possible to their foothold in West Berlin. Any interruption of their normal pattern might have weakened their grip on what they had come to regard almost as a piece of diplomatic territory.

Goaded by Soviet hostility, the Western governments again discussed the possibility of unilateral action: of releasing the prisoner on their own initiative and facing the consequences. The answer, however, as expressed in March 1970 by Lord Chalfont, Minister of State at the Foreign Office, was that to free Hess without Russian consent would mean breaking "solemn international obligations", and that the British Government "would not contemplate this".

10

The Plot

ALTHOUGH I HAVE wrestled with the problem for nearly fifteen years, I have not been able to establish exactly what happened on May 10th, 1941, and I doubt if anyone will ever find out. The real Hess took off from Augsburg; a different man and a different plane reached Scotland. So much is certain. But the plot which achieved the substitution is still largely mysterious, for scarcely any clues remain to show how it was put together.

In my view, there was only one man capable of devising and executing a plot on the necessary scale, and that was Heinrich Himmler, head of the S.S. Evidence survives to show that in the spring of 1941 Himmler was already scheming to supplant Hitler as Führer, and my guess is that he deliberately got rid of Hess in an attempt to increase his own stature, his aim being to secure peace with England and at the same time to take over as leader of Nazi Germany. Although this theory is only guesswork, it is based on the facts that remain.

First, it is worth considering the roles and motives of the others who played leading parts in the Hess affair. It is tempting to see Goering – who, as Commander-in-Chief of the Luftwaffe, certainly had the power to get one aircraft shot down and organise a substitute – as the architect of the plot. The fat, sybaritic, and superficially jovial former fighter-pilot certainly disliked Hess and referred to him as a *Piesl*, a contemptuous term for a half-bred gentleman. The Deputy Führer, in turn, regarded Goering with a cold, superior disdain. The animosity between the two was such that at Nazi Party conferences in the 1920s and 1930s they sometimes had almost to be physically kept apart.

By the spring of 1941 Hess no longer appeared, on the face of things, to be a serious rival to Goering. By creating Goering his number one deputy the year before, Hitler had put him ahead of Hess in the line of succession: the Reichsmarschall thus had nothing further to fear from Hess, and no reason for disposing of him.

And yet, if Hess's mission had succeeded and he had returned in triumph, with peace proposals worked out, his prestige would at once have been immensely enhanced. He would again have gone ahead of Goering in the struggle for power. Is it possible that this danger was enough to make Goering engineer his removal?

Hardly. In spite of his physical bulk and undoubted intellectual gifts (which were formidably displayed at Nuremberg) Goering was always something of a political lightweight. For example, though he had once commanded the S.A. (the Party's strong-arm group), he had given up the job because it interfered too much with his social life. Hess was simply not a real enough threat to his position.

Even so, he was obviously involved in some way. This is shown not only by his telephone call to Galland on the evening of May 10th, but also by the astonishing laxity with which he treated Willi Messerschmitt when the aircraft manufacturer was summoned before him in Munich on May 12th. Goering was ordered by Hitler to find out how Hess had had access to an aircraft, but according to Messerschmitt there was no interrogation, only the following merry exchange:

> Goering pointed his baton at me and shouted: "As far as you are concerned, I suppose anybody can come and fly off with one of your machines!"
>
> I pointed out that Hess was not "anybody", but was the *Stellvertreter*.
>
> "You should have known that this man was crazy."
>
> I replied dryly: "How could I be expected to suppose that one so high in the hierarchy of the Third Reich could be crazy? If that were the case, Herr Reichsmarschall, you should have procured his resignation!"
>
> Goering thereupon roared with laughter and exclaimed: "Messerschmitt, you are quite incurable! Go back to your factory and get on with your construction. I will help you out of the mess if the Führer shall seek to make trouble for you."[1]

Why was Goering content to roar with laughter and sweep the matter out of sight? His whole attitude shows the self-confidence of a man who knew well what was going on.

Further suspicion attaches to Goering because of his manner with the prisoner known as Hess at the Nuremberg trial. As I have shown, the tense, sparring relationship which had existed between himself and the real Hess vanished entirely. Instead, he treated his fellow accused with a mixture of incredulity and pitying sarcasm. His jocular suggestion that "Hess" should tell the court his "big secret" still tantalises with its ambiguity. Did Goering *know* that the man in court was the double? And was he daring him to reveal the fact, secure in the knowledge that he could not?

Just as Goering was more heavily involved than standard accounts relate, so also was Willi Messerschmitt. It may only be that because of his friendship with Hess he became innocently caught up in an affair that embarrassed himself and his firm; yet in retrospect almost all his own and his firm's actions in this matter look suspect.

First, there was the fact that the dossiers of every single 110 disappeared from the Messerschmitt factory, even though the records for all other types of aircraft remained and survived the war. Who destroyed them, and why? Second, no records were apparently kept of Hess's multiple training-flights. Third, Messerschmitt claimed that for his final mission Hess had entered his flight under his wife's maiden name and put his destination down as Stavanger – although no one else recalled this strange combination. Fourth, three days after the flight, a long and unconvincing exculpatory memorandum went up on the notice boards of the Messerschmitt factory in Regensburg. It was signed by Theo Croneiss, one of the firm's chief executives, who had been even closer to Hess than Messerschmitt himself, and its aim was to exonerate the company – with which, as all its workers knew, Hess had been on special terms. "Fellow workers, men and women," began the memorandum:

> The close association of the Deputy Führer, Reichsminister Rudolf Hess, with the work of our Professor Messerschmitt, with myself personally, and in the final analysis with each of you on the staff of the firm's factories in Augsburg and Regensburg, gives you the right to an explanation of the events of the past few days.

The notice then gave the text of the Party announcement, and went on:

> To us – Professor Messerschmitt and myself – the Deputy Führer repeatedly made it clear that his sole reason for wanting to train in the Me 110 was so that he could ask the Führer permission to do his share as a fighter pilot at the front. As at every stage of his life, he wanted to make a personal contribution to his fatherland and to set an example to his fellow countrymen at the front . . .[2]

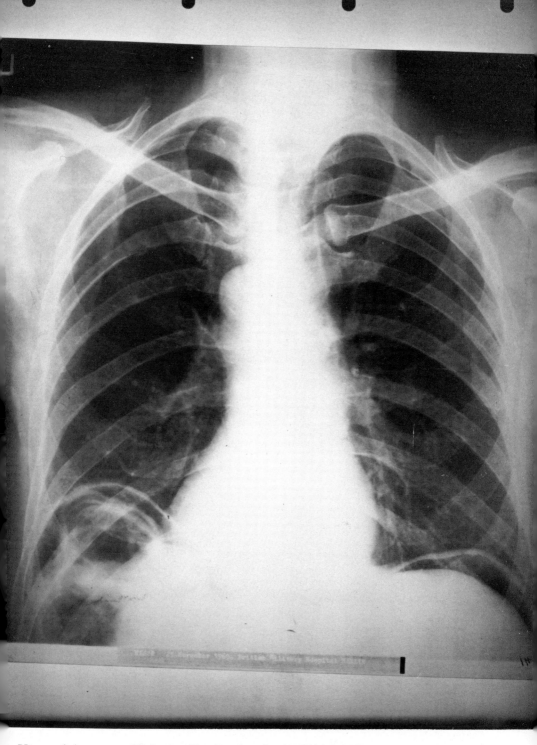

X-ray of the torso of Prisoner No. 7, taken in the British Military Hospital, Berlin. The left side of the chest – to the right in the photograph – shows no sign of damage to the ribs, and no dead-tissue track through the lung, which the passage of a rifle-bullet would inevitably have left behind.

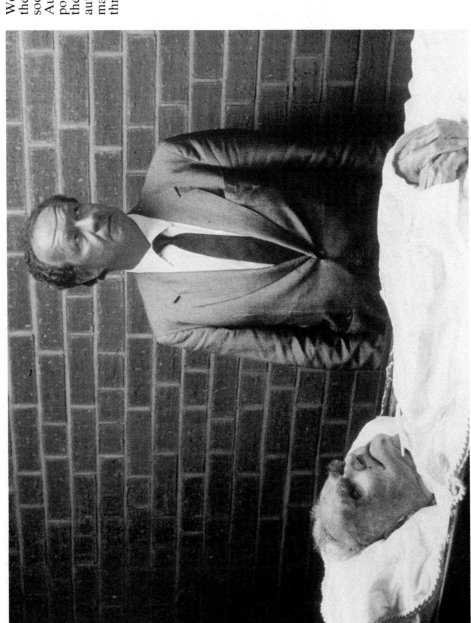

Wolf Rüdiger Hess with the body of the prisoner, soon after his death in August 1987. A German post mortem confirmed the findings of the British autopsy: that the dead man had never been shot through the left lung.

This high-flown waffle was not difficult to see through. Yet neither Goering nor Hitler himself appears to have made any effort to extract from Messerschmitt an explanation of how Hess had enjoyed the regular use of an aircraft. Messerschmitt was not even arrested: he escaped with nothing worse than Goering's jovial reprimand.

Another central figure, Albrecht Haushofer, was less fortunate. Arrested by the Gestapo on May 12th and flown to Berchtesgaden, he was interrogated and ordered to dictate immediately all possible background information on the kind of contacts Hess might try to make in England. His twelve-page report – typed out on the *Führer-maschine*, a special typewriter with letters large enough for Hitler to read without his glasses – summarised the Haushofers' ideas and negotiations to date, and gave a list of prominent Englishmen who, the author thought, might be sympathetic towards the idea of an Anglo-German peace, including Sir Samuel Hoare, Lord Derby, Lord Astor and Lord Dunglass (later Sir Alec Douglas-Home).

None of this was very new. Haushofer was kept in prison for two months, then was allowed to resume his teaching at Berlin University.[3] Neither he nor Messerschmitt, both essentially friends of Hess, had any motive for getting rid of the Deputy Führer. Neither, in consequence, could possibly be considered as the ringleader of any conspiracy against him.

In all the turmoil that convulsed the Nazi hierarchy after Hess's departure, the one man who acted consistently out of character was Himmler. As head of the S.S. he was in charge of the main investigation that followed. It proved such a fiasco that for the first time in its history the S.S. was condemned as being too soft. No culprit was unearthed. No member of Hess's former staff was convicted of any misdemeanour.

The only real revenge taken was the so-called *Aktion Hess*, a purge of astrologers, faith-healers, fortune-tellers and so on, which was launched on June 9th, 1941. This was provoked by Hitler's discovery that Hess had frequented unqualified practitioners of various kinds, and was no more than an attempt by the Party to save face. Having failed to find individual scapegoats, the régime fell back on the expedient of a general round-up. But just as Hess's "progressive illness of long standing" was invented by Party propagandists after his departure as part of the campaign to blacken his reputation, so his reliance on quacks was grossly exaggerated. In fact he was not alone among the Nazi leaders in toying with astrology; Hitler himself also showed interest. And no doubt most of the victims of *Aktion Hess* were perfectly innocent.

In other circumstances, the S.S.'s failure would have infuriated Himmler. Yet on this occasion he seems to have remained quite unmoved; indeed, far from looking for scapegoats, he took positive steps to use his powerful position to protect several of the people involved.

First, he prevented the arrest of Frau Hess, even though Hitler announced that it had taken place. Then he saved his personal masseur, Felix Kersten, from the clutches of the vicious S.S. general Reinhard Heydrich, who was carrying out a separate investigation of his own and had arrested Kersten because he was known to have treated Hess recently.[4] For Heydrich, Himmler's subordinate, to arrest Kersten was extremely rash, but symptomatic of the general dissatisfaction which the official S.S. enquiry produced. Not only did Heydrich launch his own investigation; Martin Bormann set up yet another and, once again, it was Himmler who intervened to resist Bormann's attempts to have Hess's adjutant Pintsch condemned to death. Himmler's concern for the Hess family lasted several years, as his surviving letters show: if anything happened to Frau Hess, he told her in one, he would make sure that her son, Wolf Rüdiger, was looked after.[5]

To adopt so lenient – even tender – an attitude was exceedingly unlike Himmler, especially when confronted, as in the case of Hess's defection, by a major insult to the Reich. This small, fastidious man, who was so obsessive about details that he recorded every occasion on which he shaved and had a bath, and whose only weakness was for stroking the heads of blond Aryan children, conceived it his duty to eliminate every opponent of Nazi ideology. Wielding his gold pen with totally impersonal calm, he signed the death warrants of millions. Yet after the Hess disaster he behaved like a benevolent uncle. Linked with another odd circumstance, this softness becomes extremely significant.

On April 28th, 1941 – as described in Chapter 4 – Hess had sent Albrecht Haushofer to Geneva, to discuss the possibilities of an English peace with Dr Burckhardt, the President of the Swiss Red Cross. Soon after this Burckhardt was visited also by an *agent of Himmler*, who asked specifically whether the British would be willing to discuss peace terms on the same basis as those proposed by Hess, but with *Himmler, not Hitler, in the seat of power*.

From this initiative two facts emerge: first that Himmler already had ideas of supplanting the Führer; and second, that he knew about Hess's peace plan at least by the end of April 1941. How he had discovered the plan's existence it is no longer possible to tell. Perhaps through the loquacious Kersten, whom he had planted on Hess; perhaps through Carl Langbehn, a friend of Albrecht Haushofer whom Himmler often used as a contact-man; perhaps through Gestapo agents. For as early as September 1940 Albrecht Haushofer mentioned in a letter to his parents that Hess seemed "to have given pretty clear instructions to our friends in black uniform"[6] – in other words, Hess had given orders that the Gestapo were not to interfere with any peace moves which he or the Haushofers might make. And what the Gestapo knew, they did not fail to pass on to Himmler.

Later in the war Himmler's overtures to the Americans made his ambitions increasingly obvious,[7] but even in early 1941 it was no secret among his own circle that he had ideas of taking over from Hitler. In May 1941, after a talk with Langbehn, Ulrich von Hassell, in Berlin, reported in his diary that Himmler might be seeking a separate peace with Britain.

Himmler seldom asked important questions except with good reason, and it can now be seen that there *was* a good reason for his approach to Burckhardt in April 1941. Agents in the eastern spy network run by Colonel Reinhard Gehlen reported direct to Himmler, and through them he began to receive ominous indications that the military strength of the Soviet Union was far greater than anticipated. Hitler believed the reports to be exaggerated, but Himmler did not. It was thus very much in his interest to get a peace initiative with England under way as soon as possible – and as far as possible ahead of the launch of Operation Barbarossa. (The final decision to invade Russia was taken in early May, and the invasion itself began on June 22nd.)

Nor would Himmler have exposed his intentions – as he inevitably did in the question put to Burckhardt – unless he had had some means of implementing them: in other words, unless his plan for the elimination of Hess, and the sending of a substitute peace envoy, was complete.

I believe that Hess's preparations, his friendship with Albrecht Haushofer, and his views on peace in general, gave Himmler his opportunity for eliminating a powerful rival who was also a true ally of Hitler. Here was his chance not only of removing the Deputy Führer, but also, at the same time, of sending to England a counterfeit Hess – a *Doppelgänger* – who would start by making peace overtures as though they came from Hitler, but then, when some progress had been made, would put forward the very proposals that Himmler himself had been cultivating – namely, that peace should be made with himself rather than Hitler as Führer.

The whole business of finding and training a double sounds fantastic when first considered. Yet on a purely physical basis doubles are more common than is often supposed. Also in the Second World War, for instance, Field-Marshal Montgomery's double, the actor Clifton James, was so perfect a replica in voice as well as in appearance that he was able to fool close friends, besides the more distant Germans. In 1944 he sustained an important part in the deception scheme which preceded the Normandy landings: he flew to Gibraltar, stayed with the Governor and went on to North Africa. His movements were faithfully reported by German agents, and the German High Command was persuaded that some major Allied operation was imminent in the Mediterranean.

Similarly in pre-war Germany, when the Nazi Party was young and struggling, there was the well-known case of Gauleiter Schemm, who would apparently speak at two widely separated Party meetings simultaneously. He himself would be in one place, and in the other his unknown double would read out a copy of the same speech, making identical gestures, with the result that most people had no idea which was which.

It may even have been the discovery of a man closely resembling Hess that gave Himmler his idea. However the double was found, his training clearly took some time. He had to learn not only the details of Hess's family, background, career, habits, mannerisms, likes and dislikes; he had also to acquire some grasp of his ideas, and in particular of his relationship with the Haushofers, since it was their negotiations which had led to the peace initiative.

As I hope I have shown, the man was reasonably well trained in matters of fact. Also, he had one great built-in advantage, in that his audience in England was not very discriminating: nobody there knew the real Hess well, and anyone who *had* met him at all often was prevented from seeing him anyway. Nor could the British communicate with Germany to check up on details. But though the man learnt to *impersonate*, he never grasped how to *negotiate*, and it was this shortcoming that condemned Himmler's scheme to failure.

Whether he knew it or not, the *Doppelgänger* was doomed from the start. There is every indication that Himmler regarded him as expendable, a non-returnable envoy. If he *had* returned to Germany with the outlines of a peace plan, he would not have been able to sustain his pretence for five minutes, and it seems certain that Himmler would have arranged a fatal accident to prevent anybody else in Germany recognising the true state of affairs. As it was, the mission had exactly the opposite effect to the one Himmler wanted, for it (and the German invasion of Russia) closed ranks behind Churchill, effectively putting paid to the existence of the peace group in Britain.

As to the mechanics of the actual substitution, Pintsch was the one person placed centrally enough to have been the link-man in the conspiracy. Frau Hess maintains with some insistence that Pintsch's relationship with her husband was no different from that of his other adjutants, Leitgen and Winkler.[8] All three lived together in a house not far from the Hesses and shared the Deputy Führer's staff-work. Yet the fact remains that it was Pintsch who was on duty not merely on May 10th, 1941, but also on the day of the alleged earlier attempt to reach Scotland, when Hess is said to have given him the letter for Hitler, but then returned after four hours in the air.

Pintsch had the knowledge of his master's job, household, family, relatives and correspondence. In and out of the Hesses' house all the time, he could furnish all the information needed to equip a double with a convincing knowledge of the background. It was he who produced the story of the earlier failed attempts, he who handed Hess the weather forecast on the fatal day, he who took the photographs of the departure, he who made the peculiar telephone call at nine p.m. that evening, and he who delivered the last letter to Hitler.

Afterwards he spent three years in gaol without trial. Then he was released: he rejoined the army and fought on the Eastern Front, being taken prisoner by the Russians who, knowing his background, tortured him by breaking all his fingers in an attempt to discover more about Hess. Eventually he returned to Munich, and lived again in the same house as during the war. He died some years later.

If Hess's Deputy, Martin Bormann, had had his way, Pintsch would have been executed. Bormann demanded the death penalty, and only the intervention of Himmler prevented it. Again, why the leniency? Perhaps because Himmler feared that the supreme penalty would loosen Pintsch's tongue at the last moment, so that the truth would be revealed.

It is impossible to know how much of the story that Pintsch later told was true. Equally, it is impossible to reconstruct Hess's real motives on May 10th, 1941. He may, as he told his wife, have planned to go for a training-flight on his way to Berlin; but it is possible, also, in spite of the various considerations that make it unlikely, that he was indeed planning to fly to Scotland, as Pintsch claimed. If this was so, it makes the rest of Pintsch's story in some ways more credible. It means, for instance, that Hess did write the explanatory letter for Hitler, which Pintsch delivered next day. If, however, the flight was intended as no more than another training sortie, the letter can only have been forged by Himmler or one of his agents.

At all events, someone was needed to remove Frau Hess's Leica from the house and the leather flying-suit from the airfield in time for them to be transferred to Aalborg. Someone was needed to collect the Haushofer visiting cards and the photographs of Hess as a child with which the substitute pilot was equipped. (For obvious reasons it was impossible to abstract the everyday identity documents which Hess carried on his person – and this was why the man who came to Scotland had none.) On the day itself, someone was needed to alert Himmler's men to the fact that the flight was on, to report the time of take-off, to confirm that the plane was on its way, and to relay details of its route. Only Pintsch, in my view, could have managed all this.

If Pintsch did act as link-man, he can hardly be blamed, for, like the *Doppelgänger* and thousands of other people, he had fallen victim to one of Himmler's favourite weapons – *Sippenhaft*, or the responsibility of kinship. This classic dictator's concept, exploited, if not actually invented, by Himmler and wielded by him with devastating effect, meant that not only an individual, but his or her relations, too, bore responsibility for any deed that the person might have done. Thus if somebody failed to carry out orders, or committed an alleged crime against the State, not just that person but his or her entire family stood to be liquidated by the S.S. After the July 1944 plot against Hitler, for instance, the S.S. brutally murdered every member they could find of the family of Count Schenk von Stauffenberg, the ringleader, including at least six people over seventy. As a threat to ensure silence, *Sippenhaft* was the perfect device. Nor did its efficacy by any means end when the war came to a close. After the death of Himmler and the cessation of hostilities, there were, it is estimated, five million active members of the S.S. still at large in Europe;[9] and even today, when trials of former Nazis are held in Germany, many people refuse to come forward as witnesses for fear of reprisal. More than thirty years later, the sinister power of *Sippenhaft* is still alive.

Sippenhaft explains the malleability of Pintsch. It also accounts, in part, for the fact that Prisoner No. 7 was unable to reveal his true identity. If his peace advances had met with even a guarded welcome from the British, and he had returned to Germany for further consultation, he would have been quickly exposed as an impostor and eliminated. If the British had released him from gaol and sent him home at any later stage of the war, the same would have happened.[10] But if, on the other hand, he had defaulted in his mission – if he had let it be known that he was *not* Hess, and had sought to escape justice by proclaiming his true identity – not only would he himself have been liquidated but a terrible retribution would have fallen on his family. A man is unlikely to fail in his duty if he knows that failure will mean the end not merely of himself but of his nearest and dearest as well.

In the event, he played his cards with almost pathetic craft and doggedness and ended up with a sentence of life imprisonment at Nuremberg – the safest verdict he could have hoped for. No wonder, as he wrote to Frau Hess, he felt calm.

As for Frau Hess, her apparent ignorance of the deception is puzzling. But in this connection, three crucial facts should be borne in mind. First, the prisoner's early letters to her were extremely cautious, and volunteered scarcely any comment about the past: only when he had acquired information from incoming mail did he expand a little.[11] Second, he refused to see her for twenty-eight years, by which time his physical appearance had changed substantially with age. And third, she never spent a moment alone with him, since at every meeting in Spandau she was chaperoned by representatives of the four Allied powers. Just as he grew into acceptance of his prison life, so she apparently grew into acceptance of the fact that he was the man she always thought him to be.

A final reason for the success of the deception was the extraordinary physical similarity between the double and Hess himself. There is no doubt that the two men were essentially alike. It is probable that if measurements of the prisoner's face had been taken professionally when he arrived, and the ratios of height to width had been compared with those of the original, some discrepancies would have been observed. But in everyday life the likeness was more than good enough to pass muster. Nor can any differences be seen when pre-war photographs are compared with those taken later, except for changes wrought by loss of weight and age.

It is time to recapitulate the main conclusions of this book so far. The real Hess bore major scars on his chest and back as a result of his First World War wounds. The man in Spandau bore none.

The fact that the real Hess never reached England is corroborated by many details of the events that took place on May 10th, 1941. Pintsch's photograph shows that the plane in which Hess took off carried no underwing fuel-tanks. The plane that reached Scotland did have such tanks. Even if Hess's aircraft *had* been fitted with drop-tanks, it still could not have covered the distance the pilot claimed to have flown. The radar records show that the pilot did not fly the route he said he had followed. All this is confirmed by the leading British aviation experts of the period, by serving officers of the R.A.F. and the Luftwaffe, and by the Historical Department of the Messerschmitt firm itself. Add to these anomalies the fact that the man who arrived in Scotland carried no identity papers, and wore a leather flying-suit different from the one in which the real Hess had set off, and the whole story of the flight, as accepted convention, collapses like a house of cards.

Everything else follows as one would expect. The strange behaviour of the prisoner, hitherto inexplicable, is now easily understood. No wonder his personal habits were so much at variance with those of the real Hess: no wonder he ate all kinds of food with the manners of a peasant, instead of being a fastidious vegetarian; that he did not know how to score at tennis instead of being a skilled and enthusiastic player; that he failed to recognise Hess's secretaries at Nuremberg and refused to see Frau Hess for more than a generation.

His silence before the international military tribunal and in Spandau suddenly makes sense. At last it is obvious why he offered the court no defence. At last it is obvious why, in gaol, he almost invariably declined to join Speer and his other fellow inmates in their interminable reminiscing – and why, when he did (according to Speer himself), he seldom if ever made a truly informed contribution. At last it is clear why he feigned loss of memory and consistently refused to talk about his past.

11

Sudden Death

THE FIRST EDITION of this book received serious reviews, some of them highly favourable, when it came out in 1979. It also led to a question about the prisoner's identity in the House of Commons, but as usual the British Government brushed the matter under the carpet, saying that they had no doubt that the prisoner was Hess. Some people cast doubts on my veracity, others on my powers of observation, convinced that on the two occasions when I saw the prisoner's chest, I must have made a mistake. Frau Hess was openly contemptuous, and remarked of me to one newspaper, "*Dieser Kerl hat nicht alle Tassen im Schrank*" – "This fellow hasn't got all his cups in the cupboard", a new variation (to me) of having a screw loose. The family did not waver in its belief that the old man in Spandau was their kith and kin; Wolf Rüdiger, still firmly convinced that the prisoner was his father, campaigned with admirable pertinacity for his release, petitioning governments and Heads of State, as well as human rights organisations, but with no success whatever.

Evidence from both London and Berlin suggests that some sort of crisis briefly disrupted life at Spandau in 1979. Whether or not this was the result of my book's appearance, I cannot say; but a leak from Whitehall revealed that great alarm was caused in the Foreign Office by messages from Berlin, which reported that the prisoner had become confused and distressed and started to say extraordinary things. From Spandau itself came confirmation that security had suddenly been stepped up and the staff reminded of the need for total secrecy. Prisoner No. 7 had been taken to the British Military Hospital with bladder-neck obstruction, and there sedated.

Early in 1988 I learnt from Wolf Rüdiger that word of my book had indeed reached No. 7, and that in a letter the prisoner had told Frau Hess not to worry, as he certainly still had the wound scar on his chest, although he could not be certain about the one on his back, as he did not have a second mirror with which to observe it. Here was a fascinating innovation: for the first recorded time in forty-seven years, the prisoner *himself* claiming to have the tell-tale scars.

Over the years, however, nothing much changed inside Spandau, except that towards the end the prisoner's life was made slightly less spartan. He was moved from cell No. 23 to a larger one, No. 17, which had once been the prison's chapel. He was given a more comfortable bed, brought by lorry from the British Military Hospital; but he took with him his old brown table, on which he kept a jar of instant coffee, a mug and spoon, and an AEG electric water heater for brewing hot drinks. He had hooks on which to hang his coat, jacket and two towels, and on some shelves he kept an enamelled plate, two enamel cups, a spoon, salt, pepper and a roll of lavatory paper. From 1969 the door of his cell was left unlocked, and he was allowed to go to the lavatory, along the same corridor, without calling for the warder. (Nevertheless, a warder was present in the corridor, twenty-four hours a day, and the prisoner was never left unaccompanied when he went out into the garden or anywhere except his own immediate surroundings.)

For a few months after he had tried to cut his wrists with a table-knife in 1977, he was watched twenty-four hours a day; but gradually this was found to be intolerable both for him and for the warders, and supervision was once more slackened. As with his other apparent attempts at self-destruction, this one was more for show than in earnest, and after it the Russian warders heartlessly mocked him by asking why, if he really wanted to kill himself, he did not get on and make a job of it with the electrical apparatus in his cell or in the washroom.

In spite of the relaxations, there was one area in which maximum security was maintained to the bitter end: his contact with the outside world. Never, in all the forty-seven years of his captivity, was he alone with any member of the general public. Even the visits which he received every month from one or other of the Hess family were closely chaperoned by at least two, and often all four, of the prison directors, sitting on a row of chairs along the wall. The meetings took place in a room on the first floor of the gaol, described by Wolf Rüdiger Hess as "of unsurpassed bleakness", and divided in two by a plywood partition from floor to ceiling. In the middle of this wooden wall, in an opening six feet wide, stood a table. The prisoner would be led in to sit at one side, and his visitor sat at the other, not allowed even to touch him, still less to kiss or embrace him, forbidden to make any enigmatic sign or gesture, to mention the Nazi era, the Third Reich, the Nuremberg trials or Hess's flight to England. If any breach of security seemed imminent, one of the directors would immediately intervene.[1] One author, Jack Fishman, claims that Frau Hess did once bring up my theory about a double – at which he is said to have laughed and told her not to worry, because his "old bullet wounds" were still there[2] – an echo of what he had said in his letter.

Equally tight censorship was maintained on newspapers, television and the prisoner's letters, both incoming and outgoing. He was allowed to receive one letter of 1,300 words each week from a member of the family, and to write one of the same length; but his access to paper (kept in a drawer in the library) was strictly controlled, and he could not simply write in his cell whenever he wanted to. In any case, he never showed the slightest inclination to write memoirs, as Speer had – for the simple reason that his own history was not what most people supposed.

Of course he chatted a good deal to his warders, but whenever one of them asked him anything about the past, he almost invariably answered that he had forgotten. Even Pastor Charles Gabel, who for nine years was military chaplain to the gaol, and paid the prisoner regular visits, could get no sense out of him when he asked about old times. His standard response, Gabel recalled, was "I can't remember."

On purely physical grounds, it is unlikely that this was true; for, as can be constantly observed, the normal characteristic of very old people is to retain clear memory of the distant past, even if they forget things that happened a day before. The part of the brain dealing with recent events atrophies, but the centre of deep memory remains intact. Yet, at the same time, cerebral *control* also decays, making it more likely that elderly people will involuntarily say things which in earlier days they would have suppressed. Thus, the older No. 7 grew, the greater became the risk that he would start to speak the truth.

Even in very old age, his daily routine altered little. On waking he would call through the half-open door to the warder on duty, who would be sitting in the corridor. The man would then accompany him to Cell 19, once occupied by Baldur von Schirach and now the lavatory. After that he would go over, again accompanied, to Cell 8, where he used his Braun electric razor to shave before washing. He would then walk the twenty-eight yards back to his own cell, again – officially – accompanied. Thereafter, much of his day was spent merely pottering, in his cell, in the garden or in the library. In practice the quality of supervision varied immensely, from the slack approach of the American régime, under which he was allowed more or less to look after himself, to the obsessive attitude maintained by the

Russians, who never left him for a moment and recorded every syllable he uttered. It is not surprising that, of the four nations who guarded him, he felt most relaxed with the easy-going Americans.

It is important to remember that by August 1987 he had become extremely debilitated. His exact age is still a matter of doubt. Hess, had he still been alive, would have been ninety-three (having been born in April 1894); on several occasions, including once at Nuremberg, Prisoner No. 7 had inadvertently given what I believe to have been his own birth-date – 1899 – and this would have made him eighty-eight. Either way, he had grown very frail and decrepit: much of his physical strength had gone, and he was capable of only the most modest effort.[3]

He had earlier suffered a slight stroke, and during the 1980s he was beset by cerebral circulatory problems. As a result he lost visual acuity in both eyes, and the field of vision in his left eye was severely curtailed. This meant that he could read very little, and wrote only with difficulty. The grip in his left hand was recorded as barely enough to hold an object up – a child of six could have unwrapped his fist without difficulty, against his will. (His grip was assessed on the neurological scale used for such measurements as the grip of a child, about half that of a normal man.) His left arm, in fact, was of little use to him, for a frozen shoulder meant that he could not lift it above the horizontal in front, and not even as high as that out to the side. (The pain and disability caused by a frozen shoulder can scarcely be imagined by someone who has never suffered them.) When he wanted to take his coffee-jar and mug off the shelf, he would reach out with a bent left elbow and push them across into his right hand, to make sure they did not fall on to the floor. The warders watched him go through this little performance every day.

His right hand and arm had lasted better. He could raise them straight above his head to comb his hair, but he had to have an outsize comb, and to control it properly he held it not in his fingers but with his whole hand gripping its back. Even when he tried to write, his right hand quickly grew tired; after a few minutes he would put down his pen and rub his hands together, to ward off stiffness and cramps. Ever since 1979 he had found his coffee mug too heavy to hold by the handle, so he had taken to gripping it with his hand round the barrel. His sense of balance had been badly impaired, partly by the failure of his eyesight, but mainly by arteriosclerosis in the blood vessels of his brain-stem. His left knee was liable to give way beneath him, and he could no longer walk upstairs without help.

To the men who looked after him, his most obvious physical

feature was a pronounced stoop. His spine, affected by arthritis, had developed a hump: the vertebrae at the top of his back had collapsed into wedge-shaped bodies, and this had the effect of thrusting his head forward and limiting its traverse to either side. He could turn his head no more than a few degrees to the left, and halfway to the right – and this only with pain and difficulty. Yet, for the purposes of this enquiry, the most significant feature was his inability to raise his head backwards and look up. If he tried to do this, the effort instantly made him dizzy: he felt that he was going to fall over backwards, and, to compensate, at once threw himself forwards. If he raised his arms in front of him, it made these symptoms worse – and this had two direct consequences on his toilet: he could not wash the back of his neck, especially on the left side, without some help, and because he needed both hands to manipulate an electric razor – one to hold the implement, the other to pull or steady the skin – he took to shaving sitting down. In 1984 the authorities decided that it was no longer safe for him to stand up to inspect his own appearance, so they lowered the mirror in his washroom to waist-height, and the British warders had orders to watch him carefully, both there and around the main wing of the prison, in case he fell.

His combination of weaknesses – uncertainty of gait, limitation of vision, lack of balance and bad posture – meant that once he had set himself moving in a particular direction, he would lurch forward on that bearing. Altogether, although he was not suffering from Parkinson's disease, his various debilities produced effects not dissimilar.

It would be unseemly thus to enumerate the defects of a very old body if they had no bearing on what happened. But in fact they were of crucial importance, for in my view the prisoner, in his advanced state of decrepitude, could not possibly have committed suicide in the way which has been suggested.

My enquiries reveal that the even tenor of the old man's days was disrupted during the last week of July 1987. Messages reaching the Foreign Office in London warned that one of the Soviet warders on duty that month had reported "loose talk" by Prisoner No. 7. The warder had taken notes, and these were sufficiently strange for the Soviet representative to make some jibe during the regular, Thursday-morning, administrative meeting held by the four Prison Governors in their room on Spandau's first floor.

Obviously, official sources will never reveal what the prisoner said. They will never disclose whether, his endurance finally exhausted, he had tried to reveal that he was not Rudolf Hess at all. But although he had begun to speak frankly at least once before, he had never done so to a Russian; and now, it seems, somebody decided that the risk of him surviving for another month of Soviet custody was too great. Within three weeks of his outburst, whatever it was, his life had been brought to a sudden and brutal end.[4]

On the morning of August 17th his breakfast was taken to him as usual on a rubber-wheeled trolley, which was left standing outside his cell for him to help himself. He had some black coffee, dietary bread, apricot jam and half a glass of milk, and although he left his boiled egg untouched, he took a tangerine and an apple into his cell to eat later.

At ten ten a.m. the American warder on duty tapped on his door and called him to go out for his morning exercise; but he did not emerge till ten twenty-five. Then he was escorted down the spiral, wrought-iron staircase that led from the main cell block to ground level, and out into the garden, straight to a chair near the ramshackle garden seat made out of wood by his former colleague Albert Speer. There he was allowed to remain for most of his allotted exercise time, and the guard in the tower immediately opposite the end of the main prison block (Tower B in the accompanying diagram) observed him sitting with his hands in his pockets.

At eleven thirty a.m. he was led to the main prison entrance and given a routine search before being helped back to his cell. The warder's report for the morning in the Occurrence Book was the usual "Nothing Found".

Lunch, normally at midday, was served a quarter of an hour late. The first course – afterwards found partially digested in the prisoner's stomach – was shrimp cocktail; but he scarcely touched his main course of fish, mashed potato and beans. There was nothing unusual in this: like many old people, he had for years only picked at his food, and sometimes, in a reversion to the strange behaviour which had characterised his early captivity, he sent away a whole meal and demanded a replacement, as though suspicious that the food was poisoned.

After lunch he lay on his bed and took a nap. Then at two thirty he awoke of his own accord, put on his jacket and was again escorted down the steps to the garden by his warder. He did not – and this is important – ask for writing materials or attempt to use the adjustable hospital table that swung out over his bed. He certainly did not write a letter or note during this period.

Shortly after two thirty the guard in Tower B saw him emerge and walk slowly, bent forward at an acute angle, led by his escort, along the main garden path. The last specific notice that the guard took of

SPANDAU PRISON

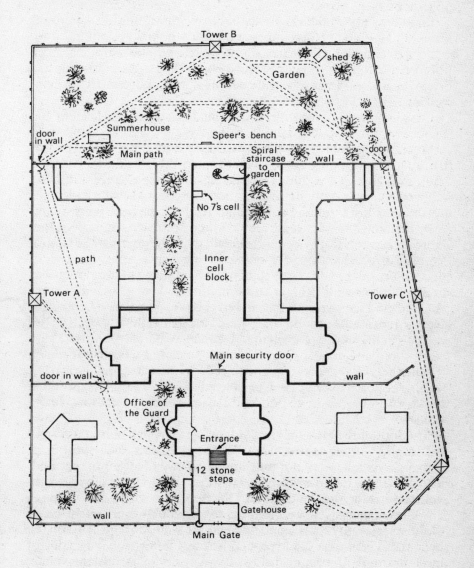

him was at three fifteen p.m., when he saw the two men sitting together on a garden seat.

Only the duty warder knew that at some time after this – perhaps three thirty – he took his charge to the garden shed or summerhouse which stood under a large tree at the junction of the paths. There he sat with him for a few minutes before – according to his own testimony – leaving him alone briefly while he was summoned back to the main cell block to answer a telephone call.

Over the years the security inside Spandau had become lax, and the prisoner was not watched anything like as closely as he might have been. The perimeter towers had originally been built mainly so that the guards could maintain surveillance on the outside walls of the gaol, and cover each other; but inside the prison, trees had been allowed to grow without thought for the cover they provided for anyone moving about the compound. By 1987 the trees were higher than the watch-towers, and they created so many blind-spots that large areas could not be observed at all; even the guard in the central tower (Tower B) had no view of the summerhouse, and did not know that the prisoner had gone to sit in it. His command of the garden was limited to the sector straight ahead of him, and the guards in Towers A and C had their view of the garden completely blocked by foliage. Only a man on the ground could have seen beneath the trees.

The shed itself, a rectangular wooden building, was used as a work-room and depot by the gardener. In earlier days the prisoners had not been allowed into it, but since No. 7 had been on his own, he had, as a special favour, been permitted to go in and sit on a wooden bench during his exercise period if rain came on or if he was feeling tired.[5]

The roof of the little building sloped up to a pitch more than eight feet high, but the eaves over the door, carried on a substantial transverse beam, were not much more than six feet off the ground. The place was full of clutter, its most obvious fixture being a work-bench along the wall on the left of the door. Above it was a window, and on the bench itself was mounted a sharpening-wheel, and two sets of shears, recently sharpened, hung on the wall above it. Also on the bench were some rags, and several heavy, folding wooden chairs; at least one more of these chairs was standing folded against the bench, and more were stacked outside (they were used by the cooks to sit out during off-duty periods). There was also a coil of garden hose. The floor was covered with dust, wood-shavings and metal-filings; but also, inside the door, to the right, were several coils of yellow electrical flex, apparently left there by workmen from the firm of

Frohberg Elektrobau, who had been working in the gaol that day. I presume they had been repairing the 4,000-volt killer-wire which ran round the gaol's perimeter; but why the Prison Director had brought in a German firm, rather than use British Army electrical engineers, who were on hand close by, I cannot make out. (A telephone call to Frohberg's office earlier this year produced a complete refusal to answer; a director, asked to confirm that his men had been in the gaol on August 17th, would only say, "Absolutely no comment."

It was in this modest hut, with its smells of oil and wood, that the prisoner's life came to a sudden end. The warder, returning from his brief absence, found him on the floor in a crumpled position, half sitting, half lying, bent forward, with his knees drawn up to his chest, propped against a folded chair, on which the right side of his head was resting. Round his neck was a length of flex, and his face had turned dark blue.

Immediately the warder felt certain that Prisoner No. 7 was dead. But he yelled loudly for help, and almost at once people came running. For a few moments confusion reigned. Someone got the flex off the prisoner's neck, straightened out the body and dragged it into the open. By the time it was outside, several people had handled the flex, and one of them later remarked that his hands felt oily and smelt of the nail-polish remover used by his wife.

The prisoner's face was clean, but the right side of his jacket, and the right leg and seat of his trousers, were covered with dust and shavings. There, on the grass beside the path, they desperately tried to revive him by mouth-to-mouth resuscitation and external massage of the heart.[6] But these men were not medically trained, and their efforts were so violent that they fractured six ribs on the left side of the prisoner's chest and three on the right.[7]

Already, as they laboured, rumours began to fly: that the prisoner had been found hanging; that he had tried to hang himself, but that the flex had broken and he had fallen to the floor; that he had not tried to hang himself, but had managed to throttle himself by tying a knot in the flex and pulling it tight.

Spandau's antiquated telephone-system was instantly put at full stretch. The first call, to the Captain of the Guard's office, brought the officer in charge racing through the inner cell block into the garden. The single sergeant on duty, not bothering with the telephone, yelled an alarm message through the main security door to the Prison Director's office. There it was instantly decided that, even if they had no police escort (which normally would have been deemed

essential), the stricken man must be taken at once by ambulance to
the British Military Hospital, two miles away.

Less than two minutes after the initial discovery, the resuscitation
party was ordered to move. Shovelling the body on to a stretcher,
they ran with it to the outer door, struggled up the spiral staircase,
through the inner cell block, through the central block to the main
security door, and finally down the twelve stone steps to ground level
at the front of the gaol. As they hustled through the ancient building,
they restarted their frantic pumping of the chest whenever they
paused to negotiate a corner. Spandau, built with sloping floors so
that blood would run away easily, had witnessed some desperate
struggles in its time; but most of them were death-throes, and
probably the old gaol had never seen the opposite – men jostling
frenziedly to prolong or restore life.

As the stretcher-bearers ran, a telephone call from the Prison
Director's office, logged at fifteen fifty-three, startled the duty cor-
poral at the front desk of the British Military Hospital: he was told to
expect an ambulance within minutes, as one was on the point of
leaving. The Commanding Officer of the hospital, Colonel J. M.
Hamer-Philip, immediately began to assemble a guard, and put out
an alert on the Tannoy summoning all military staff to reception.

Away went the ambulance from Spandau, a sluggish, under-
powered Land-Rover, escorted by two other Land-Rovers. It
screamed through its gears along Heerstrasse, and then laboured in
third all the way up the long incline of Dickensweg. In the back one of
the three-man-crew struggled to insert a red rubber endotracheal tube
into the prisoner's windpipe; but the forward set of his head was so
pronounced, and the ride over cobblestones and tramlines so rough,
that, without realising what he had done, he pushed the tube into
his oesophagus by mistake, and so pumped oxygen into his stomach,
rather than into his lungs, blowing the stomach up like a balloon.

After a journey lasting barely seven minutes, the ambulance swung
right through the guarded hospital gates and roared to a halt outside
the doors. The body was rushed straight in to a waiting team of
doctors. The time was exactly four o'clock.

The Consultant Surgeon, Major Price, was on leave, and for some
reason his locum was not brought in, even though he was available.
Instead, Major Carabot, a specialist grade physician, who happened
to be on duty, took charge, along with his colleague Colonel Ross.

The team must have seen that their chances of success were
minimal. Nevertheless, they made valiant final efforts at resuscitation. They resited the throat-tube correctly and tried to establish an

intravenous drip in the right wrist. When this failed, because they could not set up a flow into the vein, they tried the same thing in the left ankle – again without success. Finally they inserted a large, hollow needle into the left subclavian vein, beneath the collar-bone – a last-resort technique developed with great success by the Americans in Vietnam. All the time further cardiac massage was being administered. But every effort was in vain, and at four ten p.m. they were forced to declare the prisoner dead. Shortly after four twenty-five the body was wheeled down to the hospital's mortuary in the basement, where it remained guarded and fully clothed, with the endotracheal tube still in place.

Everyone was left in a state of shock: the junior medical staff by the loss of a patient, the hierarchy (who had collected *en masse* in the outside corridor) by the acute diplomatic problems which the incident had suddenly created. Messages were already pouring in – from the Four Powers in Berlin, from the Ministry of Defence and Foreign Office in London – and the man under greatest pressure was the British Military Governor, Lieutenant-Colonel A. H. Le Tissier.

Clearly an immediate meeting of the Four Powers was essential, and as there were too many people to fit into the Commanding Officer's small office on the ground floor, the hospital's library was thrown open. Sandwiches and drinks were hastily brought across from the Officers' Mess, through the back door.

The meeting was short and, by all accounts, bad-tempered. Recriminations broke out at once, the Soviet representatives blaming the Americans for their slapdash methods. The Russians, as always in strange surroundings, were ill at ease, for they did not like meeting anywhere in the West except in their familiar sanctuary of the Governor's room in Spandau – a bare rendezvous, containing nothing but a scruffy wooden table, a few chairs and a hatstand, which they knew was not infested with listening devices; and now, to make things worse for them, there had been no time for them to take advice from their military headquarters outside Berlin, so that they could not shoulder any responsibility.

The Russians left at six twenty, but the meeting went on for somewhat longer. Its most important conclusion was that a post-mortem examination should be held to establish the cause of death. The British insisted that the examination should be carried out by one of their own Army pathologists, rather than by the panel of four experts called for by both the Americans and the French. They also managed to persuade everyone concerned that it would be unwise for still photographs of any kind to be taken of the body, either before or during the post mortem. (The reason advanced was that any such pictures might fall into the wrong hands and be used as propaganda by latter-day Nazi groups; but the veto was an uncanny echo of Churchill's absolute refusal to have the prisoner photographed in 1941.) Further, in spite of American objections, they insisted that the enquiry into the apparent suicide should be carried out solely by the Special Investigation Branch of the Royal Military Police. Thus, at the impromptu meeting, the British managed to keep things well under control, and although no official statement announced that the prisoner had committed suicide, this was the message which quickly found its way into the world's media.

A crack S.I.B. investigation team of three warrant officers and a sergeant, under the command of Major J. P. Gallagher, was summoned at zero notice from Düsseldorf and the British Army Headquarters at Rheindalen, in the Federal Republic of Germany. But before they could reach Berlin, a preliminary investigation was carried out by members of the local Royal Military Police, who took charge of the hut and the various objects inside.

When the S.I.B. team did arrive, they had to work extremely fast, and my impression is that the brief which they were given was strictly circumscribed. They were obliged to confine their investigations within limits that now seem extraordinary. For instance, when the team was first granted access to the corpse, and one of the warrant officers asked permission to take fingerprints, he was told that this was unnecessary – even though fingerprinting is standard practice in such enquiries.[8] Again, the American warder who had been on duty was not detained for questioning; nor was the team allowed to follow up the mysterious telephone call which had allegedly summoned him away and left the prisoner unprotected.

Even so, they raised some awkward questions, pointing out that their task had been made more difficult by three unfortunate facts:

1. The garden shed had been invaded and trampled by several people.

2. Vital exhibits had been handled indiscriminately.

3. No effective security had been imposed on the site immediately after the incident.

The team discovered the main exhibit, the electric flex, lying on the floor. It was unmarked, and there was no evidence that it had ever been stapled or nailed to any structure (the Four Powers' official statement later said that the prisoner had killed himself with the flex of a reading-lamp; but although an extension-flex may still have been stapled to the wall, the lamp itself had been removed years earlier, when the prisoner's eyes deteriorated.) The flex used for the throttling showed no sign of having been knotted, or of having been pulled taut over the sharp corners of a beam. Yet the team found the relative positions of the body and the flex consistent with strangulation, and came to the conclusion that Prisoner No. 7 had managed to throttle himself. This, they thought, he must have done by passing the ends of the flex through the roof structure, putting his head through the loop, and pulling down hard enough on the ends to cut off his breathing – until he blacked out and collapsed, dragging the flex down clear of the roof in his fall.

Had they known how weak the old man had been, how feeble his grip, and how impossible he found it to straighten up his torso, let alone to raise his hands above his head without toppling backwards, they would have realised immediately that their scenario was physically impossible. But this was the only way they could explain what had happened.

For some reason they did not list as an exhibit a rag soaked in acetone (a fat- and oil-solvent) which had been found on the workbench in the hut. The flex had apparently been wiped with it (hence the smell which one of the prison staff who went to the rescue thought was nail-polish, and the rumours that the victim had been chloroformed). The S.I.B. assumed that the rag had been used by the Frohberg electricians to clean grease off their flex; but later one of the warrant officers did ask the pathologist if acetone would work as an anaesthetic when held over nose and mouth (it would not), and in consequence the pathologist called for a toxicological sample of the dead man's blood.

In retrospect it is clear that the conduct of the American Captain of the Guard raises awkward questions. Why, as soon as the body was on its way to the hospital, did he not make certain that the scene of the incident was sealed off and kept intact? With the prisoner gone, there was no longer any point in maintaining full guard in the perimeter towers; why did he not bring men down to cordon off the summerhouse during the time – probably at least half an hour – that it took the detachment of Military Police to arrive from their headquarters at the Olympic Stadium? Yet it seems that the hut was not made fully secure for several hours, and no clear record could be given to the S.I.B. of who had been allowed into it. Also, it would surely have been a sensible precaution to detain – for the time being, at any rate – the warders who had been on duty at the time; but instead of being kept back, they were all allowed to go home.

12

The Post Mortems

THE PATHOLOGIST CHOSEN to make the post mortem examination was Professor J. M. Cameron, Professor of Forensic Medicine at the University of London since 1973 and Chief Pathologist to the Army since the retirement of Professor Francis Camps. A jovial, ruddy-faced man of sixty-eight, Cameron had known for some time that he would eventually have to perform this task, for the Ministry of Defence had put him on standby and asked him to make himself ready several years before.

When the call at last came, it caught him in Strasbourg, where he had been accompanying a swimming team (sports medicine is one of his hobbies). Arrangements were at once put in hand for him to fly to Berlin, and he arrived on the evening of August 18th, in time for a briefing and dinner.

The state of affairs there was not what he had expected. In all his years of waiting he had understood that any post mortem he conducted would concentrate only on any evidence of former wounds that he found on the prisoner's body.[1] He further understood that his report would be for the eyes of the British Military Governor alone. In other words, his findings would be secret – and so would the fact that he carried out the examination at all, for the other three Powers would never have agreed to being excluded. Yet now, as he reached Berlin, he learnt that he was required to carry out a full, formal post mortem, and that his report on it would go to all four Powers.

I find it almost inconceivable – and yet it appears to be true, for he told me so himself – that Dr Cameron arrived in Berlin without having read the first edition of this book, and without even knowing what I had claimed in it. I say this not in any spirit of self-importance, but out of sheer amazement; for, whatever the merits or faults of the book, it was indispensable reading for anyone with a medical interest in the case, and absolutely essential for someone who had, in effect, been put on standby to produce an authoritative refutation of my claims. How could Cameron possibly refute my theory if he did not know what I had said? He had, so far as I can judge, been vaguely briefed on my views, but his knowledge was hopelessly inexact.

In any case, by the time he reached the scene, absolute security had been established in and around the British Military Hospital, and X-rays had been taken of the body. But everyone concerned was so keyed-up by the highly-charged atmosphere, and so nervous of making a mistake, that a ridiculous misunderstanding had been perpetrated.[2]

The radiographer, finding that the endotracheal tube was still in place and the body still fully clothed in white shirt, grey jacket, white long johns, boxer shorts and grey flannels with braces, asked permission to remove the tube and the clothes. The anaesthetist, whom he consulted, advised that the tube should be left where it was for the first X-rays, and then removed for more pictures to be taken. (This procedure was considered correct both medically and legally, since everyone had had such difficulty introducing the tube in the first place.) Permission to remove the clothes, however, was refused: the radiographer was told that they might be opened, but not taken off, and he had difficulty getting good pictures, for he found the dust and debris from the floor of the garden shed intrusive, and tried to brush it away.

Not until later did anyone realise how utterly misleading the prohibition on undressing made some of his X-rays. Pictures of the dead man's pelvic region showed a number of small radio-opaque spots, which were tentatively described as "possible gun shot residue", in his buttocks and the backs of his thighs. Yet, whatever else had happened to the prisoner, he had certainly never been shot in the backside: the spots were neither on nor in his person, but merely flecks of metal which had stuck to the seat of his trousers when he fell to the floor.

On Wednesday, August 19th, proceedings opened before eight a.m. as the four Prison Governors and their medical representatives began to gather in the hospital. The British were represented by Lieutenant-Colonel A. H. Le Tissier and his medical adviser Lieutenant-Colonel R. C. Menzies, the Professor of Military Pathology at the Royal Army Medical College in London, who had just flown out from England. The French Prison Governor M. Planet was backed up by *his* medical adviser, Colonel Ailland; for the Americans Mr D. Keane was seconded by Lieutenant-Colonel Wilkerson, and for the Russians, Mr I. V. Kolodnikov by Lieutenant-Colonel Koslikov.[3] Besides all these, there was the Commanding Officer of the hospital, Colonel J. M. Hamer-Philip, the five-man S.I.B. investigation team, and of course Cameron himself, who was armed with a preliminary report from the S.I.B. and with the recent X-rays, but with only one of the four available volumes of the prisoner's medical records.

At eight fifteen the whole assembly crowded down to the mortuary for a formal identification of the body, and Colonel Hamer-Philip handed Cameron a Certificate of Authority to proceed with his examination. Again, it was confirmed that no still photographs would be taken, but closed-circuit television made it possible for the Prison Governors to withdraw into another room and watch progress from there.

The examination itself began with the undressing of the body. The task of removing the clothes fell to one of the S.I.B. team, Warrant Officer N. Lurcock, who was made Exhibit Officer for the occasion, and whose initials, N.L., together with numbers, were used to identify the various exhibits. Thus the dead man's sports jacket became N.L.1, his trousers N.L.2, his shirt N.L.3, his long johns N.L.4, his boxer shorts N.L.5, and so on. More macabre (from the warrant officer's point of view) was the fact that organs removed from the body were labelled in the same way: a lock of hair, for instance, became N.L.6, the left lung N.L.16, and the larynx N.L.17.

As each garment was removed, it was carefully searched – and lo and behold, what should be found, in the presence of so many august witnesses, but a "suicide note" – or at least a note which was interpreted as such. Scribbled on the back of a letter to the prisoner from Hess's daughter-in-law were the words, "Please would the Governors send this home. Written a few minutes before my death. Dear Ilse, Thank you for what you have done for me and for what you tried to do." Like many other people, I find it incredible that any message could have sat undiscovered for two days in the dead man's right-hand jacket pocket. The S.I.B. team had had access to the body; had none of them thought of searching its clothes?

With the body naked, Dr Cameron made a careful examination of its surface, and in particular of the marks on its skin, first under normal illumination, then by ultra-violet light, which gave the whole scene a surrealistic air and stuck in the minds of the observers without medical training. Many forensic experts, among them the distinguished Home Office pathologist Professor Bernard Knight, believe that ultra-violet light affords no advantage, and that scars can be seen perfectly well without it; but Cameron clearly wanted to give himself every chance of spotting any scars that the prisoner carried.

Of the many points recorded in his report, I refer here only to those directly concerned with the death and with possible earlier wounds.

Running across the left side of the neck Cameron found a "fine linear mark", about 3 inches (7 centimetres) long and ½ inch (.75 centimetres) wide – the pressure-mark left by the electric flex; but he failed to give a precise – and crucial – description of the angle at which this mark lay; and, in the absence of any photograph, the world would now no longer be certain of its alignment, had a German pathologist not produced a much more exact account of it soon afterwards.

Next Cameron recorded "an old scar on the left side of the chest, 126 centimetres from the heel, 7 centimetres from the midline". A measure of this kind – peculiar as it sounds to laymen – is a standard formula used by forensic pathologists to give the height of a scar above ground in case the information is relevant in a case of stabbing. The fact that Cameron used this formula showed that he immediately ascribed the chest scar to a stab wound – and in this he was quite correct, for the mark was one of the two small parallel scars left after the prisoner had pushed a kitchen knife through his skin at Maindiff Court, Abergavenny, on exactly the site now pinpointed, over the apex of the heart (see page 117). This scar – and its neighbour, which Cameron missed – were also soon described again in greater detail by a German pathologist.

One curious fact is that Cameron did not record the size of the scar, which was one inch or 2.5 centimetres long. Was his omission designed to give the British Government a loophole – a chest scar of *some* sort on which an explanation, however misleading, could be built? Yet Cameron, being an honest man, and furthermore surrounded by a battery of curious eyes, could not invent scars which did not exist – *and he recorded no other scars on the dead man's torso*. As I had known since 1973, there was no sign of an entry- or exit-wound caused by a rifle bullet, no sign of the scar left when Sauerbruch operated to save Hess's life, no sign (in short) of the marks which Frau Hess had repeatedly insisted her husband carried on his chest and back.

Whether Cameron realised it or not, he was the fifty-eighth surgeon to examine the prisoner's torso since the man had fallen into British hands, and all fifty-seven of his predecessors, from the meticulous Dr Gibson Graham on, had recorded the same history-defying enigma: that the prisoner had never been shot through the chest. His torso had stood the test of time.

When Cameron measured the corpse, from the tip of the head to the heel, he recorded a height of 5 feet 9 inches, or 175 centimetres; but although this figure was no doubt accurate, it clearly did not represent the height of the man before old age withered him and curved his spine. In his youth he had been about 6 feet 1 inch tall. Cameron also noted the severe kyphosis or stooping already familiar to the prisoner's warders.

Of the various bruises which he reported, most had been caused by the desperate attempts at resuscitation; but there was one of particular significance, on the back of the top of the head. By the time Cameron saw it, the hair had been shaved off this area for easier examination, and he recorded it only as "a circular bruised abrasion". But an independent witness who saw it described it as a central bruise about two inches in diameter, raised half an inch from the level of the scalp, with the discoloured area extending beyond the visible swelling. Although the skin had not been broken, the bruise could only have been caused by a blow of considerable force from, or against, a blunt object.

Proceeding to operate, Cameron next reflected, or peeled back, the scalp. This revealed that the skull had not been fractured, but there was "deep bruising over the top of the back of the head". Investigation of the throat showed "excessive bruising" in the upper-right part of the voice-box, and in general appearances was "consistent with compression of the neck". There was further deep bruising behind the voice-box, and two further X-rays revealed a fracture of the right upper horn of the thyroid cartilage.

The chest yielded no positive information of any significance. Cameron found multiple fractures of the ribs on both sides, but, as he recorded, all the fractures had been caused at the time of resuscitation, "and had no bearing on the cause of death". He placed some emphasis on the fact that the left lung was "firmly adherent to the chest wall and diaphragm, with extensive old adhesions", and he removed the lung for dissection; but, because he had not been furnished with relevant X-rays taken in earlier years, or with all the prisoner's medical records, he seems not to have realised that these adhesions were the result of the perforated duodenal ulcer which No. 7 had suffered in 1969.

Cameron's examination of the chest was immensely more significant in terms of its *negative* information, for it showed beyond all doubt that the prisoner had never been shot through the lung. There was no old damage of any kind to the ribs and muscles which formed the thoracic cavity. The lining of the chest was virgin. There was no track of fibrous tissue through either lung, such as would have been left by the passage of a bullet. There was no major scarring or evidence of sepsis. The linear scar which Cameron had noted on the outside of the chest was only skin-deep, and in the lung itself were nothing but the small marks left by tuberculosis.

When Cameron came to examine the buttocks and backs of the thighs, he must have been truly bewildered, as he was looking for the "possible gun shot residue" which had showed up as opaque spots on the X-rays taken before he arrived. Of course he could find no such residue, on either external or internal examination – because the removal of the prisoner's trousers had done away with it.

Nine samples – of hair, urine, blood and so on – were taken, and later handed by Cameron himself to Dr P. A. Toseland of Guy's Hospital, in London, for toxological analysis. This showed no abnormalities, and there was no indication of any volatile substances, "particularly there was no evidence of acetone". Twenty-three microscopic sections were prepared and sent for examination. These revealed no evidence of natural disease " which could have caused or contributed to death at that moment in time", and in his summary, Cameron concluded:

"Death was not due to natural causes.

In my opinion the cause of death was:

a. Asphyxia.

b. Compression of the neck.

c. Suspension."

Cameron could not, of course, write up his report until later; but he finished his examination of the body at eleven thirty-five a.m. on August 19th, and the main lines of his findings were clear enough. By four p.m. that day the British Military Government – greatly helped by the note so conveniently found on the corpse – had persuaded the other powers to agree that death had been due to suicide. It should be emphasised, however, that Cameron did not even suggest suicide, and nowhere considered the idea in his report. Nor did he mention the severe bruise on the back of the dead man's head as having any special relevance. At six p.m. local time an official statement went out declaring that

while some laboratory tests are still to be completed, the primary cause of death has been determined to be asphyxiation. The note which was found on the body – the contents of which have been released to Hess's family – clearly implies that Hess planned to take his own life.

Earlier, the Allied Powers had recommended that when Prisoner No. 7 died, his corpse should be cremated; but by now international pressure was so great that the idea of cremation was abandoned, and it was decided to return the body to Hess's family. The decision led to frenzied speculation in Germany about where it would eventually be buried, and the press quickly discovered that its intended resting-place was the village of Wunsiedel, in the Fichtel Mountains of Upper Franconia. Not surprisingly, the Mayor of Wunsiedel, Karl Walter, at once issued a protest, fearing that the grave would become a shrine for neo-Nazis: he pointed out that Hess had never lived in the village, and had no links with the place except that he had been made an honorary citizen of it in 1933.

Nevertheless, on August 20th the body was taken under a heavy escort of the Gloucestershire Regiment through the streets of West Berlin to Gatow airport, where forty years and thirty days before the prisoner had landed to begin his Spandau sentence. From Gatow it was flown in an R.A.F. Hercules to the United States air base at Grafenwohr, and there Wolf Rüdiger was waiting to receive it. The handover was completed by noon.

Next day, however, events took a lively turn when Wolf Rüdiger and his lawyer, Dr Seidl, declared themselves totally dissatisfied with the Allies' verdict; they called it "unimaginable" that the prisoner could have committed suicide, and announced that they had commissioned a second autopsy. This was carried out that same morning, August 21st, by the distinguished pathologist Professor W. Spann of Munich University, assisted by three other specialists, in the presence of Dr Seidl and of the Munich Chief of Criminal Police, Herr Nefzger, together with some of his officials.

Spann was hampered by several difficulties, among them the facts that he had none of the prisoner's medical records or X-rays, and that the body had already been opened, and some organs, including the whole block of tissue surrounding the tongue and larynx, removed. Even so, his examination – conducted without the benefit of ultra-violet light – was more thorough and perceptive than Cameron's, and his report more descriptive.

The corpse, he recorded, arrived in a wooden coffin. "After taking the lid off, a tin coffin was found inside. The lid of the tin coffin was missing. The body lay under a white coverlet, wrapped in a shroud . . . The hair on the head was brown/grey, thin above the forehead and on the crown, with distinct balding . . . The eyebrows were exceptionally bushy, the eyeballs sunken, the left eyelid still showing a slit-like opening . . ."[4]

On the left side of the chest Spann found not one but two "single, old scars, lying parallel to each other, the lower one 2.5 centimetres long, the upper 2 centimetres". Moreover, in the neighbourhood of the scars he found "traces of stitching". His description exactly mirrored that of the American doctor Ben Hurewitz, who examined the prisoner at Nuremberg in 1945 (see page 126). Like Cameron, Spann recorded no trace of a gunshot wound. Yet his findings did show an important variation from those of the British doctor when he came to examine the neck.

Here he found a clearly apparent red-brown mark running obliquely from behind the left ear down round the throat to the bottom of the right side of the neck. The breadth of the mark varied from 6 millimetres to 20 millimetres, and it was thickest in the middle, over the point where the Adam's apple had been. Across the back of the neck were two parallel marks running almost horizontally, described as "stripes of reddish discoloration 1 millimetre broad, separated by other discoloration 6 millimetres broad". (These had been made by a single cord or flex being pulled tight – for the characteristic pattern left by such a ligature is two lines of bruising marking the outer edges of the cord, with a slightly less bruised area between.)

The rest of Spann's findings did not differ in any important way from those of Cameron, and he, too, concluded that death had not been natural: "There is incontrovertible evidence of the fact that death was caused by a strangling implement around the throat."

The significance of the marks which he recorded on neck and throat is hard to exaggerate, for they show categorically that the prisoner was throttled rather than hung. Cameron was certainly correct in deciding that the man had died from asphyxia and compression of the neck; yet, no less certainly, he was wrong in saying that the final factor causing death was "suspension".

When a man is hung, the weight of his body, dragging down on the noose, inevitably pulls the knot round so that it is at the highest point of the loop, usually against the back of his neck, or slightly to one side. This entails three facts about marks left on his neck:

1. Under the knot itself, there are usually no marks, as the ligature rises and draws away from the flesh at the so-called suspension point.

2. The mark on the throat will be of equal width all along its length.

3. The marks at the front and back will be parallel.

On Prisoner No. 7, the marks were exactly the opposite:

1 The double, tramline mark across the back of the neck was horizontal and of even width.

2. The mark on the front of the neck was steeply oblique, falling away from beneath the left ear.

3. This mark was not of even width, but thickest over the Adam's apple, indicating that maximum pressure had been applied there, either by a knot or by a twist in the flex held tightly in someone's hand. No suspension point was anywhere apparent.

In other words, the marks recorded by Spann made it physically impossible that the man had been hung – and it should be emphasised that this is not a matter of opinion, but of scientific fact. Had Cameron read the marks as clearly as Spann did, he would surely have ruled out his third finding, suspension, as a factor contributing to death. Fortunately Dr Seidl, the lawyer, had photographs taken of the body, so that no one would be able to say that any finding had been falsified. Seidl also asked Spann to make a special examination of the prisoner's hands, and this showed that he had certainly not wound the cable round his hand – the only way in which, with his enfeebled grasp, he might conceivably have been able to exert pressure on his own neck.[5]

Being already familiar with the prisoner's medical records, and having studied both post mortem reports at length, I can come to only one conclusion: that he was murdered. To test this idea further, and to confirm the practical possibilities involved, I employed a gang of four tough, young would-be assassins – all serving soldiers, one of them a leading karate instructor – to carry out attacks on my own throat. After some practice with a length of flex identical to the one found in Spandau, they made assaults on a not-altogether-willing dummy – and the result of each attack was to leave on my neck and throat marks precisely similar to those reported in Berlin. It was almost uncanny to see that every one of the attackers instinctively adopted the same method and attitude, pulling up with the right hand and down with the left, to achieve a quick stranglehold on a victim below waist level, slumped on the floor.

Experiments showed that the savage blow which the prisoner received on the back of the head could have been delivered from behind or from the side. Equally, the same stunning effect could have been achieved by slamming the old man bodily backwards against the wall of the shed; obviously he was not expecting any assault, and a sudden push would have made his head swing back and hit the wall first, in spite of the curvature of his spine.

Once he had slumped unconscious or semi-conscious to the floor on his backside (thus covering his trousers and parts of his jacket with shavings and shreds of metal), the assailant – who was probably right-handed – must have slipped the flex over his head from in front, crossed it over on his Adam's apple and jerked it tight, pulling up with his right hand and down with his left, legs braced apart to achieve greater traction. A short grip of the flex with the right hand would have produced the severe bruising which both doctors reported in the angle of the prisoner's left jaw – and in no more than two or three minutes, his life would have been snuffed out.

His death was certainly achieved with brutal efficiency, and it shocked almost all the men who had looked after him in Spandau. Obviously the key question is, Who killed him, and why?

I would lay a very large bet on the fact that it was not one of the warders. Like their English counterparts, the Americans were gentle old-timers, chosen years before for their steadiness. They all knew each other, and it seems inconceivable that one of them would suddenly have gone off his head and violently killed the man whom he had looked after for so long. Equally improbable, to me, is the possibility that one of them had been planted there long ago as a sleeper-assassin, to do the deed whenever the call came.

Nor could the killer have been one of the guards, for they went everywhere in pairs, and none of them had any chance of reaching the summerhouse alone. It is conceivable that one of the cooks or other domestic staff could have done it – but they, too, had been working in the prison for years, and were not violent criminals. By far the most likely candidate was some outsider who had gained access to the gaol that day, and who was ready to strike when the warder on duty was decoyed away.

All that can be said with certainty is that the only party to gain from the prisoner's death was the British Government, which must certainly have been glad when he was silenced for ever, and which, in my view, has been covering up the truth about him ever since 1941. This they did once again in a press release put out by the British military Government in Berlin on September 19th, which claimed to be "a final statement on the death of Rudolf Hess", and, in blatant contradiction of the facts thrown up by the post mortems, said:

"Investigations have confirmed that on August 17 Rudolf Hess hanged himself from a window-latch in a small summerhouse in the prison garden, using an electrical extension cord which had for some time been kept in the summerhouse for use in connection with a reading-lamp . . ."

Describing the so-called suicide-note, the release made an extraordinarily feeble attempt at authentication:

"The senior document-examiner from the laboratory of the British Government Chemist, Mr P. A. M. Beard, has examined the note, and concluded that he can see no reason to doubt that it was written by Rudolf Hess."

The release concluded with a piece of utterly useless information: "The investigations confirmed that the routine followed by staff on the day of Hess's suicide was consistent with normal practice." Of course, everyone had done everything perfectly, by the book.

Even so, the Press release was remarkable for its omissions. It did not quote any evidence from Dr Spann's report, or even reveal that a second autopsy had taken place. Nor did it state what the British post mortem had shown, except to say that "the report noted a linear mark on the left side of the neck consistent with a ligature".

Dr Spann's report has not yet been published – and before it had even been completed, Wolf Rüdiger, who had been under tremendous strain, was rushed into intensive care at a hospital in Munich, reported to be suffering from a stroke which caused slight paralysis. In spite of the contentious nature of my ideas, I have always been on good terms with him, and when he had recovered, I wrote to ask for a copy of the Spann report. The fact that he readily sent me one seemed tantamount to an admission that I had been right all along.

When Cameron returned to England, and I telephoned him to compare notes about the post mortem, I was astonished to hear that he had been required to compile not one report, but two: his general account of the autopsy, copies of which went to the other powers and to Wolf Rüdiger, and a separate report which went to the British Military Governor only. When I wrote to Colonel Hamer-Philip to ask about this second report, he denied that it existed; but Cameron has confirmed to persons other than myself, that he wrote it, and I can only conclude that it went more fully into the possibility of murder.

Cameron, in turn, seemed amazed when I told him that Rudolf Hess had been shot through the left lung by a rifle bullet. He appeared not to have known that before, and agreed that the body which he had examined in Berlin bore no trace of any such wound.

Thus in death, as in life, Prisoner No. 7 continues to create mystery. But on February 28th, 1988, my fifteen-year quest for the truth almost reached its goal. In a calm and friendly telephone conversation, Wolf Rüdiger agreed that he and Dr Spann had no doubt that murder had been committed: far from challenging my verdict, he sought my help and advice in preparing an action against the British Government or the Four Powers. Further, he agreed that no scars of a bullet-wound had been found in the chest or lung; he agreed that my diagnosis had been correct all the time; he agreed that

I had done right, as a doctor, to bring the matter to light. And yet he could not draw the inescapable deduction from what he was saying. He could not accept this final proof that the dead man had not been his father. It was as if he thought that by some magic the old wound scars had disappeared. "I must still consider that it is my father," he said. "My mother couldn't have been wrong after all those years."

In clinical terms, he was expressing a selective hysterical repression of the truth. The condition is often seen in patients, who appear to acknowledge the facts about their illness, but do not really take them in or understand them. Wolf Rüdiger was the same: he could not make the jump from one part of the truth to the other.

Nor, it seems, can the British Government. Imagine my surprise when, in February 1988, I telephoned the Foreign Office in London to ask the state of play in the Hess affair and heard an official read out to me *the proposed answer to a Parliamentary question due to be put in the House of Commons by the Labour Member for Workington, Dale Campbell-Savours*. Until then I had had no idea that Campbell-Savours was planning a question – but here already was an answer, and a highly mendacious one at that, claiming among other things that the body did bear major wound-scars on the chest.

The parliamentary question, however, was never asked, and the draft answer never given. Investigation revealed that although Campbell-Savours had *tried* to table a question in the House, he was told that such a procedure was inadmissible in view of the sensitive nature of the subject. He therefore put a series of eleven searching questions about the prisoner's identity and the post mortem in a letter to the Foreign Secretary, Sir Geoffrey Howe, dated January 26th, 1988.

On February 15th, 1988, he received from Mrs Lynda Chalker, Minister of State at the Foreign and Commonwealth Office, an extraordinarily inadequate reply. Only four of the questions had been answered at all. The replies concocted by her department were at best evasive and at worst downright dishonest. Thus Question No. 4 had been: "Could you confirm that one of the post mortem reports . . . indicates no bullet scars on the left part of the torso of the prisoner?" And the answer to it was:

No. Both the interim report and the full report drawn up by the pathologist [Cameron] indicated scarring on the left part of the torso consistent with bullet wounds.[6]

It takes my breath away that a Minister of the British Government can sign her name to a statement so patently false – and one whose falseness was bound to become apparent in due course.

Already, as I write, Spandau Gaol is passing into history. On August 24th the American guard stood down for the last time, and the place was handed over to a caretaker detachment of the First Battalion, the King's Own Scottish Borderers. On September 2nd workmen began removing the tiles from the roof. Two weeks later demolition work started, and by the end of the month the old prison had gone for ever.

The publication of an extract from this book in the *Mail on Sunday* on March 13th, 1988 had several dramatic and precipitate effects. The first was an ill-advised statement made to *The Times* reporter Andrew McEwan by a British Military Government spokesman, Mr Purdon, in which it was accepted that my account of the prisoner's frailty was correct, and that it had possibly been a mistake not to describe the bang he had sustained on the back of his head.

It was claimed, however, that the electrical flex had already somehow been attached to the window-latch, when the prisoner found it, looped it round his neck, and fell backwards, thus injuring the back of his head on the floor. *The Times* quoted my reply, that the claim was self-contradictory, since the very fact of hitting his head on the floor meant that the man could not have been hanging.

This statement was no more than a hasty, indeed a panicky, attempt by the British Military Government to explain away the anomalies I had pointed out. It ran contrary to the S.I.B.'s report of the position in which the body had been found, and also to plain common sense. Further, it again illustrated how non-professional people fail to understand medical facts.

The prisoner's diseased state made him involuntarily jerk his torso forwards whenever he felt himself starting to sway backwards. His legs were almost permanently flexed to balance his inclined torso, and all that could possibly have resulted – had he tried to execute the movement described – would have been for him to totter backwards and collapse on to his rump. Had he rolled back further, on his grossly-curved spine, it is unlikely that he would have hit his head at all, and inconceivable that he would have sustained severe deep bruising. But even if he had managed to deal himself a severe blow, he could only have done so with the flex completely slack, and exerting no pressure on his throat.

Quite apart from the injury to the head, the degree of deep-bruising in the neck tissues was far beyond anything that could have been caused by an attempt at self-strangulation, and totally out of keeping with this new scenario.

The second event of note was the hurried burial of the body at

Wunsiedel on the morning of Thursday, March 17th, four days after my article appeared, and roughly seven months after the intended burial date of August 25th, 1987. The official reason for keeping the body in the mortuary, and delaying the burial, was to prevent the interment becoming a neo-Nazi focus and the grave a neo-Nazi shrine. Yet the sight of 200 police cordoning off the cemetery was not, perhaps, the most successful way of ensuring anonymity.

Dr Seidl, the Hess family lawyer, obviously appreciated the significance of the post mortem findings to the full. In 1979 he was so confident about the famous gunshot wounds that he officially asked for the prisoner to be examined, so that my claims about his identity could be refuted. Nine years later – presumably at the wish of the family – he maintains an understandable silence about these very same claims, now proven in both post mortems.

The third event of note came on Friday, March 18th, when it was revealed that, after receiving information in February, the West Berlin State Prosecutor had instituted a murder investigation into the prisoner's death. The Justice Department spokesman, Herr Christoffel, declared that the files remain open. With no possible cooperation from the Four Powers, there seems little chance that they will ever be satisfactorily closed.

The cover-up by the British Government strikes me as one of the most disgraceful crimes in history: the most prolonged, deliberate and cynical evasion of responsibility that one can possibly imagine. It is understandable that Churchill should not have exposed the deception in 1941, at the height of the war; but the truth should certainly have been revealed before the prisoner went to Nuremberg. Then, in 1979, it was inexcusable that the authorities should continue in collusive denials after my evidence had been published; and it is still more unforgivable that they should go on lying now.

Notes

ABBREVIATIONS

I.M.T.   International Military Tribunal. Record of the Nuremberg War
         Criminals' Trial.
P.R.O.   Public Record Office, London.
P.S.F.   Prisoner No. 7's Spandau File.

1 THE DISCOVERY

1. Airey Neave, *Nuremberg*, p. 315. The text of the book reads: "But if
   you are looking for Convict Number —", but the prisoner gave his own
   number, 125.
2. Rees, *The Case of Rudolf Hess*, p. 9.
3. P.S.F. Also quoted in Rees, op. cit., pp. 136–7.
4. A conversation between the author and Hurewitz held in 1978 confirmed that the American surgeon saw no other scars.
5. The proceedings were in no way expedited by the behaviour of the
   Russian radiologist, whose presence was also considered essential.
   Although a quick, clever man, he was extremely suspicious of the
   modern processor that developed the X-ray films automatically. Being
   used to the old method, in which the X-ray plates were put on a metal
   screen in a developing tank and washed, like ordinary film, he was
   furious at losing sight of the films as they went into the new machine, and
   kept darting from one end of it to the other to make sure we were not
   substituting different X-rays halfway through.
6. Experiment recorded by Rees, op. cit., pp. 84–90.
7. Manvell and Fraenkel, *Hess*, p. 19.
8. Conversation with the author, October 1978.

2 THE SURGICAL EVIDENCE

1. Details kindly provided by the Rumanian Embassy in London.
2. A comprehensive survey of the effect of bullet wounds, from the earliest
   use of rifles in war until the 1970s, is given in *Projectile Trauma*: *An
   Enquiry into Bullet Wounds* by the military surgeon Lt.-Col. Robert
   Scott, R.A.M.C. (Crown Copyright, 1977).

3. There is no documentary evidence to show that Hess *did* have an operation. But family tradition related that he was operated on by the famous surgeon Sauerbruch; also, judging from my own experience, and from the length of time that Hess spent in hospital, I consider it almost certain that an operation must have been performed.

4. It is often supposed that very high-velocity rifles, such as the Armalite, inflict more damage than those firing slower and heavier bullets. But Scott, among others, confirms that this is not so:

> "The experimental observations which I have made under widely-varying circumstances do not indicate that lightweight rifle bullets inflict more serious wounds than those caused by rifles in use since the early part of this century" (Scott, op. cit., p. 45).

3 THE FLIGHT

1. Radar evidence supplied to the author by a communications expert serving with the German Air Force.

2. A full account of the aircraft's arrival appears in Derek Wood's *Attack Warning Red*.

3. Leasor, *The Uninvited Envoy*, pp. 82ff. Also confirmed in conversation between Leasor and the present author.

4. Conversation with the author, November 1978. Kaden also claimed to remember that drop-tanks *were* fitted to the aircraft, giving it a total fuel complement of 3,000 litres, and therefore a range of nearly 1,200 miles.

5. Green, *The Warplanes of the Third Reich*, pp. 573ff.

6. The map, which the present author has examined, is now in the possession of Mrs Ellis Jones, widow of one of the doctors who cared for the prisoner during the war.

7. Information from source quoted in Note 1 above. Two kinds of radar were being used in conjunction: the mobile scanners known as Freya and the larger, more accurate apparatus called Würzburg. The Freya sets picked up aircraft first, and two Würzburgs then analysed their height as well as their flight-path. (The Würzburg could also direct interceptor aircraft if necessary.) The system became known to the Luftwaffe as the *Himmelbett* (heaven bed), and a *Himmelbett* zone covered the whole section of coast that Hess crossed, keeping a constant watch at least forty miles out to sea. The zone as a whole was divided into smaller, circular areas. Hess's aircraft was plotted as it crossed the fringes of the Tiger and Salzhering zones.

   The German Air Observer Corps (*Flugmeldendienst*) was also on duty at the time, but in general it was not nearly so well coordinated as its British counterpart. In this area it was linked mainly with the searchlight batteries which extended all down the North Sea coast in a belt twenty-five miles wide, known as the Kammhuber Line.

8. Testimony of Sidney Clifford, former medical orderly at Maindiff Court, Abergavenny.

9. For many years after the war air historians were baffled by the markings
   of German military aircraft; but then, in 1961, there came to light a
   directive issued in 1936 by the Supreme Commander of the Luftwaffe
   which gave the key to the puzzle. (See Karl Ries, *The Markings and
   Camouflage Systems of the Luftwaffe*, pp. 6ff.)
   To understand the system, one must first know the units in which the
   Luftwaffe was organised:

   Three aircraft   = one *Kette* (literally chain) or flight
   Three *Ketten*   = one *Staffel* or echelon (nine aircraft)
   Three *Staffeln* = one *Gruppe* or group (twenty-seven aircraft)
   Three *Gruppen* = one *Geschwader* or squadron (eighty-one or more
                      aircraft).

   The letters carried by Messerschmitt 110s on their flanks were designed to give a complete account of each aircraft's status. The two
   before the *Balkenkreuz* (or cross) indicated the *Geschwader* (squadron); a white line (if any) between the letters and the cross showed the
   Gruppe (group). The first letter after the cross identified the actual
   plane within its *Staffel* (echelon), and the last letter or number gave the
   Staffel.
   The plane that crashed in Scotland had been destined for one of the
   NJ or *Nachtjagd* (Nightfighter) squadrons.
10. Galland, *The First and the Last*, pp. 108–9.
11. I first wrote and explained what I wanted, but got no reply, and tried
    without success to telephone his house in Bonn. I then again contacted
    the German Military Attaché in London, who gave me telephone
    numbers for the office and suite which Galland rented in the Inter-
    national Hotel at 136 Koblenz Strasse, also in Bonn. A pleasant and
    helpful secretary said he would be there that evening. Yet when I rang
    the hotel at the suggested time, I was given the brush-off in no uncertain
    fashion: the switchboard denied that Galland had a room or office there
    in such exaggerated terms that it was clear they had instructions to get
    rid of me.
12. Ironically enough, Goering himself later came close to being shot down
    by Galland, in not dissimilar circumstances. In his biography, *Hitler's
    War* (p. 810), David Irving relates how in April 1945, when Hitler was in
    his bunker in Berlin, Goering, in Obersalzberg, tried to assume overall
    control of the Reich and end the war. His plan was to fly to General
    Eisenhower, the American Supreme Commander, and ask for peace
    terms.
    Hitler, however, still had enough fight left in him to react vigorously
    to the telegram that Goering had sent, and ordered him to be placed
    under house arrest. The same day, Hitler's munitions chief, Albert
    Speer, wrote to Galland (by then a general and in command of a
    jet-fighter squadron in Bavaria) saying, "I request you and your com-

rades to do everything to prevent an aeroplane flight by Goering as discussed."

Irving himself remarks, "Speer does not refer to this in his memoirs. The only acceptable explanation is that if Goering tried to fly to Eisenhower, Galland was to have him shot down."

Galland's memoirs do not refer to the incident either.

Goering's own ruthlessness in despatching opponents by air is illustrated by his attempt to get rid of Ernst ("Putzi") Hanfstaengl during the Spanish Civil War. In his book *Zwischen Weissem und Braunem Haus* Hanfstaengl recorded how he was ordered to fly to Spain to protect the interests of German correspondents. When the aircraft was on its way, the pilot revealed that his orders, signed by Goering, were that Hanfstaengl was to parachute over the Red lines between Barcelona and Madrid. Hanfstaengl shouted out that this was a death-sentence, and after some help from the pilot, who put down with alleged engine trouble, he eventually escaped to Switzerland.

13. Messerschmitt related this episode in an interview printed by the *Frankfurter Neue Presse* in May 1947. Recalling the interview in her book *Prisoner of Peace* (p. 18), Frau Hess assumed that Messerschmitt made a mistake, and that the call from Goering had in fact come on the evening of May 11th. But since there is independent evidence for Goering's call to Galland on the evening of the 10th, there seems no reason to doubt Messerschmitt's original date.
14. In theory it should still be possible to find the remains of the Messerschmitt – and salvage experts are indeed considering the idea. One of the main practical difficulties is that the sea-bed off the Dutch coast is littered with hundreds of aircraft-wrecks, and identification would be extremely difficult.
15. *Prisoner of Peace*.

4 THE REAL HESS

1. Adolf Hitler was a despatch-runner in the same regiment, but did not meet Hess till after the war.
2. Hanfstaengl, *Hitler: the Missing Years*, p. 114.
3. Ibid, p. 115.
4. Calic, *Unmasked*, p. 68.
5. Gisevius, *To the Bitter End*, p. 150.
6. Shirer, *Berlin Diary*, p. 194.
7. Manvell and Fraenkel, *Hess*, p. 35.
8. Shirer, *The Rise and Fall of the Third Reich*, p. 270.
9. Lüdecke, *I Knew Hitler*, pp. 519–20.
10. *The Kersten Memoirs*, pp. 88–9.
11. Rees, op. cit., pp. 137–8.
12. Conversation with present author, November 1978.

13. The best account of the Haushofers and their relationship with Hess is given in Douglas-Hamilton's *Motive for a Mission*.
14. Douglas-Hamilton, op. cit., p. 134.
15. Ibid, p. 137.
16. Ibid, p. 137.
17. Ibid, p. 137.
18. Ibid, p. 140.
19. Ibid, p. 139.
20. Nuremberg Documents, I.M.T. 6, p. 150.
21. *The Von Hassell Diaries*, p. 176.
22. Schwerin-Krosigk, *Es Geschah in Deutschland*, pp. 239–42.
23. The remark was witnessed by the police officer on duty, and reported to the present author by Frau Hess, November 1978.
24. Although almost everyone who witnessed Hitler's reaction considered it to be genuine, it is possible that it was a superb piece of acting. The consensus, however, was that the Führer received a severe shock. See also Chapter 5, pp. 174–6.
25. Paul Schmidt, broadcast printed in *The Listener*, April 16th, 1970.
26. Conversation with the author, November 1978.

5   DESTINATION – WHERE?

1. Leasor, *The Uninvited Envoy*, p. 71.
2. Ibid, p. 18.
3. Pintsch's version is given in *The Uninvited Envoy*, p. 81. Kaden's testimony was given in conversation with the present author, November 1978.
4. Leasor, op. cit., pp. 88–9. The incident is also recorded in *Prisoner of Peace*, p. 12.
5. Leasor, op. cit., p. 91.
6. Baur, *Hitler's Pilot*.
7. Udet died in peculiar circumstances during November 1941. At first it was claimed that he had met with a fatal accident while testing a new weapon. Then he was said to have committed suicide. Neither account struck contemporaries as convincing – especially when Udet's death was followed by those of many other senior Luftwaffe officers and civil servants, the series culminating in the demise of Udet's successor Gablenz.
8. Leasor, op. cit., p. 71.
9. Quoted by David Irving in the London *Evening Standard* of January 10th, 1970. It seems odd that when so many of the firm's records disappeared, this memorandum should have survived. In retrospect, all Messerschmitt's reactions to the Hess affair seem suspicious. For a fuller account, see Chapter 10.
10. Rosenberg was a frequent visitor to the Hess household, so his meeting on May 10th has no special significance.

11. *Prisoner of Peace*, p. 14.
12. Giving evidence at Nuremberg, Messerschmitt claimed that Hess had entered the flight under his wife's maiden name (Pröhl) for a trip to Stavanger, in Norway. This seems highly improbable, for several reasons, not least that Hess made no mention of any such plan to Piehl.
13. Leasor, op. cit., p. 93.
14. Ibid, p. 95.
15. Irving, *Hitler's War*, p. 244.
16. Speer, *Inside the Third Reich*, p. 174.
17. Schmidt, *Hitler's Interpreter*, p. 233.
18. Quoted by Manvell and Fraenkel, *Hess*, p. 110.
19. Ibid.
20. Irving, op. cit., p. 245.
21. From Ley's private papers. Quoted by Irving, op. cit., p. 845.
22. Speer, op. cit., p. 175.
23. Leasor, op. cit., p. 102. Frau Hess claimed to have memorised the final paragraph of the letter.
24. Schmidt, op. cit., p. 234.
25. Von Hassell's *Diary*, p. 176.
26. Weizsäcker, *Memoirs*, p. 168.
27. Frank, *Im Angesicht des Galgens*, p. 401.
28. Semmler, *Goebbels*, p. 32.
29. Ernst Bohle, the Gauleiter in charge of all Germans living overseas, and a close friend of Hess, confessed to Hitler after the flight that he had helped the Deputy Führer to compose a letter for the Duke of Hamilton in English, and that the document had been finished on January 7th, 1941 (Irving, op. cit., p. 250).
30. Douglas-Hamilton, *Motive for a Mission*, pp. 150–1.
31. *The Yorkshire Post*, November 1969.

6 THE BRITISH REACTION

1. *Prisoner of Peace*, pp. 31ff.
2. P.R.O. War Office file. Report by the Officer Commanding Third Battalion Renfrewshire Home Guard.
3. A detailed account of the identification of the Messerschmitt, and the reception of the pilot, is given in Derek Wood's *Attack Warning Red*.
4. *Documents in German Foreign Policy*, Series D, Vol. XII, pp. 38–40.
5. This was not true. Hamilton had never met Hess. But the idea that he had done so was given widespread credence when Duff Cooper, the Minister of Information, inadvertently passed it to the B.B.C. Later it was denied in the House of Commons by Sir Archibald Sinclair, the Secretary of State for Air.
6. This was a most curious request. Frau Rothacker was Hess's aunt; but since he had not even bothered to tell his wife what he was doing, why

should he have told his Aunt Emma? There is no evidence to show
that she was in Zürich at the time, or that the name Horn would have
meant anything to her. When Frau Hess visited her in 1949, neither the
alias nor the message was ever mentioned. (Testimony of Frau Hess in
conversation with the author, November 1978.)

Even the significance of the name Alfred Horn is not clear. The first
half is supposed to have come from Hess's brother, and the second from
a relation of his mother; but the prisoner never confirmed this.

7. Kirkpatrick, *The Inner Circle*, pp. 173–4.
8. Ibid, p. 175.
9. P.R.O. P.M.'s file. The account given in Kirkpatrick's memoirs is
   sloppy and inaccurate. He says, for instance, that the pilot jettisoned his
   extra petrol tank in the North Sea, whereas the tank which was
   recovered came from the Clyde, on the opposite side of Scotland.
10. *The Inner Circle*, pp. 175–6.
11. Ibid, p. 178.
12. *The Eden Memoirs*, Vol. 2, pp. 255–7.
13. Harold Nicolson, *Diaries and Letters, 1939–45*, pp. 166–7.
14. A. P. Herbert, *Let Us Be Glum*.
15. Churchill, *The Grand Alliance*, p. 45.
16. *The Inner Circle*, p. 180.
17. Information given to the author in conversation with Sir Roger Chance,
    1980.
18. *The Grand Alliance*, p. 47.
19. Lord Haw-Haw was the derisive nickname bestowed by the British on
    William Joyce, an Englishman who made propaganda broadcasts from
    Germany.
20. Hansard, May 1941.
21. P.R.O. P.M.'s file.
22. Conversation with the author, 1980.
23. Leasor, op. cit., pp. 149–50.
24. Rees, op. cit., p. 37.
25. Ibid, p. 39.
26. Ibid, p. 43.
27. I.M.T. Documents in Evidence. Hess 15, pp. 281–2.
28. *The Inner Circle*, p. 184.
29. Rees, op. cit., p. 61.
30. P.R.O. P.M.'s file.
31. Eden, op. cit., p. 257.
32. P.R.O. P.M.'s file.
33. "Historical Responsibility of the Psychiatrist" by Maurice N. Walsh.
    Archives of General Psychiatry, Vol. 2, October 1964.
34. In November 1978.
35. *The Inner Circle*, pp. 184–5.

7   A CASE FOR TREATMENT

1. P.S.F.
2. Rees, op. cit., pp. 29–30.
3. Conversation with present author, November 1978.
4. Rees, op. cit., p. 30.
5. Ibid, pp. 28–9.
6. Ibid, p. 16.
7. See also Chapter 10.
8. Rees, P.R.O. P.R.E.M. 3/219-3. He suppressed this early report when he came to write his book.
9. Rees, op. cit., pp. 20–1.
10. Ibid, p. 6.
11. Ibid, p. 21.
12. Ibid, p. 25.
13. Ibid, p. 25.
14. Ibid, p. 31.
15. Ibid, p. 7.
16. Ibid, p. 65.
17. Ibid, p. 68.
18. Ibid, pp. 87–9.
19. *Prisoner of Peace*, pp. 65–6.
20. Eden, openly contemptuous of Goering's pretentiousness, snubbed him pointedly at a State banquet in Berlin in 1935. The incident set off an anti-Eden newspaper campaign, and was common knowledge in Germany. Eden refers to the smear campaign in Vol. 1 of his memoirs, *Facing the Dictators*, p. 508.
21. Conversation with James Reigate, autumn 1978.
22. Rees, op. cit., p. 15.
23. As already mentioned (p. 108) there was a substantial difference between what Rees wrote for the official record and what he himself believed. See also Chapter 8, p. 128.
24. Rees, op. cit., p. 15.
25. Testimony of former medical orderlies, given in conversations with the author, autumn 1978.
26. *Prisoner of Peace*, p. 47.
27. Rees, op. cit., p. 13.
28. *Prisoner of Peace*, p. 100.
29. Speer, *Inside the Third Reich*, p. 176.

8   NUREMBERG

1. Airey Neave, *Nuremberg*, pp. 79–80.
2. Captain Hurewitz confirmed in conversation with the author that he had excellent facilities for the examination: good lights, equipment and ancillary services. He also had plenty of time. What he did *not* have,

however, were records of the real Hess with which to compare his findings.

3. P.S.F. Report also published in Rees, op. cit., pp. 136–7.
4. The quotations in this passage are from Rees, op. cit., pp. 140–4.
5. The apparent failure to recognise Rees was clearly part of the prisoner's overall deception scheme, designed in the first instance to slow down the procedure of questioning and in the longer term to fit in with his genuine non-recognition of Hess's secretaries and colleagues.
6. Goering hid two cyanide capsules about his person, one in his rectum and one in his navel. (Information culled from inmates of Spandau by warders in the gaol.)
7. See Chapter 6, Note 35.
8. Rees, op. cit., p. 134.
9. Ibid, p. 135.
10. Andrus, *The Infamous of Nuremberg*.
11. Kelley, *Twenty-two Cells in Nuremberg*, pp. 26–7.
12. Rees, op. cit., p. 161.
13. Andrus, op. cit.
14. This behaviour is typical of a patient trying to cope with the pain of a duodenal ulcer: sitting forward and putting pressure on the abdomen do help relieve discomfort. A properly qualified medical or surgical opinion should have been sought at this stage. The fact that the patient broke off his demonstration to talk about the pain does not necessarily mean it was false.

    His refusal to take medicine reflected his fear of poisoning. In Scotland, England and Wales he had been extremely suspicious, and reluctant to take medicine. At Nuremberg he was terrified of doing so, no doubt because he thought that he was more likely to be poisoned in Germany than in Britain. In Spandau his fear gradually subsided until, by the time he was the only inmate, he showed definite interest in new medication and was almost eager to try new remedies, especially if they were explained to him with sympathy and understanding.
15. I.M.T. I, pp. 305–6.
16. *Prisoner of Peace*.
17. Rees, op. cit., p. 167.
18. *Prisoner of Peace*, pp. 50–1.
19. Gilbert, *Nuremberg Diary*, p. 35.
    Ribbentrop's remarks are profoundly ambiguous. On the surface, it sounds as though he could not believe that the Hess he had known before would behave like the man in court. Yet it is possible that the former Foreign Minister knew about the plot to get rid of Hess. (See Chapter 10.) If he did, what did he mean by "the Hess we have here"? Did he suddenly wonder whether the whole plot had misfired, and whether this was not the double after all, but the real Hess? He seems to have been amazed that the man should put himself in line for the death sentence by proclaiming his own guilt in the way the prisoner did.

20. Rees, op. cit., p. 169.
21. Gilbert, op. cit., p. 89.
22. That the prisoner liked Goering is confirmed by Colonel Eugene Bird, American Commandant of Spandau in the 1960s, and by former members of the staff at Maindiff Court, Abergavenny.
23. Rees, op. cit., p. 183.
24. Ibid, p. 183.
25. Gilbert, op. cit., p. 129.
26. I.M.T. XXII, pp. 384–5.
27. *Prisoner of Peace*, p. 56.
28. After the trial it became clear that the Soviet demand for the death sentence had been inspired by political rather than criminal or judicial considerations, and emanated directly from Stalin.
29. Gilbert, op. cit., p. 271.
30. Neave, op. cit., p. 315.
31. *Prisoner of Peace*, p. 55.
32. Rees, op. cit., p. 133.
33. Ibid, pp. 170–1.
34. Bird, *The Loneliest Man in the World*, Chapter 5.
    The prisoner might have realised that the real Hess was anything but sophisticated in sartorial matters, and would hardly have worried about the details of a new uniform. Unlike some of the other Nazi leaders, the real Hess did not much care for dressing up, and showed no special reverence for uniforms.
    The prisoner should also have remembered that Hitler had always regarded Esser as a dangerous man, and that Hess, who shared the Führer's views so intimately, would hardly have selected him for the new administration.
35. *Prisoner of Peace*, pp. 86–7.
36. Ibid, p. 82.

9 SPANDAU

1. The Russians had already demanded, during the war, that Hess should be tried before hostilities ceased, but Churchill had rejected the idea.
2. The full report is in the prisoner's Spandau file (P.S.F.).
3. "Historical Responsibility of the Psychiatrist", *Archives of General Psychiatry*, Vol. 2, October 1964.
4. Ibid.
5. *Prisoner of Peace*, pp. 107–8.
6. Bird, *The Loneliest Man in the World*, pp. 180–1.
7. Ibid, p. 182.
8. Ibid, p. 211.
9. Ibid, p. 211.
10. Ibid, p. 219.
11. Ibid, p. 216.

12. Ibid, p. 253.
13. Bird was ill-rewarded for his efforts to capture the prisoner's definitive history. When the authorities discovered that he was compiling his book, he was arrested and dismissed from his post.
14. Wolf Rüdiger Hess in conversation with the author, November 1978.
15. *Pravda*, January 7th, 1970.

10   THE PLOT

1. *Prisoner of Peace*, p. 18.
2. Memorandum from the Messerschmitt Company's Historical Section.
3. The war brought both the Haushofers to tragic ends. After the plot against Hitler of July 1944 Albrecht, rightly suspected of having been involved in the resistance movement, was hunted by the Gestapo. After some months of freedom he was captured in December 1944 and confined in the Moabit Prison in Berlin, where he composed a series of moving poems which became known as the Moabit Sonnets. At one o'clock in the morning of April 23rd, 1945, he was brutally murdered by the S.S., without trial, along with fourteen of his fellow prisoners.

   After the July Plot Karl Haushofer was also imprisoned, in Dachau concentration camp. Late in 1945 he was brought to Nuremberg, not to stand trial, but in an attempt to spur the memory of the prisoner known as Hess. By then the old general was sadly disillusioned, both by the fate that had overtaken Germany and by the fact that his dead son had denounced his ideas. On March 11th, 1946, he and his wife went out into the woods, where they both committed suicide by taking poison, Martha also being hanged from the bough of a willow tree.
4. *The Kersten Memoirs*, pp. 88–9.
   On May 15th, the masseur recorded in his diary:

   > After an interrogation lasting five hours Heydrich had to let me go. I've just heard that all doctors who had treated Hess in recent years have been arrested. I also heard from a trustworthy source that during Heydrich's interrogation Himmler rang up and ordered my immediate release. That must be right, for towards the end of it Heydrich was called from the room and I was left alone for ten minutes. Then he said that the Reichsführer had guaranteed me, but that I should hold myself at their disposal.

   Kersten's account is unconvincing. A five-hour interrogation would have been a tremendous ordeal, yet he makes little of it. All the same, it is clear that he was rescued from further punishment by Himmler, who really had no business to intervene, as he was supposed to be in charge of the main enquiry.
5. Manvell and Fraenkel, op. cit., p. 215n.
6. Washington National Archives File No. C002196. Quoted by Bird, op. cit.

7. Himmler's plots against Hitler were manifold. Later in 1941 he several
   times contacted the Allies with consistently similar proposals. He
   continued to negotiate secretly with the Americans, mainly through
   Switzerland, until the end of the war. At one stage he arranged with S.S.
   and American contacts to have Hitler kidnapped and smuggled out of
   Europe alive. The plan broke down when vital papers were stolen by a
   courier, who sold them to an Allied secret service.
      Himmler was also closely associated with several of the attempts on
   Hitler's life. In the one by Popitz, his excuse was that he had been
   keeping the group under surveillance. As for the plot of July 1944, it has
   often been asserted that Himmler cannot have known about the Stauffenberg group's intentions. In fact it was Himmler who recommended
   Stauffenberg for promotion in June that year, and so enabled the Count
   to take his place at Hitler's conference table and deposit beneath it his
   expanding briefcase containing the bomb. Was this a coincidence? (See
   Eberhard Zeller: *Geist der Freiheit*, Munich, 1963, p. 246.)
8. In conversation with the author, November 1978.
9. Frischauer, *Goering*.
10. Hitler told several of his colleagues that if Hess returned to Germany he
    would be executed for treason.
11. The present author has seen copies of the prisoner's early letters from
    England in the file at Spandau.

11 SUDDEN DEATH

1. An excellent account of these meetings is given by Wolf Rüdiger Hess in
   My Father Rudolf Hess, pp. 331–8.
2. Fishman, *Long Knives and Short Memories*, p. 436.
3. My account of the prisoner's physical state is based partly on my own
   knowledge of his medical history, and partly on up-to-date information
   from contacts in Berlin.
4. The account of the prisoner's last day is built up from eye-witness
   reports.
5. Although I myself often saw the shed, I never went into it, but have
   reconstructed details of its layout from people who did go in.
6. Details of the resuscitation attempts are from eye-witnesses.
7. This was revealed by the post mortem examinations.
8. To me this is strangely reminiscent of an incident in 1979. After the first
   publication of my findings, an amateur historian who had a flying mask
   that he claimed had belonged to Hess asked the authorities for leave to
   compare fingerprints found on it with those of the prisoner. Permission
   was of course refused.

12   THE POST MORTEMS

1. Author's conversation with Professor Cameron, September 1987.
2. Details from eye-witnesses.
3. Autopsy Report by Professor J. M. Cameron on Allied Prisoner No. 7. Examination carried out in the British Military Hospital, Berlin, on August 19th, 1987. Report issued from the London Hospital Medical College.
4. Autopsy report by Professor Dr Med. W. Spann of the Institut für Rechtsmedizin der Universität München. Examination carried out on August 21st, 1987.
5. Information supplied to the author by Wolf Rüdiger Hess.
6. The letter, and the answer, were made available to representatives of the Press by Dale Campbell-Savours.

Bibliography

Andrus, Burton C., *The Infamous of Nuremberg*, Leslie Frewin, London, 1969.

Avon, Earl of, *The Eden Memoirs*, Vol. 2: *The Reckoning*, Cassell, London, 1965.

Baur, Hans, *Ich Flog Mächtige der Erde*, Kempton, Pröpster, 1956. Translated as *Hitler's Pilot*, London, 1958.

Bird, Eugene, *The Loneliest Man in the World*, Secker & Warburg, London, 1974.

Calic, Edouard, *Unmasked*, Chatto & Windus, London, 1971.

Churchill, Winston S., *The Second World War*, Vol. 3: *The Grand Alliance*, Cassell, London, 1950.

Ciano, Count Galeazzo, *Ciano's Diary*, edited by Malcolm Muggeridge, Heinemann, London, 1947.

Deacon, Richard, *A History of the Secret Service*, Muller, London, 1969.

Dornberger, Walter, *V.2*, London, 1953.

Douglas-Hamilton, James, *Motive for a Mission*, Macmillan, London, 1971.

Fishman, Jack, *Long Knives and Short Memories*, Souvenir Press, 1986.

Frank, Hans, *Im Angesicht des Galgens*, Beck Verlag, Munich, 1953.

Fraser-Smith, Charles, *The Secret War of Charles Fraser-Smith*, London, 1981.

Frischauer, Willi, *Goering*, London, 1953.

Galland, Adolf, *Die Ersten und die Letzten*, Darmstadt, 1953. Translated as *The First and the Last*, Methuen, London, 1955.

Gilbert, G. M., *Nuremberg Diary*, Eyre & Spottiswoode, London, 1948.

Gisevius, H. B., *Bis Zum Bitteren Ende*. First published in Germany, 1948. Revised edition, 1960. English translation: *To the Bitter End*, Cape, London, 1948.

Green, William, *The Warplanes of the Third Reich*, Macdonald, London, 1970.

Hanfstaengl, Ernst, *Hitler: The Missing Years*, Eyre & Spottiswoode, London, 1957.

Hansford, R. F., *Radio Aids to Civil Aviation*, Heywood, 1960.

Hassell, Ulrich von, *The Von Hassell Diaries, 1938–44*, Hamish Hamilton, London, 1948.

Henderson, Sir Nevile, *Failure of a Mission*, Hodder & Stoughton, London, 1940.

Hess, Ilse, *Prisoner of Peace*, edited by George Pile, Britons Publishing Co., 1954.

—— *Gefangener des Friedens*, Druffel Verlag, Leoni, 1965.

—— *England-Nürnberg-Spandau*, Druffel Verlag, Leoni, 1968.

—— *Antwort aus Zelle Sieben*, Druffel Verlag, Leoni, 1968.

Hess, Rudolf, *Reden*, Eher Verlag, Munich, 1938.

Hess, Wolf Rüdiger, *My Father Rudolf Hess*, W. H. Allen, London, 1986.

Hildebrandt, Rainer, *Wir Sind die Letzten*, Berlin, 1950.

Hutton, J. Bernard, *Hess: The Man and His Mission*, David Bruce & Watson, London, 1970.

Irving, David, *Hess: The Missing Years, 1941–1945*, Macmillan, London, 1987.

Kelley, Douglas M., *Twenty-two Cells in Nuremberg*, W. H. Allen, London, 1947.

Kersten, Felix, *The Kersten Memoirs*, Hutchinson, London, 1956.

Kirkpatrick, Sir Ivone, *The Inner Circle*, Macmillan, London, 1959.

Leasor, James, *The Uninvited Envoy*, Allen & Unwin, London, 1962.

Lüdecke, Kurt, *I Knew Hitler*, Jarrolds, London, 1938.

Manvell, R., and Fraenkel, H., *Goebbels*, Heinemann, London, 1960.

—— *Heinrich Himmler*, Heinemann, London, 1965.

—— *Hess*, MacGibbon & Kee, London, 1972.

Masterman, J. C., *The Double-Cross System*, Yale University Press, 1972.

Neave, Airey, *Nuremberg: A Personal Record*, Hodder & Stoughton, London, 1978.

Nicolson, Harold, *Diaries and Letters, 1939–45*, London, 1967.

Nuremberg War Criminals Trial, English edition. Proceedings, Vols. 1–23. Documents in Evidence, Vols. 24–42. H.M.S.O., London, 1947–49.

Rees, J. R., *The Case of Rudolf Hess*, Heinemann, London, 1947.

Ries, Karl, *The Markings and Camouflage Systems of the Luftwaffe*, Mainz, 1972.

Sauerbruch, Ferdinand, *Die Chirurgie der Brustorgane*. First published 1919. English edition, *Thoracic Surgery*, in cooperation with Laurence O'Shaughnessy, Edward Arnold, London, 1937.

Schmidt, Paul, *Hitler's Interpreter*, Heinemann, London, 1951.

Schwerin-Krosigk, Count Lutz, *Es Geschah in Deutschland*, Tübingen, 1951.

Semmler, Rudolf, *Goebbels, the Man Next to Hitler*, Westhouse, London, 1947.

Shirer, William L., *Berlin Diary, 1934–40*, Hamish Hamilton, London, 1941.

—— *The Rise and Fall of the Third Reich*, Secker & Warburg, London, 1960.

Simon, Viscount, *Retrospect*, Hutchinson, London, 1952.

Speer, A., *Inside the Third Reich*, Weidenfeld & Nicolson, London, 1970.

Strong, Sir Kenneth, *Intelligence at the Top*, Cassell, London, 1968.

Thyssen, Fritz, *I Paid Hitler*, Hodder & Stoughton, London, 1941.
Weizsäcker, Carl von, *Memoirs*, London, 1951.
Wood, Derek, *Attack Warning Red*, Macdonald & Jane's, London, 1976.

Index